MAKING AMERICA POORER

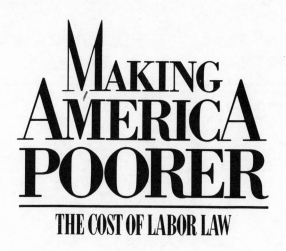

MAKING AMERICA POORER

THE COST OF LABOR LAW

Morgan O. Reynolds

INSTITUTE

Library of Congress Cataloging-in-Publication Data

Reynolds, Morgan O., 1942–
  Making America poorer.

  Bibliography: p.195
  Includes index.
  1. Trade-unions—United States.   2. Industrial
productivity—United States.   3. Wages—United States.
4. Labor laws and legislation—United States—Compliance
costs.   I. Title.
HD6508.R435   1987   338.5′1′0973   87-6569
ISBN 0-932790-63-1
ISBN 0-932790-64-X (pbk.)

Printed in the United States of America.

CATO INSTITUTE
224 Second Street, S.E.
Washington, D.C. 20003

To Suzie

Contents

Acknowledgments

This book began in October 1982 when Edward Crane, president of the Cato Institute, asked me if I would be interested in doing a monograph-length study of the air traffic controllers, strike and its implications for labor legislation and the U.S. economy. A potential conclusion was that without the rigidities imposed by current labor law there would be a substantial reallocation of resources and liquidation of malinvestments. I said that while I approved of the idea I was swamped for the next 12 months and could not get to it.

One year later I wrote to Ed Crane suggesting that I could undertake such a monograph. The mandate was broadened to include the economic drag caused by artificially high union wages, overmanning imposed by unions, and the obstacles to capital mobility caused by union power. While neither of us was opposed to labor unions per se, we were opposed to legal privileges or immunities that might advantage unions in negotiations.

I agreed to deliver a first draft of the manuscript by the end of summer 1984. In 1985 I submitted it—one year late, due to the common frailties of writers. While the manuscript was in reasonable shape, it had a number of deficiencies. Catherine England, William Niskanen, and David Boaz of the Institute made careful corrections and insightful suggestions. I was not too happy about this turn of events initially, but by August 1986 I had incorporated all of their suggestions. The monograph lengthened considerably but improved enormously. Now that those costs have been sunk, I can genuinely thank my reviewers. Thanks. I am grateful. The book is a much better product as a result of your efforts.

MORGAN REYNOLDS
College Station, Texas

I. American Labor Unions

> Consumption is the sole end and purpose of production; and the interest of the producer ought to be attended to only so far as it may be necessary for promoting that of the consumer.
>
> —Adam Smith, *The Wealth of Nations*

Labor unions and labor legislation continue to be sensitive subjects. Although unions and union leaders are unpopular in public opinion polls, a substantial undercurrent of good will still exists toward them. This ambivalence rests on a widespread perception that labor unions once improved material conditions for downtrodden workers, but that unions today are greedy and obstructive. Economists and other scholars are still reluctant to be openly critical of unions and the government policies that support them. Understandably enough, people want to be seen as pro-labor. However, the key question is whether American unions and the labor laws that support them actually improve the wages and working conditions of American workers.

A professor in my department recently told me that the reviewers of his textbook on price theory loved his analysis of business monopoly but objected to the same treatment being applied to labor unions. Yet, many economists do recognize the similarity between labor combinations and other interest groups that try to raise their prices by restricting access to markets.[1] The standard analysis is not "balanced" by other material in the case of business cartels, but some economists want such a balance in the case of labor cartels. As Murray Rothbard (1983, p. 44) observes, "It is curious that even economists who subscribe to a general theory of prices, balk whenever the theory is logically applied to wages, the prices of labor services."

---

[1] The terms "trade union," "labor union," "labor combination," and "labor cartel" are used interchangeably throughout this book.

Unions claim to be the vehicle for improving the economic well-being of the masses. Certainly there is much to celebrate in the situation of the American worker. If we trust the national income accountants, our standard of living is six times higher than it was for our ancestors a century ago. Most jobs formerly done by human muscle are now done by machine. The work week averages 35 hours instead of 65. Three- and four-week vacations have replaced no vacations. Air conditioning is commonplace. Retirement in good health at age 62 has replaced death in harness at age 52.

But who gets the credit for today's higher wages and better conditions? Trade union leaders have claimed it so often that most people hesitate to challenge them. After all, everybody knows that unions press for higher wages for their members and that companies resist these pressures. Nevertheless, unions are no more the source of today's high wages than are minimum wage laws.

Gaining a hearing for rational analysis of unions and their effects and public policy toward unions has long proven difficult. At a time of heightened labor turbulence in the 1940s, for example, Henry C. Simons's classic article on syndicalism (1944) began, "Questioning the virtues of the organized labor movement is like attacking religion, monogamy, motherhood, or the home. Among the modern intelligentsia any doubts about collective bargaining admit of explanation only in terms of insanity, knavery, or subservience to 'the interests.' " Things have changed since then, but not all that much.

Along with other disinterested observers, I share many of the noble aims of unions, such as expanded opportunities for all, improved well-being for the masses, and a free society that relies as much as possible on voluntary consent rather than privilege, status, and the use of force. Good intentions, however, are not enough; the debate must focus on whether the prescribed means promote the ends. These are technical, scientific issues. As the son of a blue-collar father—a union man—I have worked in factories and in both union and nonunion jobs. I consider myself at least as pro-labor as any union leader. Being pro-labor need not coincide with being pro–organized labor, pro–American Dairy Association, pro-OPEC, or pro–collective bargaining laws. Disagreements over economic policy do not stem from quarrels over ends as much as from quarrels over the proper means to achieve them. Sound analysis is inherently pro-labor because knowledge is essential to advance the interests of working people (and all others).

The purpose of this book is to evaluate the impact of trade unions in U.S. economic performance: Do the unions, under existing labor law, increase or decrease U.S. output and the real flow of labor earnings? Do the unions of the American Federation of Labor–Congress of Industrial Organizations (AFL-CIO) and other unions raise or lower the standard of living of the common man? How large are the economic effects of unions? Do such unions help or harm the poor and disadvantaged? Are these economic effects caused by unions per se or do they reflect the legal privileges and immunities that government has bestowed on unions?

The Counterfactual

To assess the economic impact of unions under existing labor law requires a counterfactual, in the language of economic historians. The counterfactual for this study is a U.S. legal system that effectively would allow only "competitive unions" (in H. Gregg Lewis's words)—that is, free-market unions without legal privileges or immunities and therefore without the ability to sustain monopoly prices for their members' services. Under current federal and many state labor policies, we basically have "monopoly unionism"—government has granted labor cartels legal immunities and privileges that allow them to wield market power to affect ("fix") wage rates and other terms of employment. What government has given, however, government can take away.

A return to common and criminal law to govern labor relations in the United States would generate different output, employment, and wage results from what we now observe. One purpose of this book is to estimate what output and wage rates would look like. Based on U.S. history prior to the 1930s—a period when employment relations in peacetime were governed by common law—it can be predicted that unions would not disappear if today's collective-bargaining laws were repealed. Instead, labor organizations would decline in membership, and more of the survivors would be based on a cooperative theme, as the independent (so-called company) unions were, and fewer would be based on the adversarial ideology of labor versus capital (or labor versus management, in today's vernacular). From an economic perspective, powerful unions would

3

virtually disappear and the production, employment, and wage results of the U.S. economy would be nearly indistinguishable from a competitive (or union-free) labor market system.

The idea of an explicit counterfactual is troublesome to some people. A counterfactual certainly is an imaginary construction, but any "with and without" comparison involves comparing what actually happened with an estimate of what would happen "without" that factor. Although unobserved, a counterfactual can be a well-constructed prediction of what would happen if (in this case) public policy were to repeal the legal privileges and immunities that support the economic clout of labor unions. If public policy were to deregulate labor markets, the predictions would be tested. In sum, an estimate of the impact of adversarial unions under existing labor laws implies constructing an estimate of what the economy would look like under deregulated labor markets (for example, restoration of the "employment at will" doctrine that once held in labor contracts).

The Background

Organized labor is now in its biggest slump since the 1920s and early 1930s, when major unions flirted with expiration in this country. The slide in union influence is conspicuous in many dimensions: fewer unions, smaller memberships, weaker union finances, shrinking employment in unionized industries, failures to organize workers in new industries, givebacks and concession bargaining, competition from domestic and foreign nonunion enterprises, deregulation in product markets, adverse court decisions, bolder employer resistance to unions, and declining public esteem for unions. The difficulties of organized labor in the marketplace have been paralleled by an erosion of organized labor's influence in the political arena.

It should be remembered, however, that the U.S. economy has always been predominantly nonunion. We can divide the history of U.S. unionism into five periods: (1) pre-1850, (2) the agitation of 1850–89, (3) the union growth of 1890–1917, (4) the rise and fall of 1917–33, and (5) the modern era since 1933.[2]

---

[2]The following account is based on Reynolds (1985c).

4

Pre-1850

Before 1850, organized labor was trivial in extent. Unions were largely failures, having relatively little economic clout and disbanding whenever business downturns occurred. Contrary to popular impression, unions did not originate among the lowest wage earners, who presumably were the most exploited by capitalists, but among the educated, urban workers in such high-income crafts as printing and other skilled trades. Nor did unions form at large firms, whose corporate size presumably gave them a powerful bargaining advantage over their workers. Consistent with economic theory, unions were mostly groups of craftsmen because they met the two general conditions for profitable organizing: (1) large potential gains in wages because of inelastic demand for services (hard to replace), and (2) low-cost organization of the labor market (small numbers of workers in the trade, low turnover rates, and employers being few in number or geographically concentrated). In business language, it was profitable to organize (cartelize) labor in some markets and not in others. In the modern era, unions are still found in crafts and industries where the labor market is concentrated or regulated by government rather than in decentralized industries such as wholesale and retail trade, services, and agriculture.

1850–89

Nearly everything was tried in some form or other during the 1850–89 era: socialism, syndicalism, anarchism, cooperatives, political unionism, and the most seductive idea of all, welding everybody into one giant union. Unions and unionists were a diverse lot. Some unions, for example, were here one day, gone the next. Some were secret societies that adopted names such as the Knights of St. Crispin, the Molly Maguires, or the Knights of Labor and had secret membership rolls, secret rites, and secret membership campaigns.

An aura of collective protest, high-pitched emotion, and revolutionary fervor accompanied unionism everywhere. And with it came the specter of union violence. Bombings and killings in the anthracite fields during the 1870s (attributed to the Molly Maguires), the anarcho-syndicalist flavor of the Haymarket riot in 1886, the violence of railroad and steel industry disputes, and many other incidents helped create a public image of unionists and organized workers as a threat to peace, prosperity, property rights, and liberty itself. Although union accounts tell of the oppression of capitalism and worker protest, unionism commanded little allegiance or respect in the 19th century because individualism and liberty, not collectivism, were the ethic of the day. American capitalism was in its heyday (as was British capitalism), and the concepts of free enterprise and individual freedom had a grip on popular opinion that is hard to imagine from our contemporary vantage point. The United States was not fertile ground for planting union doctrine—or for other forms of collectivism, for that matter. The main adhesive of European unions—easily aroused class resentments—was absent in America, and Marxist-style sentiments about the plight of the working class never became a dominant mood here, contrary to some historical accounts. More often, Americans were horrified and alarmed by outbreaks of labor violence and union disruption of production, especially if the outbursts had revolutionary overtones.

1890–1917

Eventually, one form of unionism emerged as a survivor in this unfavorable environment. Experiments with political radicalism gradually gave way to business unionism—that is, the notion that unions must pursue immediate, material gain for their members within a private-enterprise system. The underlying idea was to accept capitalism—the wage and political systems—and to achieve marginal gains for members within it. Consequently, the ambitions of social visionaries and reformers who saw unions as a vehicle for comprehensive change fell by the wayside.

The tradition of 20th-century American unionism was largely the work of the American Federation of Labor (AFL) and especially its leader, Samuel Gompers. The AFL was founded in 1881 as a federation of national trade unions, each composed of a particular craft. Unions in single crafts could survive in a private-property, market order by banding similar workers together and bargaining monopoly-style for their services as an undifferentiated lump.

Union membership in the early 1890s was barely 200,000. As the economy recovered from the panic of 1893, unions found effective methods of organization, and their membership hit 447,000 in 1897. Once the formula of national craft unionism was in place, unions grew to a modest share of the labor force without much government help. Membership rose to 2.7 million by 1913, 7 percent of the labor force. But it then fell to 2.5 million in 1915 on the eve of the U.S. entry into World War I.

Only the railroad and postal unions were direct beneficiaries of pro-union federal legislation, although 17 state legislatures passed laws during the 1880s and 1890s prohibiting employers from firing employees for belonging to or joining unions. The laws may have temporarily boosted union membership; if nothing else, they may have reflected a more favorable political climate for organized labor during this period. However, the courts subsequently struck down these laws as being infringements on the liberty of contract.

1917–33

Many historians identify World War I as the watershed of the 20th century, and it certainly was pivotal for government policy toward unions. The national emergency doubled union membership to 5 million, or 12 percent of the labor force, by 1920. Not only was labor scarce, but the federal government set up wage and labor boards—which included union leaders as board members—to promote labor unions and collective bargaining and thereby ensure "labor peace." The government proclaimed its support of unions, ordered the establishment of work councils of employee representatives in nonunion plants, forbade interference with union activities, ordered companies to reinstate union members with back pay, seized defiant companies such as Western Union and Smith & Wesson, and in one case created a union, the Loyal Legion of Loggers and Lumbermen. The greatest union growth occurred in industries directly managed by government, such as the railroad and shipbuilding industries. Some of the federally ordered employee organizations later became company unions.

After wartime orders were filled, there was an end to the federal measures to force companies to recognize unions as exclusive agents of employees, and the legal regime reverted to prewar standards. In other words, the labor market was deregulated. Although unions had gained more than 2 million members during World War I and its aftermath, membership plummeted by 1.5 million by 1923. Union losses were concentrated in the government-run war industries, thereby suggesting how dependent unions were on intervention for membership. Additional factors were the general return to private management and the 1920–21 depression. From 1923 to 1930 union membership stabilized at 3.5 million, but by 1933 the Great Depression had reduced membership to 2.8 million and unions were in a condition of free fall.

Since 1933

The New Deal legislation of the 1930s reversed the decline and created the framework that persists today. The first durable help for unions was the Railway Labor Act of 1926, which basically mandated collective bargaining on all interstate railroads and set up the machinery for government intervention in labor disputes. The act was declared constitutional in 1930.

The national emergency of World War I provided much of the experience and precedent for the 1926 railway act (Watson-Parker Act) and for six major pieces of labor legislation passed during the confusion of the Great Depression: Davis-Bacon, the Norris-LaGuardia Anti-Injunction Act, the National Industrial Recovery Act, the National Labor Relations Act of 1935 (Wagner Act), the Public Contract Act (Walsh-Healey Act), and the Fair Labor Standards Act. Three of these acts—Davis-Bacon (1931), Walsh-Healey (1936), and Fair Labor Standards (1938)—authorized direct federal fixing of minimum wage rates, maximum working hours, and other working conditions in various sectors of the economy; the other three acts empowered labor unions to fix terms of employment and are discussed in chapter 2 below.

Spurred by federal protection, new Congress of Industrial Organizations (CIO) unions advanced into the mass-production industries, while the old-line AFL unions also gained members. From a trough of 2.8 million members in 1933, total union membership rose to 7.2 million by 1940, then to 13.2 million by 1945. The decline that unions suffered after World War I failed to occur after World War II because the pro-union federal framework sustained the union gains of the 1930s and World War II. After 1945, union membership continued to rise to a peak of 25 percent of the civilian labor force in the early 1950s. Since then, however, the union share of private employment has eroded in a nearly straight line to its current 15 percent and promises to fall below 10 percent within the next few years.

Public-sector unions grew rapidly from a total membership of 900,000 in 1960 to almost 6 million by 1976, concealing organized labor's overall weakness from public perception. The union share of government employees during the same period also rose from 11 to 40 percent, but by 1983 the union share had slumped to 34 percent and 5.4 million members (Troy and Sheflin, 1985).

Even more than in the private sector, the rise of large unions in government owes less to employee demand through private choice than to pro-union legislation, rulings, and orders handed down by way of legislative choice. Membership in both private- and public-sector unions has not grown steadily but in leaps following specific changes in public policy. Even at the peak of union membership strength in 1953, 75 percent of the labor force was nonunion. Today, 83 percent is nonunion and the proportion continues to rise. Organized labor has never been synonymous with labor in the United States, despite all the careless talk to the contrary.

The history of U.S. labor law and unionism puts the current troubles of the unions in perspective. Their problems do not seriously impair the ability of well-placed unions to impose their will in their industries, as evidenced by the 10-day strikes by the United Automobile Workers (UAW) against the General Motors Corporation in 1984 and the Chrysler Corporation in 1985. The fundamentals of pro-union collective-bargaining laws have remained intact. Unions have had their ups and downs in the past and they have suffered some unfavorable legal rulings in recent years, but unions remain a potent force both in the marketplace and in politics (Kirkland, 1986).

Unions and Ideas

Along with increasing public attention to the changing labor relations, there has been a dramatic revival of interest in labor unions by the academic community, especially among economists. In the 1930s and 1940s, "the labor problem" was the most popular area for scholarly studies in applied economics, but beginning in the 1950s it became a neglected portion of the research agenda in economics, largely abandoned to institutionalists and industrial relations specialists. In the late 1940s, for example, economist Kenneth E. Boulding (1949, p. 52) said that everywhere he turned he found labor economists and industrial relations specialists jumping

9

up and down on what they thought was the corpse of supply and demand, proclaiming, "The labor market is dead, long live human relations."

The renewed interest of modern economists in unions began in the late 1970s. New books, scholarly research, and journals now abound. Instead of dampening enthusiasm for the topic, the ongoing deunionization of America has raised both questions and research money that attract serious economists to the issues of unions and collective bargaining. Major shifts in U.S. labor relations raise fundamental questions about unions and labor legislation, including the impact of unions on the ability of American workers to compete in a global economy.

The remaining years of this century are crucial to the future of unionism and collective bargaining because what counts for unions is not so much where they are as where they are going. Unions really cannot tolerate a sustained period of membership decline because it produces an adverse psychological aura. Employees in nonunion firms are reluctant to unionize if unions continue to decline in their old areas of strength. A dwindling minority also looks more and more like a labor elite. Its claims, demands, and stridency begin to look increasingly like the pleas of a narrow interest group rather than the demands of labor. Organized labor's image as a special-interest group has made a public endorsement by the AFL-CIO more of a political curse than a blessing in many political circles. Unions appear to be on a slippery slope, akin to their decline in the late 1920s and early 1930s.

Why did unions arrive at this situation? The ultimate answer lies in the realm of ideas. Toward the end of the 19th century, the world began to receive the ideas of unionism sympathetically; these sympathies eventually found their way into labor law. Collectivist ideas generally triumphed among intellectuals in the 20th century and thereby transformed government policy; labor law followed the same pattern. Writers as diverse as David Hume, John Maynard Keynes, and Friedrich A. Hayek have pointed out that all governments rule by public opinion. In the long run, public opinion is guided by the active intellectuals. Ideas are crucial in sustaining the legitimacy of any institution, and their potency can scarcely be exaggerated in the case of labor unions and pro-union government interventions. The ability of unions to win economic concessions

10

and maintain their privileges rests on community acceptance of the idea of labor as an underdog and unions as benefactors of society.

The key idea sustaining acceptance of adversarial unions, their techniques, and their government support is the belief that they help working people to get their fair share of the economic pie. Dignity in the workplace and better wages, hours, and other conditions are supposed to be the social benefits that unions deliver. Unions and their allies in academia, the press, and government bureaus constantly appeal to our best instincts, arguing that unions help the underdog. An articulate segment of opinion continues to believe in what is called labor's disadvantage, that popular if unverified inequality in bargaining power between labor and capital that unions allegedly remedy. Public support for the New Deal labor legislation that continues to frame employer-employee relations rests on a belief that pro-union rules rectify a labor-market imbalance so as to create a level playing field on which labor and capital can fight it out more fairly. While many economists steeped in the analysis of exchange for mutual advantage find the doctrine of the oppressed worker a myth, the myth's political acceptance undergirds all modern systems of government interference in labor markets.

Unions remain controversial private organizations in American society, despite 200 years of experience with them and more than 50 years of federal protection of unions and collective bargaining. As Douglas V. Brown and Charles A. Meyers (1962, p. 17) have stated, "Basically, we are impressed by what seems to have been before 1930, and what seems to exist today, a feeling of 'unease' in the presence of unions on the part of large segments of the population." Why? Probably because it is hard to shake the ideas that (1) unions are adversarial rather than cooperative organizations, and (2) unions harm productivity and U.S. competitiveness.

If union power means control over the supply of labor, it always poses serious questions for public policy. How far can unionists go in interfering with the peaceful activities of other people? Under a system that put unions and union members on the same legal footing as the rest of us, their special privileges would disappear and only competitive (nonmonopoly) unionism would exist.

The use of force in labor disputes is a chronic problem for public policy, but this and other issues surrounding unionism ultimately collapse to the central economic question of this study: Do adversarial unions and their actions improve the standard of living for working people as a whole, especially the conditions of the poor? If rational thought demonstrates that the answer is no—that unions cannot raise the general standard of living or help the poor—and if the public were to accept this conclusion, then all the ingenuity that legislators, jurists, and bureaucrats have demonstrated in helping unions would dissolve. Economists long ago recognized that the question of whether or not unions help labor is primarily a matter of discovering the overall impact of unions on the productivity and efficiency of the economy. If unions reduce or hamper the growth of real national income, all the redistributive effort of unions is unlikely to offset the decline in wage income suffered by the working population in general and the poor in particular.

The impact of unions on productivity is an area of basic agreement among economists, despite superficial appearances to the contrary. For 200 years, economists have argued that the actions of unions do not raise the standard of living for working people as a whole, although their reasons for so arguing have changed over time. Most of the quarrel has been over how much unions *reduce* national output. Even Adam Smith, in a muddled treatment of unions, thought they could be tolerated but in no way should they be encouraged or granted special privileges.

The standard economic view has long been that unions hamper national production for the same reasons that other anti-competitive producer combinations do: they restrict the supply of labor services in their markets, distort the structure of relative labor prices, and induce misallocations of productive resources. Unions also limit managerial flexibility on the job, oppose new technology, compel excessive use of labor (so-called featherbedding or overmanning), foster adversarial attitudes, and disrupt production through strikes, strike threats, and other tactics that leave bitterness in their wake.

Within the economics profession, the major dissenting voices on this view come from Harvard University. In a celebrated book entitled *What Do Unions Do?* labor economists Richard B. Freeman and James L. Medoff (1984) claim that unions increase productivity through their collective-voice/institutional-response role. They conclude that "unionism on net probably raises social efficiency, and that if it lowers it, it does so by minuscule amounts except in rare circumstances" (p. 247). They argue that unions, on balance, increase

12

productivity within unionized enterprises (not necessarily in the economy as a whole) by reducing labor turnover, enhancing worker morale and cooperation, providing an efficient collective voice in negotiating workplace characteristics and grievance resolution, and pressuring management into stricter efficiency. The work of Freeman and Medoff and that of many others receives attention in the chapters that follow. Suffice it to say here that the theory and evidence from Freeman and Medoff are unconvincing.

The Plan of the Book

Understanding the impact of unions on U.S. economic performance calls for investigation by nondogmatic methods, not ideological disputation. In particular, estimating the economic impact of U.S. unions requires a counterfactual, so chapter 2 specifies an alternative legal regime to replace the labor codes that rule labor relations today.

Chapters 3 and 4 discuss productivity and the sources of economic growth in order to place unions within the proper general context. Specifically, chapter 3 states the 10 principles of productivity and summarizes the theory of production. Chapter 4 describes how productivity is measured and analyzes the U.S. growth experience.

Chapter 5 estimates the union-nonunion wage differential and analyzes the impact of these wage distortions on national output. Chapter 6 looks at the wage inflexibility introduced by unions and estimates the cost of this form of price rigidity. Chapter 7 studies work rules and absenteeism at unionized work sites and estimates the nationwide expense.

Chapter 8 studies the cost of strikes and the direct expense of administering the strike-threat system. It focuses on the 1981 air traffic controllers' strike and the 1983 and 1986 American Telephone & Telegraph Company (AT&T) strikes. Chapter 9 examines the debate among economists over the Harvard school's contention that unions raise rather than harm productivity. The chapter also considers the impact of unions on dynamic change, investment, and entrepreneurship. Chapter 10 analyzes unions by output sector in the U.S. economy. The automobile industry receives special attention. The chapter also looks at the international evidence to see if unionism lowers national output in other countries too. Finally, chapter 11 summarizes the evidence and presents a numerical tally of the cost of American unionism. The chapter also returns to the key policy issue: the legal treatment of unions and their actions.

II. The Legal Privileges and Immunities of Labor Unions

> It is the system of government, the situation in which they are placed, that I mean to censure; not the character of those who have acted in it.
>
> —Adam Smith, *The Wealth of Nations*

> The federal labor laws as a whole appear to have a remarkable consistency and intelligibility when viewed as a legal regime for fostering (though not to the maximum possible extent) the cartelization of labor markets.
>
> —Richard A. Posner, "Some Economics of Labor Law"

We live in an era of deregulation.[1] In telecommunications, trucking, railroads, financial services, airlines, oil and gas, advertising in the professions, and perhaps other industries to come, the straitjacket of government regulation has been loosened. Price and service competition have progressively increased in the newly freed markets, much to the benefit of consumers. Long-distance airfares have fallen by 50 percent, the price of trading common stocks has fallen by 70 percent, and truck-load rates are lower than they were in 1980. Perhaps less noticed have been the efficiency and employment gains in these industries. In the airline industry, for example, productivity increased 20 percent between 1981 and 1983 (U.S. Department of Labor 1985b) and airline employment shot up 100,000 between 1983 and 1985, by far the largest two-year gain in history. Deregulated industries offer a growing array of new products and services.

If product markets can be deregulated, so can markets for labor services and other factors of production. The current wave of dereg-

---

[1] This chapter is based on Reynolds (1986a). For a more detailed analysis of the Norris-LaGuardia, Wagner, Taft-Hartley, and Landrum-Griffin acts, see Reynolds (1984a), especially chapter 5.

ulation is a promising environment in which to rethink the fundamentals of regulation in all areas of the modern administrative state.
Of all the interventions wrought by the New Deal, none is a better
candidate for reexamination than the National Labor Relations Act
of 1935. This law, popularly known as the Wagner Act, is the
centerpiece of a vast labor code that has grown up outside the
common law.

To appreciate the extent of the regulatory and bureaucratic rules
that govern labor relations, we need only look at the Decisions and
Orders of the National Labor Relations Board, a series occupying
more than 50 feet of shelf space and over 400,000 pages. Has this
effort by the National Labor Relations Board (NLRB) brought tranquility and order to labor markets? The answer is no. The NLRB's
Annual Report for 1979 (NLRB 1979, p. 1) understated the situation
when it declared, "The uninterrupted growth of the NLRB case
load underscores that the field of labor relations in the United States
remains controversial and volatile, an area of national importance
and concern, forty-four years after the labor relations statute was
enacted and the Labor Board established."

Labor policy can move in any of three directions from the current
situation. It can retain the status quo, impose stronger federal controls, or move toward deregulating labor markets.

The threefold purpose of this chapter is to (1) describe and analyze
the legal privileges and immunities that current labor law grants to
unions, (2) suggest that these privileges be repealed (deregulation),
and (3) postulate deregulation and the resulting demise of monopoly unions as a counterfactual.

The analysis may seem radical because the status quo exerts a
powerful influence and unions long ago identified themselves with
the social interest. Nevertheless, on its merits, deregulation is superior to continuing down the path of the last 50 years or imposing
more federal control on labor relations. This conclusion follows
whether the criterion of choice is justice, liberty, equality of income,
or general prosperity. The ultimate goal should be repeal of all the
special-interest legislation supporting unions and restoration of the
rule of law in labor relations. The common law has the crucial
properties of generality, impartiality, and predictability that labor
legislation does not: "A free field and no favor," as Woodrow
Wilson summed it up in a phrase then common in the sporting

16

world. Indeed, repeal would weaken the power of unions with favorable results for the economy and freedom.

Privileges and Immunities

Privileges grant special prerogatives (or rights) as peculiar advantages or favors to particular persons, classes, or groups at the expense of others. Immunities relieve particular persons, special classes, or groups from the duties and obligations required by law of other people. In other words, privileges are positive acts conferred by the state on behalf of favored groups, whereas immunities exempt favored persons from legal obligations (negative privileges). Legal privileges and immunities traditionally have been regarded as repugnant, but as Roscoe Pound (1958, p. 122) observed, "because of a deep-seated feature of human nature they have been a fairly constant phenomenon in legal history."

The unsavory character of privileges and immunities stems from their obvious violation of the principle of equality before the law, their partiality, and their arbitrariness. The statue of Justice—with its blindfold, scales, and sword—peeks and plays favorites. Some observers would claim that any law that is not intended to apply impersonally to everyone cannot be a worthy law. Others would not be so uncompromising, although sharing the community's skepticism about privilege and immunity.

The current privileges and immunities of labor unions are of such long standing that they have come to be taken for granted. In fact, the privileges are so extensive that it is hard to sum them up with both economy and accuracy. In a characteristically blunt assessment, economist Ludwig von Mises (1922, p. 435), years before the New Deal ushered in the modern era of labor law, said: "The long and short of trade union rights is in fact the right to proceed against the strikebreaker with primitive violence, and this right the workers have successfully maintained." Mises and a handful of other writers such as W. H. Hutt, Henry C. Simons, and Sylvester Petro have emphasized that threats and violence are involved in making strikes effective. To convince buyers (that is, managers and ultimately their customers) to pay more than necessary for labor services, trade unions must induce most if not all labor suppliers to withhold their services.

This is an inherently unpromising task, especially in a market

17

economy with 4.5 million firms employing labor on the demand side and 118 million people in the civilian labor force on the supply side. Unions implicitly ask the unemployed and other outsiders to abstain from competition so that strikers can be subsequently overpaid for their services. This unattractive situation needs considerable propaganda to be sold; therefore, unions invest heavily in hoopla about solidarity, the moral duty of everyone to respect union picket lines, the evils of undercutting union demands, and the subhumans they label as scabs and union-busters. The mystique fails to convince everyone, however, so vandalism and violence usually lurk in the background of labor disputes. Among those to be ostracized are former strikers who return to work before the union leaders give their approval.

In 1958, two decades after the New Deal transformation of labor relations law, Roscoe Pound (1958, p. 145), former dean of the Harvard Law School, wrote as follows:

> The substantially general privileges and immunities of labor unions and their members and officials [are] to commit wrongs to person and property, to interfere with the use of highways, to break contracts, to deprive individuals of the means of earning a livelihood, to control the activities of the individual workers and their local organizations by national organizations centrally and arbitrarily administered beyond the reach of state laws, and to misuse trust funds—things which no one else can do with impunity.[2]

Sen. Barry Goldwater summed up the privileges of unions in an address to the American Bar Association in 1962. What the following list loses in complexity and subtlety, it gains in basic truth (see Reynolds 1984a, p. 265):

1. Almost total immunity under antitrust laws.
2. Immunity from taxation.
3. Ability to use union funds for purposes not directly related to collective bargaining, even if union dues are compulsory

---

[2]Pound also emphasized the fact that labor unions persistently and successfully resisted suggestions that they be incorporated. As unincorporated associations, unions are unsuable or, if they are suable, enforcement of the judgment is complicated and a doubtful remedy. Although unions occasionally lose in civil damage suits, there are chronic problems in suing unincorporated associations and applying the "implied authorization," or doctrine of agency, to the acts of union officials and members. For more on this issue, see Reynolds (1984a, p. 285).

(a less clear privilege today than in 1962 owing to subsequent court decisions).

4. Immunity from injunction by federal courts.
5. Power to compel employees to pay union dues as a condition of keeping their jobs.
6. Power to represent all employees in a bargaining unit, no matter how small the majority of those voting and including those compelled to join and those denied membership.
7. Power to compel employers to bargain in good faith with "certified" union officials.
8. Power to deny membership to employees in a bargaining unit.
9. Power to compel employers to make their private property available for use by union officials.
10. Comparative immunity from payment of damages for personal and property injury inflicted on anyone by union members engaged in strikes, picketing, and other tactics in disputes.
11. Power to strike for objectives not related to a collective-bargaining dispute.
12. Power to examine an employer's books and records, including confidential data on costs, earnings, and prices.
13. Relative immunity from state labor law under the doctrine of federal preemption.

While the summaries offered by Mises, Pound, and Goldwater suggest the nature of the privileges of unions, precision demands that we examine the details to confirm their analyses. Consider the Norris-LaGuardia Anti-Injunction Act, signed by President Hoover on March 23, 1932, after it had passed the House of Representatives by a vote of 363 to 13 and the Senate by 75 to 5. It was the culmination of a 50-year campaign against government by injunction.

The threefold purpose of the act was to (1) declare nonunion agreements (so-called yellow-dog contracts) unenforceable in U.S. courts (section 3); (2) relieve labor organizations from liability for wrongful acts under antitrust law (sections 4 and 5); and (3) give unions immunity from private damage suits and nullify the equity powers of federal courts in labor disputes (sections 7 through 12). The overriding object of the act was to allow unions to be freer of the constraints that bind businessmen and everyone else, thereby allowing unions more latitude to use their aggressive tactics. An immediate result was that the number of strikes suddenly doubled between 1932 and 1933 to 1,695 and then continued climbing to a 1930s peak of 4,740 in 1937. This was during a period of deep depression and massive unemployment—conditions that normally diminish strike activity.

During the 1920s and 1930s, it was widely and mistakenly believed that high wages caused prosperity (the reverse is true) and interventionists mistakenly regarded wage and price deflation as the causes of the depression, rather than recognizing it as the only method by which to restore employment and income after monetary deflation. Among the wage- and price-boosting interventions (sustaining unsold goods and unemployment), the National Industrial Recovery Act—the New Deal system of industry codes intended to push up prices throughout the economy—was struck down by the Supreme Court in the *Schecter Poultry* case of 1935 on the grounds that the act had delegated virtually unlimited legislative power to the president. Congress then adopted almost identical labor regulations in the 1930s, piece by piece, in surviving legislation such as Walsh-Healey and the Fair Labor Standards Act. The most famous and important example, however, was the National Labor Relations Act of 1935 (Wagner Act), which was a rewrite of the NIRA's section 7a. The act passed by a 63–12 vote in the Senate and an unrecorded voice vote in the House, and it was signed by President Roosevelt on July 5, 1935.

The Wagner Act declared that the labor policy of the U.S. government is encouragement of the practice and procedure of collective bargaining, as well as protection of worker designation of representatives to negotiate terms and conditions of employment. All federal legislation tends to announce high-minded goals, but in the case of this particular intervention, a more apt description would be that it basically used federal power to make it easier (less expensive) to impose unionization on enterprises and employees in the private sector who would otherwise not participate in unionization and collective bargaining. The main regulatory features of the act were:

1. Creation of a political board, the National Labor Relations Board, to enforce the act.
2. Restrictions on employer resistance to unionization by specifying "unfair labor practices" by employers.

3. NLRB enforcement of majority elections for union representation.
4. NLRB determination of eligible voters.
5. NLRB enforcement of exclusive (monopoly) bargaining rights for certified representatives.
6. NLRB enforcement of union pay scales for all represented employees, whether union members or not.

In April 1937, the Supreme Court declared the Wagner Act constitutional by a 5–4 vote in the midst of Roosevelt's famous threat to pack the Court. The Wagner Act decisions marked the judiciary's general abandonment of constitutional protection of economic rights and economic due process.

Subsequent federal legislation to modify the Wagner Act—principally the Labor-Management Relations Act (Taft-Hartley Labor Act) in 1947 and the Labor-Management Reporting and Disclosure Act (Landrum-Griffin) Act in 1959—has not been so favorable to unions, but this can be exaggerated. Neither law tampered with the basic privileges supplied to labor organizations. As legal scholar Richard A. Epstein (1983, p. 1386) says, Taft-Hartley was a partial union victory because it kept the original structure of the statutes, making it more difficult to return to the rules of common law. Government regulation expanded to deal with some of the effects of union power, largely created by privileges and immunities. This is a familiar pattern in regulatory behavior because once monopoly rents (that is, transfers of income caused by intervention) are created and enforced by government (through tariffs, marketing orders, licensing, and a wide range of redistributions), the tendency is to dissipate rents in response to pressures by aggrieved groups. The ad hoc balancing of interests displaces protections of universal rights.

To illustrate the immunities of unions, consider section 602a of the Landrum-Griffin Act:

> It shall be unlawful to carry on picketing on or about the premises of any employer for the purpose of, or as part of any conspiracy or in furtherance of any plan or purpose for, the personal profit or enrichment of any individual (except a bona fide increase in wages or other employee benefits) by taking or obtaining any money or other thing of value from such employer against his will or without his consent.

The parenthetical exclusion speaks volumes about the nature of the privileges for unions since 1930.

The Wagner Act declared five employer activities "unfair labor practices." Among the employer options declared unfair in the Wagner Act, section 8(a)(2), is "to dominate or interfere with the formation or administration of any labor organization or contribute financial or other support to it." This restriction spelled the demise of most independent or so-called company unions, relieving unions of an effective competitor. During the 1920s and early 1930s, there were nearly 1,000 employee-representation plans and company unions, with a total of more than 1.5 million members. As labor historian Philip Taft (1964, p. 454) wrote, "These organizations [company unions] were not always initiated by management, and frequently employees themselves took steps to prevent the forming of outside organizations." Independent unions generally did not use force or take to the streets; section 8(a)(2) of the Wagner Act eliminated an option for interested employees and companies.

The Wagner Act does not expressly compel employers to reach an agreement with a labor representative, but their right to refuse is attenuated by the fact that they are obligated to "bargain in good faith" with union officials, a phrase interpreted by the political appointees of the National Labor Relations Board. To illustrate how the statute operates in practice, the Supreme Court ruled that in-plant food prices and services are mandatory subjects of bargaining, even if the food operation is operated by a third party (*Ford Motor v. NLRB*, 1979). Justice Byron R. White, writing for the Court, said that although "disputes over food prices are likely to be frequent and intense," national labor policy supported the conclusion that "more, not less, collective bargaining is the remedy" (quoted in Reynolds 1984a, p. 109).

Legislators and jurists have preserved the facade of law but have exempted unions from many of the rules that apply to other individuals and groups, thereby writing a fascinating chapter in the story of human affairs. A conspicuous example is the treatment of labor violence under the federal anti-extortion statutes. The Anti-Racketeering Act of 1934 proscribed the exaction of valuable consideration by force, violence, or coercion in matters of interstate commerce, "not including, however, the payment of wages by a bona-fide employer to a bona-fide employee." Congress tried to exempt unions from the federal prohibitions on coercion because organized labor feared that the term "coercion" might be applied to its traditional tactics, such as striking and picketing, that were intended to compel employers to recognize the union, pay union wage rates, or cease hiring nonunion workers.

In the *Teamsters Local 807* decision (1942), however, the Supreme Court was called upon to clarify the boundaries of organized labor's immunity. The defendant Teamsters met trucks as they entered New York City and used threats and violence to obtain the equivalent of a day's wages for driving and unloading the trucks within the city. In some cases, the defendant unionists performed partial work for full payment, but in many instances, they did no work at all. In more tortured language than in the act itself, the Court virtually emasculated the act as a check on union violence. To put it bluntly, the Court embraced the idea that the end justifies the means. The Court declared: "The history of labor disputes is studded with violence which unhappily is not yet obsolete; but, although the means employed may be the same as those here condemned, the end is always different, for it is to secure work on better terms" (Haggard and Thieblot 1983, p. 250).

The congressional reaction to the *Teamsters Local 807* decision was swift and negative, culminating in the 1945 Hobbs Act amendment to the Anti-Racketeering Act of 1934. Congress rewrote the 1934 law and took pains to eliminate the specific language on which the Supreme Court had based its decision. Judicial reluctance to apply the Hobbs Act to union violence continued to surface, however, culminating in *U.S.* v. *Enmons* (1973). The defendants were indicted for firing high-powered rifles at three utility company transformers, draining the oil from a company transformer, and blowing up a transformer substation owned by the company—all in the pursuit of higher wages and other benefits from the company. The district court dismissed the indictment on the grounds that the Hobbs Act did not prohibit the use of violence to obtain legitimate union objectives. On appeal, the Supreme Court upheld the ruling, saying "the [Hobbs] Act does not apply to the use of force to achieve legitimate labor ends" (410 U.S. at 401). The decision clearly distorted the legislative history of the Hobbs Act to justify the opinion, irritating Justice William O. Douglas, who wrote in his dissent: "At times, the legislative history of a measure is so clouded or obscure that we must perforce give some meaning to vague words. But where, as here, the consensus of the House is so clear, we should carry out its purpose no matter how distasteful or undesirable that policy may be to us" (410 U.S. at 418).

Why Unions Obtained Privileges and Immunities

Why did the political community adopt these labor policies? Political opinion had drifted a long way from the view of unions and their tactics as being antisocial toward a theory of unions as being an appropriate vehicle of worker self-help. Eventually, circumstances and politicians combined to support unionism and collective bargaining through the force of law. Ultimately, what counts is not strike threats, picket lines, boycotts, and union political spending but what people believe about unions and their impact. Unions constantly appeal to the public's best instincts, arguing that unions help the underdog.

A combination of interest-group politics, misguided idealism, and a belief in the erroneous purchasing-power doctrine led to the labor legislation of the 1930s. Labor unions historically were difficult to organize and sustain in the United States because of the various obstacles to cartelization: large numbers of people on both the demand and supply sides of labor markets, ease of entry and exit, high turnover, high mobility, geographic dispersion, active resistance among firms and workers, and differences of opinion about collectivism and the use of force. The courts also tended to restrict such union tactics as threats, violence, and interference with voluntary trade; unionists, therefore, were prominent demanders of government privilege, and they mounted persistent political campaigns for pro-union legislation.

Prior to World War I, unions had relatively little to show for their political activism. Organized labor had agitated for anti-injunction legislation and exemption from antitrust laws since 1880. As early as 1896, the Democratic party platform included a plank that denounced labor injunctions and supported restrictions on the courts. Edwin Witte (1932, p. 266) described it: "The virtual partnership of organized labor with the Democratic party continued through the congressional elections of 1910 and the Presidential elections of 1912 and led to the enactment of the Clayton Act in 1914." The Clayton

24

Antitrust Act exempted worker cartels from the Sherman Antitrust Act, restricted the use of injunctions in labor disputes, and provided that picketing and similar union activities were not unlawful. However, judicial rulings quickly neutralized the pro-union provisions of this legislation.

World War I was pivotal for government policy toward unions (as described in chapter 1). The national emergency provided much of the experience and precedent for subsequent labor legislation, as well as other cartel-like policies. The federal measures compelling firms to negotiate with unions ended after wartime orders were completed, and the labor market was deregulated through a return to the comparative neutrality of the rules of common law.

During the 1920s, anti-injunction bills and other legislation favored by unionists and their academic supporter, did not succeed in Congress, state legislatures, or the courts, despite persistent effort. More ambitious peacetime interventions, such as the Wagner Act, were politically unthinkable until the onset of the Great Depression and the National Industrial Recovery Act. Even in the midst of the Depression, the Wagner Act faced significant opposition and was widely believed to be unconstitutional at the time it was passed, especially after the Supreme Court struck down the National Industrial Recovery Act. Some senators who voted for the Wagner bill wanted to avoid antagonizing the AFL at the polls and expected the Court to nullify the act. The special nature of political conditions in the 1930s is highlighted by the swing of the political pendulum against additional legislative benefits for unionism beginning late in that decade. State legislatures began to adopt restrictive measures to control union actions, Congress passed the Hobbs amendment to include labor violence in the Anti-Racketeering Act, and Congress passed the Taft-Hartley Labor Act over a presidential veto only 12 years after the Wagner Act.

The Normative Case for Repeal

Once the privileges and immunities of labor unions have been summarized, the case for repeal is almost self-evident. Nevertheless, we should explicitly judge the desirability of repealing the privileges of unions by four standards: justice, liberty, equality of income, and general prosperity.

25

Justice

There is no universally shared standard of what constitutes the just and the unjust, but a dictionary definition refers to "the assignment of merited rewards or punishment." Friedrich A. Hayek (1976, ch. 8), among others, argues that the true rules of justice are predominantly negative. They forbid unjust conduct rather than specify what is to be considered just conduct. In the administration of criminal justice, perhaps we come closest to a consensus: people guilty of serious violence and coercion against the rights of others should be punished. It is unfair (unjust) to allow users of private coercion to escape the costs of their aggression while those with the moral character to restrain themselves from committing crimes suffer as victims. Injustice is the Darwinian jungle; the strong plunder the weak, and the advantages of peaceful cooperation and personal security evaporate.

Current arrangements allow unions to violate justice as defined here. The means—the tactics—used by unions to pursue their ends are defective; their tactics cannot pass the Kantian universalization test. A preeminent product of liberal Western thought is the conclusion that means must be evaluated on their own, that they tend to determine ends—indeed, that the means are the ultimate ends. As Milton Friedman (1962, p. 22) wrote: "To deny that the end justifies the means is indirectly to assert that the end in question is not the ultimate end, that the ultimate end is itself the use of proper means. . . . To the liberal the appropriate means are free discussion and voluntary cooperation."

Unions are pressure groups. Given their privileged status, too many of them rely on coercion or threat of coercion as a last resort. Compulsory union dues are common, but union coercion goes further. All union negotiations involve the thinly disguised question "Do you want to preserve labor peace?"

Consider the United Mine Workers of America (UMW), for example. Mining coal has always been dangerous, dirty work done by generally strong and rough employees. The UMW still relies on dynamite and intimidation to coerce acceptance of the union's demands. Unionized mines do not try to operate during a strike, so most of the violence is directed at nonunion employees (many of whom are intensely anti-union), nonunion mines, and rival labor organizations. During the 1981 strike, for example, nonunion

26

miners and mine operators armed themselves or shut down their operations for the duration of the strike. Truck convoys used lead trucks with five-foot-long magnets to sweep up nails and spikes on the road. When UMW ambushes and gun battles broke out, Governor John Y. Brown of Kentucky adopted a policy of what he termed strict neutrality, declaring, "We're not going to camp on one side or the other" (Haggard and Thieblot 1983, p. 114). This would have been seen by the public as an incredible statement by a governor, sworn to uphold the law, in any violence-laden context except a labor dispute. A nonunion operator protested, "The concept of neutrality toward breaking the law is not found in any statute or practice in our society" (Haggard and Thieblot, p. 116).

Within broad limits, government officials in many parts of the country do little to protect law-abiding citizens and their property from union threats because of the belief that their inaction helps labor. A century of intellectual effort has promoted the idea that the noble purposes of unionists justify their means. If A threatens to strike B on the head with a baseball bat to take $20 from B's wallet, it is a crime. However, if A is an organized worker wielding the bat on the picket line to prevent B—legally hired to fill a position voluntarily abandoned by A—from peacefully going to work, then the NLRB and the courts often declare it "picket line horseplay" or "exuberance short of coercion," despite the fact that access to employment opportunities is worth thousands of dollars to B. Sometimes B is a former striker.

The shadowy privilege of unions to threaten or use violence is the only important instance of the state failing to jealously guard its monopoly on coercion, as F. A. Hayek has pointed out. Union privileges and immunities violate the three ideals embodied in the statue of Justice—the blindfold, scales, and sword—because Justice peeks, tips the scales in favor of unions, and allows them to initiate violence.

Liberty

Freedom or liberty is another disputed concept. For present purposes, liberty is the state of being free of arbitrary or despotic controls imposed by other people. It is the opposite of slavery; it is the right to do as one pleases, provided that one does not actively interfere with the equal rights of others to do as they wish. Liberty is not license, because one must respect the equal rights of others; nor is it anarchy, because the state is entitled to suppress the private use of aggression and to enforce voluntarily arrived-at contracts. The rules of common law are based on this intellectual orientation in favor of individual rights, limited government, and the maximization of private autonomy.

By this definition of liberty, federal labor regulations clearly threaten liberty. Regulation, in fact, may be defined as a foreclosure of options imposed upon a market by political authorities. Restrictions on the liberty of employers are obvious; they include infringements on their First Amendment rights of free speech, their right to offer higher wage rates to their employees (for example, during a union organization drive), their right to participate in a company-sponsored labor organization, and more generally, their human right to employ people on whatever terms both parties can agree on in the unhampered marketplace. Similarly, regulation prevents employees from accepting voluntary, private arrangements that would otherwise be available for the mutual benefit of both themselves and their employers. Human rights, properly understood, are symmetrical.

These consequences of labor legislation, given the above working definition of liberty, are incontestable. Defenders of the status quo can argue, however, that the reductions in freedom are small (somehow measured) and are a worthwhile (but to whom?) trade off in terms of other improvements, especially a purported gain in equality of bargaining power and worker dignity. Putting aside the validity of such claims for the moment, the argument must be recognized as a form of social engineering. Labor relations are deliberately directed by the state, driven by the belief that workers benefit, into a form that would not have evolved through voluntary arrangements. Have employees materially benefited from these forced arrangements? The answer is in the negative, as established in this volume.

Equality of Income

Have labor unions succeeded in helping the underdog? There are strong reasons to doubt it. Unions are out to help themselves. Although unions may give the impression that they are mostly made up of disadvantaged workers and hospital orderlies fighting

28

for social justice, unions have always been disproportionately composed of well-placed and highly paid workers in mining, construction, printing, manufacturing, trucking, telephone service, and so on. Contrary to popular impression, unions did not originate among the lowest wage earners but among high-income crafts.

To the extent that unions are successful, they redistribute income toward their members, who are predominantly white, male, and well paid, at the expense of consumers as a whole, taxpayers, nonunion workers, the poor, and the unemployed—groups with lower average incomes than union members. While the unions' policy of a standard wage for each job tends to even up wage rates among union members (although diminishing employee incentives for productivity), this effect is unlikely to offset the overall disequalizing tendency of union wage effects.

H. Gregg Lewis (1986) has pointed out that we cannot observe what wage dispersion would be in the absence of monopoly unionism because we have had it for the last 50 years, thereby distorting wage distributions in both union and nonunion sectors. Nor can we infer the impact of unionism on overall dispersion by fitting wage equations. From a long-run theoretical point of view, greater competition and mobility in labor markets allows labor suppliers to pursue their highest-yielding opportunities with fewer market barriers such as unions. In the long run, this set of conditions tends to expand total output and diminish inequalities as well. As economist W. H. Hutt has put it, "The effect of competition among workers in different fields, if it had been unrestrained, would have led to far more people in the higher paid kinds of work and far fewer in the lower paid kinds of work" (quoted in Reynolds 1985a, p. 320). This effect is increasingly visible in the deregulated industries, such as the airlines, in which new firms have dramatically widened the employment opportunities for people previously shut out of unionized labor markets. Unions help the so-called ins, not the outs.

General Prosperity

Much of this book explores our knowledge about the effects of unions on the standard of living for working people as a whole. Briefly, the adversarial unions favored by the current legal regime reduce prosperity by reducing real output, although the empirical magnitude of this effect is uncertain. Union pricing, work rules, strikes, and other tactics reduce output and employment, especially over the business cycle; unions, therefore, spread poverty.

The Consequences of Repeal

All advocates believe that the good effects of their prescriptions outweigh the bad effects, and I am no different. Repeal is not only a relevant counterfactual but is meritorious because there is no sound reason to grant privileges to labor unions. As Richard A. Epstein (1983, p. 1362) has written, "There is no solid moral case for treating union members, as such, as the favored class of wealth redistribution." The present framework is defective beyond repair. It would be a mistake to build on the present structure in an attempt to outlaw unions or repress them in any special way. This would only reinforce their underdog image and sense of paranoia, would be contrary to the idea of a society of free individuals, and would be ineffective or counterproductive in practice, as demonstrated by the futility of the Taft-Hartley and Landrum-Griffin acts.

Deregulation is the answer, either piecemeal or wholesale. For example, I have proposed that the method of section 14b of the Taft-Hartley Labor Act—which allows state governments to prohibit compulsory union membership as a condition of employment (so-called right-to-work laws)—be expanded to allow states to pass laws that would permit employers and employees to cooperate, together, in labor organizations. This modest change would remove the straitjacket of federal policy and allow a wider variety of labor organizations to compete for the favor of employees. In fact, a major difficulty with the present labor-representation industry is the concentration of membership in huge unions, with rivalry among them suppressed. Today, more than 90 percent of union membership is in fewer than 50 industrywide unions with over 100,000 members each, and decision-making power is vested in national union officials. The five largest unions alone have 34 percent of union membership.

From a productivity point of view, greater regulatory freedom would allow more companies to discover superior forms of labor relations instead of concentrating on tactics least likely to play into the hands of troublemakers. The success and productivity of many Japanese companies, for example, partly rest on their freedom to develop team spirit through employee organizations without the

30

handicap of militant unions. If company unions were legalized in some states, more firms and employees would experiment with such policies. U.S. history shows that some employees would like to join an employee association based on the idea of cooperation rather than the familiar cycle of warfare-truce-warfare. Diversity among the states gradually would develop evidence about the relative effectiveness of different labor policies. Employees and companies could relocate if substantial differences occurred, and state legislatures could reconsider their decisions as time passed. Such experimentation in labor law would contribute to growth in income and jobs.

The ultimate aim, however, would be wholesale repeal and abolition of all the labor legislation supporting bilateral labor monopoly in the private and public sectors. This recommendation includes getting rid of the Railway Labor Act of 1926, the Norris-LaGuardia Act, the Wagner Act as amended, and their compulsory-bargaining counterparts in the public sector, as well as dismantling the associated commissions, boards, executive orders, state laws, rulings, administrative orders, and regulations. Unions and their members would then be treated like everyone else under ordinary contract, tort, and criminal law. There is nothing in labor relations that cannot be successfully handled under a combination of the common law—with its traditions of generality, impartiality, and predictability in contract and tort—and the criminal law.

Doubtless there would be a period of adjustment as participants learned to cope with the new opportunities. Labor disputes would be handled in the same manner as other disputes are today rather than being given special arrangements. The number of labor disputes would decline because strong unions would shrink without their special-interest protections, deunionizing the U.S. economy faster than is already occurring. Direct access to the courts in labor disputes would reduce union use of intimidation and strong-arm tactics. Experience would gradually establish that threats and violence occur in labor disputes because of the incentives associated with the immunities accorded unionism rather than because of so-called worker alienation from capitalism.

More generally, greater diversity would develop in employer-employee relations. The details are impossible to describe because we cannot know in advance exactly how a freer labor market will evolve. The marketplace is too rich and unpredictable to be typecast, although possibilities can be suggested. Just as in the 1920s, unions and collective bargaining would not disappear but unions would be under greater competitive pressure to respond to their constituencies. A different mix of union officials would gradually emerge, with lesser representation from the adversarial and aggressive schools of thought. Nonunion companies would be free to experiment with a richer menu of personnel policies, including the participatory forms of management demanded by a well-educated work force.

In economic terms, repeal of the labor codes would undermine monopoly in labor markets and would facilitate entry into these markets. Opening previously restricted markets tends to punish the guilty and reward the innocent by releasing pressures to equalize rewards. The supracompetitive wage rates of unions would be forced to adjust to competition owing to new opportunities for nonunion workers and the unemployed. The economic pie would expand, and redistribution in favor of union officials and members would erode. There would be improvement in the flexibility of the price system and its efficiency in coordinating resource flows, in the tendency of markets to clear and to fully employ labor and capital, and in U.S. competitiveness in world markets.

A Legal Conclusion

Recent experience in deregulating product markets suggests that labor relations can be successfully deregulated and that the labor codes can be successfully replaced with the common law. There is no merit to current arrangements, which are based on the tenacious myth of labor's disadvantage and assorted misconceptions from the 1930s. The scourge of our age is the political appeasement of special-interest groups at the expense of the general public, and our labor codes are a prime exhibit. Whether the criterion is justice, liberty, equality of income, or general prosperity, the labor laws fail to promote the general interest.

The common law is not perfect, merely better than current labor regulations. Scholars in the burgeoning field of law and economics argue that the common-law process tends toward efficiency in the enforcement of rights and hence promotes efficiency in the operation of markets. This proposition rests on various arguments, including relatively disinterested judges versus interested legislators, the presence of evolutionary forces tending toward efficiency, and the numerous opportunities for correcting mistaken (inefficient) rulings.

Terminating the special labor legislation that fosters adversarial unions and the practices of collective bargaining is not anti-union. It is highly likely that alternative associations of workers and non-adversarial labor leaders have been squeezed out by the current labor regimen. Similarly, some businesses have been unable to survive the threat or fact of unionization under current labor rules.

Radical repeal may appear politically unrealistic, but political reality keeps changing in unpredictable ways. A tiny but growing band of scholars, beginning with Dan C. Heldman, James T. Bennett, and Manuel H. Johnson (1981), have been analyzing, as best as their tools allow, the impacts of government policies and the possibilities for deregulation of labor law. Further, there are signs that the nation's labor laws are the subject of a growing national debate, especially in the wake of recent NLRB rulings tilting toward employers (and therefore consumers). AFL-CIO president Lane Kirkland has suggested repeal and, in his delicate expression, letting business and unions battle it out "mano a mano." Other union officials have declared that on balance, they would be better off without the Wagner Act and the NLRB. This is mostly theater, I suspect, but I see no reason not to take them up on their generous offer. Management lawyers have been cool to the idea, claiming "union leaders would repeal only certain parts of the labor law, the ones that get in their way" (Apcar 1984). This is reminiscent of a cliché in public finance that an old tax is a good tax. The policy status quo usually is attractive for those with weak imaginations and overdeveloped skills in manipulating the present system. Meanwhile, a House subcommittee has issued a report declaring that "labor law has failed," a Reagan administration official has rejected the idea of repeal as "demagoguery," and a Senate subcommittee has reviewed the labor laws (Apcar 1984).

The efficient alternative to current policy is easy to identify in this area, but the politically attainable, as usual, is hard to forecast accurately. Nevertheless, the time seems to be approaching for a fundamental reexamination of the purposes and policies of U.S. labor laws. For example, political support has eroded for the 1931 Davis-Bacon Act, which benefits the construction unions on federally financed building projects; consequently, repeal is far from being politically impossible. The U.S. Department of Labor has proposed modifying the Wagner Act to allow some degree of union-management cooperation (Schlossberg and Fetter 1986). Events and ideas may yet compel Congress to rethink labor law.

III. The Principles of Productivity

> In economics we have sunk to such depths that statement
> of the obvious has become the first duty of thoughtful
> people.
>
> —P. T. Bauer, *Rhetoric and Reality*

> No competition, no progress.
>
> —Bela Karolyi (gymnastics coach)

Unions are but one ingredient, however important, in the complex mechanism that produces the daily flow of goods and services
in the U.S. economy. Therefore, it is essential to look at the general
principles of productivity before isolating the role of unions in the
production process.

Productivity is a fundamental concept in economics because the
primary problem in economic life is how to increase the total supply
of goods and services—how to produce more from always-limited
resources. This concept was the main issue inspiring the development of economics as a scientific discipline, especially since mass
starvation was an ever-present possibility during the 18th century.
Although economists were also interested in business cycles and
income inequality, their dominant concerns during the 18th and
19th centuries were to understand how markets work and to suggest improvements in overall efficiency. Interest in these issues
decayed for much of the 20th century, but fortunately the public,
politicians, and the profession have returned to efficiency as a prime
issue, with less emphasis on macroeconomic and distributional
issues.

From the Great Depression to the early 1970s, economists paid
relatively little attention to productivity growth in the United States.
Their attitude reflected a consensus that the U.S. economic system
had worked reasonably well to generate growth over time. Since
the mid-1970s, however, the literature on the sluggish growth of
productivity and capital formation has mushroomed (Furstenberg

1980, Feldstein 1983, Darby 1984, Baumol and McLennan 1985, and Lee 1986).

Many economists, businessmen, and politicians recognize that the United States has a high percentage of obsolete plant and equipment, a low rate of domestic saving, and a low rate of growth in productivity compared to other industrial countries. Many observers explain these productivity ills by pointing to oil-price shocks, government spending, taxation, deficits, redistribution, trade barriers, and regulation as the main culprits. These explanations have merit because they are based on the theory that obstacles to business production—natural or man made—make a nation poorer. Compared to Europe and Japan, however, the United States has an acknowledged bright spot in the form of a remarkable ability to generate new employment; since 1970, the U.S. economy has generated 32 million new jobs, raising total employment from 78 to 110 million.

Unions have not received much attention in the debate over lagging productivity growth in the United States, with the exception of occasional suggestions that unionized wage costs and work rules have handicapped the steel and automobile industries. The tendency to ignore unions as an impediment to the efficient use of resources is familiar because there is a general tendency to underestimate the role of flexible prices in coordinating economic activity and promoting economic growth. As Henry C. Simons (1944, p. 18) wrote, "Much has been made of our taxes as factors inhibiting enterprise; but their effects on this score are, I think, grossly exaggerated. . . . But the bias against new investment inherent in labor organization is important and cannot be removed by changes in matters of detail."

Labor unions remain a disharmony that keeps production, employment, and growth below their potentials. Using force to fix minimum prices for labor services harms the poorest citizens in whose name these interventions are justified. The same is true if the state grants privileges and immunities that allow unions to fix premium labor prices, thereby excluding outsiders. Total output and employment are greatest and inequalities are smallest when competitive markets freely balance supply and demand across all product and factor markets.

Ten Axioms

The public image of economists is that they do not agree on anything. George Bernard Shaw was the publicist for this idea ("If all economists were laid end to end, they would not reach a conclusion"), and economists have remained a favorite public target ever since. Economist Karl Brunner has made an important distinction about the ineffectual image that plagues economists: Just as there is a difference between what physics says and what members of the Flat Earth Society say, so there is a difference between what economics says and what some people called economists say. Shaw, it should be noted, wanted to overturn the logic of economics and, failing in that, settled for discrediting economists. Like other Fabian socialists, he found orthodox economics inconvenient.

Like other scientific disciplines, economics is based on a handful of axioms. These undisputed propositions hold for all economies— past, present, future, free-enterprise, socialist, and interventionist (mixed)—and they put many controversies into perspective, including one about the role of unions in the economy. There are 10 such principles:

1. Scarcity Exists

Scarcity is the permanent human condition, the central fact of human existence. Our wants exceed our ability to satisfy them. This fact makes it easy to point out shortcomings, or problems, in life. All of us can think of something we would like to have but do not, no matter how wealthy we may be. It is much harder, however, to think of convenient and ethical ways to remedy these situations. Human beings are the product of a long biological evolution, and our constant striving for improvement in material conditions is the unavoidable consequence of membership in a surviving species.

2. People Are Self-Interested

The world offers fresh evidence for this proposition every day. People are systematic, purposeful, or rational in their daily economic activities. Socialists denounce or deny this condition or claim they could eradicate this flaw in human beings by creating a new socialist man. Few people praise the enduring trait of self-interest, but it is the basis for our prosperity and all advances in the human condition. As Adam Smith wrote in 1776, "It is not from the benevolence of the butcher, the brewer, or the baker that we expect our dinner, but from their regard to their own interest" (Smith 1776, vol. 1, pp. 26–27).

3. People Respond to Incentives

The evidence of human response to incentives is overwhelming. Socialists praise nonmaterial incentives, but all economies have money prices for goods and services (properly speaking, exchange ratios among goods) and, therefore, necessarily have material incentives. Prices are a potent subset of all the incentives facing people because they induce them (including employers) to buy or not buy, sell or not sell, hire or lay off, produce this instead of that, consume this instead of that.

4. People Like to Consume Goods

The ultimate purpose of all economic activity is consumption. Consumers are tough-minded: all of us want the cheapest prices and highest quality we can find, and we care little about how or where the goods are produced. This fact of life explains the ruthless reputation of capitalism (the system of economic freedom), which puts the customer's interest before the producer's. The persistent economizing behavior of consumers is also a major factor in the tendency for the marketplace to equalize prices for goods and services of similar value.

5. No One Can Consume What Has Not Been Produced

Consumption precedes production only in the dictionary. Consumption or redistribution of goods can only occur if the goods already exist. Many political disputes involve which policies go farthest in raising total production (efficiency), thereby raising real incomes, especially at the bottom of the economic spectrum.

6. Production Depends on Human Effort

Someone has to labor. Although this may be a self-evident truth, it is sometimes overlooked. The silence of a factory floor on a Sunday morning verifies what happens when nobody works.

7. Output Can Be Divided into Output per Hour Times Hours

The number of hours worked multiplied by output per labor hour equals the flow of output. This proposition is an accounting identity that demonstrates that output can be expanded only by working more total hours in the economy and/or by working more productively per hour.

8. Output per Hour Depends on the Amount of Capital Equipment

As Ludwig von Mises (1963, p. 492) has put it, "We are better off than earlier generations because we are equipped with the capital goods they have accumulated for us." The fact that modern buildings and machines are productive (that is, current labor does not account for all of the value added in production) explains why capital goods command rents, just as labor services command wages. At least $25,000 is invested per employee in the corporate sector, a rough measure of how much capital exists per employee. A broader measure comes from Raymond W. Goldsmith (1982, p. 197), who valued total national assets in the United States, including all natural resources, at $21.65 trillion in 1980. This is nearly $100,000 per person, or $270,000 per household.

Labor productivity depends crucially on the amount of capital goods but also on complex factors such as the quality of the equipment; the quality, skills, and motivation of the labor force; and the efficiency with which these resources are managed. Innovations in production techniques and new products allow us to accomplish more, more comfortably, and in less time than in the past. These advances explain why labor productivity has increased sixfold over the last century, thereby freeing the vast majority of Americans from backbreaking toil and dramatically raising living standards.

9. Only Human Effort Can Maintain or Increase the Amount of Capital Equipment

Someone has to save (defer consumption) to permit investment in new machinery, structures, and inventory. Otherwise, the stock of equipment and structures, which is always decaying, cannot be sustained, much less increased. Capital formation raises the marginal productivity of labor and therefore real wages. Yet investors (capitalists) have not been politically popular throughout history, and as a result, partial and total confiscations of investment returns have occurred frequently, with predictably negative consequences for capital formation and improvement in standards of living.

10. Specialization and Exchange Are the Sources of Prosperity

If everyone were forced to live as a Robinson Crusoe, cut off from human contact, most of us would soon starve to death. The isolated, self-sufficient survivors would live in grinding poverty because they would not have access to the crucial mechanism of wealth creation: cooperation in the marketplace, coordinated by the price system. A massive breakdown of trade is properly the main worry of the doomsayers who advise us about how to survive the coming (but oft-delayed) economic catastrophe.

Specialization can be defined as the production of more of a scarce good than an individual consumes. Mr. Crusoe did not specialize until Mr. Friday showed up because only a multiperson society enables individuals to enjoy the gains from the division of labor, specialized knowledge, and large-scale production and distribution.

Exchange can be defined as trading goods and services, or, more precisely, voluntarily rearranging the property rights to own, use, and transfer goods. Trade allows individuals to specialize in producing something they are relatively good at producing and yet still buy the diverse basket of consumption goods they desire. Trade is the calculation by both parties that they can do better in the marketplace than by going it alone. The attractive ethical feature of exchange is that commerce is a form of voluntary cooperation—"You do this for me, and I'll do that for you, OK?"—service for service, just like the golden rule.

Entrepreneurs and inventors have been crucial in the wealth-creation process. As Thomas Sowell (1981, pp. 42–43) has pointed out, the poor no longer wear the secondhand rags and tatters that were common in the 19th century because a man named Singer invented the sewing machine, which allowed new clothing and shoes to be bought cheaply by the masses. Similarly, Thomas A. Edison, not political crusaders and reformers, brought light to the masses. And Henry Ford and the Wright brothers, not self-styled humanitarians and political activists, ended the isolation of communities. Kodak did more to make the man in the street aware of pictures than did all the art museums put together. Middlemen named Sears, Ward, Woolworth, and Penney organized distribution in ways that cut costs. Mass markets were created for things that people could not have otherwise afforded.

One of the greatest discoveries of the human mind, in my opinion, is that one person's gain from a trade does not imply another person's loss. On the contrary, uncoerced and informed trades (the vast majority of daily exchanges) constitute mutual agreement about the terms of trade. Both parties gain, otherwise one of the parties would not participate. This proposition is general and holds for labor exchanges too. Both parties gain in labor deals, which is not to say that both gain equally.

Few people understand this proposition. Most of the general public and opinion makers remain slaves of old ideas, supporting manmade barriers, taxes, restrictions, and obstructions that deliberately interfere with trade. These obstacles inject avoidable Robinson Crusoe–style hardships into our lives. The grinding poverty in the Third World and the collapse of Rome (Mises 1963, pp. 767–69) stem from the same cause: a rejection of the spirit of liberalism and the legal system required by a market economy.

The Theory of Production

According to *Webster's New Collegiate Dictionary*, to be productive means the quality of producing desired output, especially in abundance. To economists, productivity necessarily involves a relation between outputs and inputs. Man cannot produce something from nothing. In formal analysis, these output-input relations are analyzed in both static and dynamic frameworks. The static approach provides a theory of the short-run behavior of firms in choosing input combinations under changing economic conditions. Static analysis holds technical know-how to be constant. Dynamic analysis applies to long-run situations in which technical knowledge changes, usually improving. Both static and dynamic analyses intend to measure outputs and inputs in real, homogeneous units rather than in dollar values. (Measurement problems, productivity over time, and the U.S. growth experience are discussed in the next chapter.)

Because productivity refers to an output-input relation—sometimes called an engineering relation—it has a mathematical character. Production theory is a rare instance in which mathematics can clarify an economic concept rather than befuddling it or making it appear ostentatious. Under conditions of constant knowledge about how to use inputs, economists refer to output-input relations as production functions, which are generally written as:

$$Q = F(L, K, \ldots), \tag{3.1}$$

where

41

Q = physical rate of flow of production for some homogeneous good or service,

F = symbol of general functional form, which says that level of Q depends on amounts of inputs available,

L = available hours of labor of a given type,

K = available flow of services from a given type of capital equipment or buildings, and

... = provision for including additional inputs, such as other kinds of labor, capital equipment, land, or intermediate inputs such as energy, materials, and services purchased from other businesses.

In equation (3.1), F summarizes the state of knowledge or technology about how to use inputs at a point in time. The conventional assumption is that managers are technologically efficient in the sense that managers achieve maximum output from any combination of inputs. This assumption may seem absurd, or unrealistic, to noneconomists, but it is popular among economists for two reasons: (1) it is consistent with the pursuit of maximum profit by businesses, as well as economic efficiency more generally; and (2) it is mathematically simple and necessary if a unique output level is to be associated with each combination of inputs. The assumption of technical efficiency is not far from the mark in terms of practical applications; in a market-oriented economy there is constant pressure on managers to economize on costly inputs to keep costs as low as possible.

Innovation and new technology are the sources of productivity improvement and economic growth over time, yet equation (3.1) describes a static relation. Henry Ford, to cite a famous example, achieved far more output from given amounts of labor and capital by rearranging the work flow into an assembly line. Although assembly lines were known and had been used before, Ford's great contribution was his commitment to the huge capital investment, mass-production techniques, and affordable prices required to make it work. Ford engineers achieved productivity gains ranging from 50 percent to 1,000 percent over conventional methods. Model T production grew from fewer than 300,000 cars in 1914 to 2 million cars in 1923. In a decade of rising prices (up 70 percent), Ford reduced his prices by 60 percent. An early 1926 advertisement offered the Model T at the lowest prices ever: $260 for the runabout and $290 for the touring car. Ford became a millionaire many times over while Henry Royce of Rolls-Royce fame, for instance, failed to become a millionaire even once.

In the theoretical characterization, the more-or-less persistent technological and managerial improvements that increase output without using more resources can be represented as changes in the F function (a kind of black box in most economic analyses), which summarizes the state of knowledge.

Suppose that a 10 percent change in the use of all inputs produces a corresponding 10 percent change in output. This is a common assumption behind some of the results of conventional production theory—namely, that production relation (3.1) has constant returns to scale over the relevant range of variation in output and inputs. It is plausible under many practical circumstances and also a convenient way to support the competitive model of general equilibrium (for which many theoretical economists have a fondness). Mathematically, constant returns to scale mean that the production function is homogeneous of degree one (or linear and homogeneous), which permits us to write

$$Q/L = F(1, K/L, \ldots), \tag{3.2}$$

where all variables are divided by the amount of labor hours (L) to arrive at per-hour variables. The left-hand side of equation (3.2) is the average productivity of labor (Q/L)—a key concept—and K/L is the capital-labor ratio, otherwise known as capital intensity. Alternatively, we can divide equation (3.1) by capital or other inputs to arrive at output per unit of nonlabor input. If consideration of other inputs is suppressed for the moment, equation (3.2) can be rewritten as

$$q = f(k), \tag{3.3}$$

where
q = new symbol for labor's (average) productivity, and
k = capital-labor ratio.

Equation (3.3) highlights the emphasis that economists traditionally place on capital formation as the tool of labor. As Mancur Olson (1982, p. 4) has written, "Virtually all economists agree that events, or even expectations, that discourage investment or destroy productive capital will lower the level of income." Equation (3.3) says that there are two sources of higher productivity: more capital per worker and greater efficiency due to technical, managerial, and market improvements. To be truly complete, productivity gains also depend on factors not explicitly represented in equation (3.3), such as the skill and motivation of the labor force, the quality of capital, and the introduction of new products.

New productivity ratios can be formed by dividing measured output by a measured input or a weighted sum of measured inputs. Changes in these average productivity ratios, however, should not be confused with the underlying causes of productivity gains. Average productivity ratios do not imply causation. For example, the output-energy ratio has increased in recent years, but the credit does not go to energy. Rather, it goes to the managers and engineers who economized and substituted in response to the higher relative price of energy. Similarly, if unions overprice labor in unionized industries, labor productivity in unionized firms will rise but the credit does not go to unionization per se. Nor is it a favorable event for the productivity of the economy as a whole; managers and engineers simply make substitution decisions based on the higher price of labor.

To clarify these conclusions, we must turn our attention from average productivity of inputs to their marginal productivity. The theory of production is based upon marginal analysis, as is all economic reasoning; marginal productivity explains the anomaly that union workers sometimes are more productive than equivalent nonunion workers. Suppose you own a business and someone applies for a job. Would you hire this person? Yes, if you expect the applicant to add more to your company's revenue than you must pay in wages, benefits, and employment taxes. Conversely, if you expect the applicant to add less in revenue than you must pay in wages and other expenses, then your decision will be no. The same is true in employing all factors of production. A firm increases its use of a particular input if the manager expects a larger amount to add more to revenue than to cost. Similarly, a firm reduces its use of an input if the input adds more to cost than to revenue. The key is to compare labor's marginal revenue productivity with labor's marginal cost to the company.

Now consider what happens if a nonunion firm becomes unionized. Although trade unions may be complex organizations, econ-

44

omists agree on the central feature of unions: they attempt to force buyers to pay more than is necessary for labor services. Union tactics cover a range of activities, but the traditional favorite is the strike threat, which involves not only a walkout but usually an attempt to deny other labor to the firm.

Suppose the union forces the firm, through strike threats and other tactics, to pay a wage rate 30 percent higher than equivalent labor receives in the open market. Assuming for the moment that the firm's product prices, technical know-how, and capital equipment remain unchanged, the firm will surely reduce its use of labor. This is the law of demand in operation, and production theory implies this result. The firm will be able to reduce its labor hours in a variety of more-or-less painful ways—including short shifts, normal attrition, and layoffs. In addition, the firm will attempt to eliminate the least productive workers (over union objections). Those remaining will have more capital to work with and will be the most skilled personnel. Wage increases from union activity result in unemployment among low-skill workers. Therefore, if the firm does not adjust its employment, labor will add more to cost than to production revenues. Ironically, the productivity per hour of the firm's remaining work force will be higher, assuming that the firm can survive in the marketplace with its expensive labor. A smaller work force working with the same amount of capital equipment has a higher productivity (both marginal and average). Over the longer run, the surviving firm will adjust its capital stock and use a more capital intensive production process.

What is so bad about this rise in labor productivity? Three things: (1) it often is the result of thinly disguised coercion, (2) total production in the economy is lower, and (3) some workers are squeezed into unemployment and lower-paying jobs. Although labor productivity rises in the union firm, it is nothing to applaud because previously inefficient production techniques become economical after the price of labor is boosted. From a social point of view, this is inefficient because too much scarce capital and too little labor are used to produce a lower rate of output; the lower rate results from a rise in costs and, in the longer run, a rise in output price, which reduces consumer purchases. More expensive labor and capital are used in the production of goods that otherwise would have been produced by less expensive labor and capital if free-market prices had prevailed.

The view that unions pressure all firms into greater productivity is a fallacy because no new capital is created through union wage increases. Capital is simply shifted around in the economy. The artificial scarcity of labor created by unions implies that capital and labor are not used to maximum advantage in serving private demands. The artificial abundance of labor in the nonunion sector also drags down wage rates in nonunion employments, creating an unnecessary and functionless inequality between union and nonunion wage rates. The irony is that labor unions divert labor from more productive to less productive activities, thereby impoverishing the common man.

The conventional theory of production accurately predicts the response of firms to changes other than labor prices. If the real price of output (more generally, product-demand conditions) should rise, then firms increase employment, provided that union leaders do not immediately raise the price of labor (the union tax). Similarly, new investment in the industry or technical innovation that leaves the relative prices of capital and labor unchanged generally induces more employment by increasing the labor productivity schedules.

Conclusion

Joseph Schumpeter said that science is nothing more than "refined common sense." Common sense suggests the sources of sustained productivity gain: better management practices; hospitality toward innovation and change; and a competitive, commercial spirit in the work force and management. In view of the natural indolence in man, these traits are best cultivated in an open economy, in which the application of entrepreneurship is freer and resource allocation more responsive to changing conditions.

Within a firm, alert management practices include adopting modern machinery and high-technology equipment to reduce costs; management systems that schedule, hire, invest, and account for inputs and costs in timely and accurate ways; wage systems that encourage productivity; contracting out and outsourcing to reduce costs; economizing on inventories; and generally managing resources efficiently. Over the long run, these practices imply prudent spending for technology and innovation. In terms of the work force, favorable features include the absence of both costly union work rules and resistance to technical change, pride in being a productive member of the company, and, in general, flexibility rather than rigidity of attitude in the workplace. Obviously, unions do not look good by these common-sense standards of productivity. The burden of proof remains on those who argue that unions help efficiency and productivity in the U.S. economy.

IV. Historical Perspective on Productivity

> The conditions of cowsheds and stables have improved enormously over the century with no union pressure to bring about the improvement.
>
> —W. H. Hutt, *The Strike-Threat System*

Economic analysis and sensible policies involve the long run, despite John Maynard Keynes's assertion that "in the long run we're all dead." The inheritors of short-run policies live with the long-run effects of myopic policies. The long-run productivity record of the U.S. economy is essential information in any study of unions and productivity. In recent years, the business sector has constituted about 76 percent of the gross national product (U.S. Department of Labor 1983, p. 1), a lower percentage than in the early years of the 20th century, when private production was bigger relative to government. A brief productivity history of the private U.S. economy puts the analysis of unions and productivity in perspective.

In historical studies of growth, productivity rises if measured output grows faster than measured inputs. Partial productivity ratios—such as output per hour of labor—once dominated the growth literature because capital was believed to be more difficult to measure than labor. Recently, more complicated total-factor or multiple-input indexes have superseded partial indexes.

Productivity studies have been done at the level of the plant, company, industry, and economy. Increases in a productivity index, of course, do not identify the causes of productivity change. A change in total-factor productivity, for example, is an unexplained residual not accounted for by growth in the weighted sum of measured labor, capital, and intermediate inputs. Any gain is usually attributed to subtle and gradual improvements in business practices that have been introduced by management in response to market pressures.

Over long periods of time, the impact of small differentials in rates of productivity growth is enormous. For example, if two national economies—A and B—have equal incomes per person initially and A averages 2 percent growth per person per year and B only 1 percent growth per person per year, the average person in A will enjoy a fourfold increase in the standard of living at the end of a lifetime (72 years), whereas the average person in B will only double his income. This example happens to approximate the history of the United States (A) versus England (B) since the turn of the century.

Table 4.1 compares per capita output in 25 countries as a percentage of U.S. per capita output (the highest in the world) since World War II. Western European output was generally under 50 percent of U.S. output in 1950 (Great Britain was an exception) and grew to 58–86 percent of the U.S. standard by 1980. In Asia, Burmese and Indian outputs languished at 5–7 percent of U.S. output over the 30-year period, while Japanese output rocketed from 17 to 72 percent. Similarly, Hong Kong rose from 18 to 51 percent of the U.S. standard in only 20 years (1960–80).

Although the quality of the data from communist countries is very suspect, they show less-rapid growth relative to the United States. Poland, for example, has slumped sharply since 1980 and its indebtedness to the West has increased greatly. Most of the world outside of the western Pacific basin shows little tendency to gain on the United States. No economist to my knowledge credits the economic success of high-growth countries to labor unions.

Below the economywide level, industries with above-average growth in productivity reduce cost per unit of output and the prices of their products. They enjoy higher profit margins and grow faster than the economy. By contrast, industries with below-average gains in productivity experience above-average increases in unit costs and product prices, and consequently they suffer low profit margins (or losses) and declines in output. Similarly, companies with high productivity gains have higher profit margins and outgrow competitors in the industry; companies with below-average gains in the industry eventually go bankrupt. Survival is difficult for inefficient firms if competitors are efficient, easy if competitors are inefficient. Japanese competitors, for example, pressure U.S. companies into improving efficiency or into filing for bankruptcy.

Table 4.1
REAL PRODUCT PER PERSON IN 25 COUNTRIES AS PERCENTAGE OF U.S. PRODUCT PER PERSON, 1950–80

Country	1950	1960	1970	1980
France	47	61	75	85
West Germany	40	71	79	86
Italy	31	46	56	58
Great Britain	56	65	64	65
Burma	4	5	5	5
Hong Kong	—	18	29	51
India	7	8	7	6
Iran	14*	16	19	24
Japan	17	33	64	72
Singapore	—	20	32	40
South Korea	—	12	17	25
Taiwan	10	13	20	31
East Germany	32	57	61	69
USSR	30	40	47	49
Poland	33	38	40	44
China	7	10	11	14
Argentina	41	41	41	40
Brazil	14	18	18	27
El Salvador	14	15	14	11
Mexico	24	27	30	28
Ethiopia	5	5	5	4
Kenya	9	8	7	6
Malawi	—	4	4	4
South Africa	29	29	32	30
Uganda	12	11	10	6

SOURCE: Summers and Heston (1984), pp. 220–62.
*1955 datum.

The preceding conclusions about productivity strictly follow if the marketplace forces all firms to pay similar prices for inputs of comparable quality. The firms that make better use of inputs prosper, while those that do not, die. The market economy puts a premium on productivity and cost control, thereby encouraging efficient use of available resources.

The general interest of working people lies in rapid gains in overall productivity because such gains guarantee that the real demand for labor services increases faster than the supply of labor, thereby pushing up the real labor prices. If rapidly growing companies and industries are taxed, regulated, or otherwise harmed by government and union policies for the benefit of declining companies and industries (often unionized), the total flow of real wages and salaries declines. The sectional interests of organized labor must not be confused with the general interest of working people.

The numerator in productivity indexes is output. Output must be standardized for the changing mix of products over time. This is done imperfectly—for example, by weighting outputs for a multiproduct firm by relative prices, which, in turn, reflect the marginal valuations of consumers. Similarly, the denominator in productivity indexes is an input index, often constructed to convert different types of capital, labor, and intermediate inputs into a standardized input through relative prices and other devices. In multifactor indexes, inputs are aggregated by their shares in total cost to arrive at an overall input. Under conditions of constant returns to scale (defined in chapter 3) and competitive markets for inputs, shares in total cost must equal the respective marginal products of inputs in percentage terms (output elasticities of inputs). Mathematically, growth in output is split up into a weighted sum of input growth rates plus a residual called technical change or multifactor productivity.[1]

Early productivity studies were done by the U.S. Bureau of Labor, as it was called then, in the late 19th century (Kendrick 1984a, pp. 24–25). Output per worker was compared between handicraft and mechanized operations, and changes were measured through time. The motivation for these studies was the ill-founded fear of technological displacement of workers (the implicit principle was that machines were bad because they destroy jobs), not an attempt to understand or promote productivity. In the 1920s the Bureau of Labor Statistics published a series of articles on productivity in several manufacturing industries.

In subsequent years, there were expanded efforts, involving both public and private researchers, to measure productivity growth at the economywide, industry, company, and plant levels (for more

[1]For details, see U.S. Department of Labor (1983), especially appendix A.

52

analysis, see Baumol and McLennan 1985, U.S. Department of Labor 1983, Kendrick 1984a, and Denison 1979). Researchers still differ on detailed procedures, but they have reached a consensus on such issues as the decline in U.S. productivity growth beginning in the mid-to-late 1960s.

The U.S. Growth Experience

What do these sustained measurement efforts say about the U.S. growth experience over the long run? Economic historians claim that the American Indians did not enjoy rising per capita incomes over the long term. As Stanley Lebergott (1984, p. 8) has put it, "Per capita consumption by the Indians could hardly have been much less 50 centuries earlier." Also, death by disease periodically reduced their numbers drastically.

The modest number of white arrivals between 1600 and 1700 spent their time learning how to survive in the new land. Although the arrival of the Pilgrims and others increased total output, the rate of growth of per capita output was probably close to zero (Lebergott 1984, p. 59).

Between 1700 and 1800, however, the annual rate of growth of U.S. national output per person rose to 0.4 percent, according to the crude estimates made by Robert Gallman (cited in Lebergott 1984). Although this rate is low by modern standards (at 0.4 percent, a doubling of income would take 180 years), perceptible material progress was not the common experience of mankind in those days. The 18th century—the so-called colonial century—was dominated by the major migrant streams from Ireland, Scotland, and England, although the colonies also recruited peasants from mainland Europe as settlers and sustained an influx of religious dissidents, African slaves, and a sprinkling of convicts. Working in an atmosphere of unprecedented freedom (slaves notably excepted), the colonists and subsequent citizens of the new nation created an economy whose workers and farmers outproduced those of any nation in the world. Even in 1783, real income per capita in the United States was high; it probably exceeded that in every other nation save Great Britain.

The first U.S. census, in 1790, showed that the population had reached 3.9 million, including 700,000 slaves. The new nation basically consisted of isolated settlements and coastal centers scattered from Boston to Charleston. Eighty-five percent of the labor force was engaged in agriculture and the rest was involved in fishing, mining, ocean shipping, domestic service, teaching, artisan and craft work, and merchandising. Three of every four free families owned their own farm. They settled wherever they found fertile land within tolerably close reach of military protection. Rugged individualism was not a nostalgic slogan; it was the rule of the day. Independence came from economic choice, and political independence inevitably followed. Although economic life was harsh by modern standards, Americans were accustomed to eating meat every day; in contrast, most Europeans were peasants who had meat only on special occasions. An American laborer earned from $6 to $8 a month plus room and board, and it was possible for him to buy a small farm after working and saving for a year or two; most Europeans, though, could not own their own land, nor could they realistically hope that their children would. Americans averaged less than a dollar a year in taxes, whereas Europeans suffered under steep taxes imposed by local and central governments. In addition, many Europeans were subjected to rigorous charges levied by landowners and restrictions that did not encumber Americans. And so the stage was set for the greatest material advance in human history. The prerequisite of liberty was in place.

Economic historians estimate that during most of the 19th century, total U.S. output grew rapidly but productivity per se did not increase very much. In the words of Moses Abramowitz and Paul David (1973): "Over the course of the nineteenth century the pace of increase of the real gross domestic product was accounted for largely by the traditional, conventionally defined factors of production: labor, land, the tangible reproducible capital." Table 4.2 shows that gross output grew at an average rate of about 4 percent per year during the 19th century, as rapidly as in any era in U.S. history. Most of the growth, however, was due to rapid increases in labor hours and in measured capital inputs. Advances in productivity were modest by current standards, with total-factor productivity increasing at 0.3 percent per year.

From the beginning, the U.S. economy was agricultural. By the outbreak of the Civil War, agriculture still employed more than half the labor force. Although manufacturing, mining, and other sectors contributed to the rise in U.S. incomes, it was primarily agriculture that drove incomes upward. Farming was more capital- and land-

Table 4.2

REAL GROSS PRODUCT, INPUTS, AND PRODUCTIVITY RATIOS FOR THE U.S. BUSINESS ECONOMY, 1800–1985 (average annual percentage rates of change)

	1800–1855	1855–1890	1889–1919	1919–1948	1948–1973	1973–1981	1981–1985
Real gross output	4.2	4.0	3.9	3.0	3.7	2.2	3.6
Population	3.1	2.4	1.8	1.2	1.5	0.8	1.0
Real output per capita	1.1	1.6	2.1	1.8	2.2	1.4	2.6
Factor inputs							
Labor	3.7	2.8	1.8	0.6	0.7	1.4	1.5
Capital	4.3	4.6	3.1	1.2	3.6	3.2	*
Labor productivity	0.5	1.1	2.0	2.4	3.0	0.8	2.1
Total factor productivity	0.3	0.3	1.7	2.2	2.0	0.1	*

SOURCES: 1800–1948, Kendrick (1984a), p. 87; 1948–81, Kendrick (1984b), p. 389; 1981–85, calculated from *Economic Report of the President* (1986).
*Not available.

intensive than most sectors, and it used an even larger share of other inputs than its huge share of the labor force. Farmers used their time and energy to clear the land of trees and stumps and to repair farm tools, and they saved to buy still more capital equipment. Families saved about 12 percent of their incomes to make such investments, about twice the personal savings rate of their wealthier descendants today. This statistic on thrift can be deceptive, however, because households today indirectly save more in the form of retained earnings in businesses. During the 19th century, the visible factors driving economic growth were enormous expansions in the inputs of capital and labor.

The less-visible elements were the institutional structure that allowed people to create and accept productive opportunities, as well as the values of the people themselves. Such values are crucial to economic growth. Economists often fall into the trap of being too materialistic in analyzing capital accumulation and productivity gains. Writers such as Thomas Sowell, Julian Simon, P. T. Bauer, George Gilder, and Warren Brookes have properly emphasized intangibles such as spiritual values, commercial attitudes, morale, and the mental qualities of the population. Sowell (1984, p. 7), for example, says that "the long-run prosperity of any country depends not upon physical capital but upon the ability to reproduce that capital."

Americans were willing to accept novelty in production and the associated risks during the 19th century. They were willing to bear the costs of the untidy expansion of a free economy—job turnover, migration, depreciation of machinery, and rapid obsolescence of business investments and human skills. Entrepreneurs were free to innovate in production, distribution, and consumption. Workers accepted innovation and worked with ever-changing techniques and equipment. The result was an accelerating advance in productivity and in prosperity. For example, coffee, tea, and sugar were once considered luxuries, but their use became nearly universal by the 1840s. And almost no Americans had iron stoves in 1789, but two-thirds of them did by 1890 (Lebergott 1984, pp. 69, 71).

In the 90-year period after 1889, productivity growth accelerated markedly. From an annual rate of 0.3 percent, total-factor productivity growth jumped dramatically to annual rates of 1.7 percent between 1889 and World War I, 2.2 percent from 1919 to 1948, and

2.8 percent during the golden era (as it is sometimes dubbed) from 1948 to 1966. Since 1966, however, there has been a well-publicized drop in productivity growth, with total-factor productivity growth dropping to an average annual rate of 1.7 percent between 1966 to 1973 and further to 0.4 percent between 1973 and 1981. Real output per capita, however, has maintained its post–World War II momentum owing to a rapid expansion in labor force participation.

Recent Productivity and Wage Experience

The close association between labor productivity and real hourly compensation is shown in Figure 4.1 for the years 1947 to 1985. In 1985, real wages were 2.42 times higher and labor productivity was 2.24 times higher than in 1948. That is, real wages rose 8 percent more than labor productivity did over this time period. The simple correlation between output per hour and real hourly compensation is 0.99 for these data, supporting the claim that gains in real wages depend on advances in the overall productivity of the economy. The correlation can be less than perfect (1.0) for two reasons: (1) errors in the data, and (2) the strong tendency for both labor and capital to be paid their marginal products, which are always below their respective average products but can diverge by varying amounts. Economic theory does not require a strict 1:1 relation between growth in labor productivity and real wage rates because labor's share of national income, although relatively stable, can fluctuate up or down.

From the late 1940s to the mid-1960s, real labor compensation rose at the same pace as average hourly output; in other words, labor's marginal productivity rose as fast as labor's average productivity. After 1965, real wage gains, while sluggish, exceeded the modest increases in labor productivity. More precisely, in 1965 the real wage and productivity indexes (1948 = 100) were virtually identical at 171 and 172, respectively. Then the real wage index gradually outpaced the growth of productivity, rising to 8 percent above the productivity index by 1985.

Why has this occurred? Contrary to Karl Marx, there is a long-run tendency, as capital accumulates, for the real wage to grow somewhat more quickly than labor's average product, thereby gradually raising labor's share of national income. The real price of labor rises as labor demand outpaces the growth of labor supply. As

Figure 4.1

REAL HOURLY COMPENSATION AND LABOR PRODUCTIVITY IN THE BUSINESS SECTOR, 1947–85

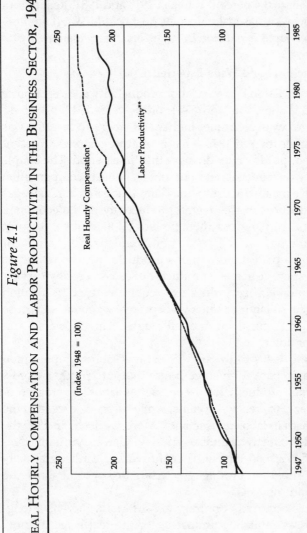

SOURCE: Calculated from *Economic Report of the President* (1986), pp. 256, 258, 302.
*Hourly compensation divided by the implicit GNP price deflator for personal consumption expenditures, 1947–59, and by the fixed-weight GNP price index for personal consumption expenditures, 1959–85.
**Output is gross domestic product originating in the business sector in 1982 dollars; hours of all persons in the business sector, based primarily on establishment data.

capital accumulates, technology advances, and markets widen, then the capital-labor ratio rises, and real wages tend to rise faster than average productivity. As capital becomes more abundant relative to labor, the real prices for capital services (capital's marginal product) tend to decline relative to the prices for labor and labor's share of gross domestic business product rises. (The appendix at the end of this chapter spells out these propositions more precisely.)

The Growth Issue

The productivity problem is more serious than many Americans imagine. Regardless of how the productivity slowdown might be explained, its existence restricts us to slow improvements in our standard of living. The relevant facts in terms of the period since the end of World War II include the following:

- Between 1947 and 1973, net investment averaged 7.1 percent of U.S. gross national product (GNP) and from 1973 to 1984, it fell to 5.4 percent.
- A Bureau of Labor Statistics (BLS) study (U.S. Department of Labor 1983) shows that from 1948 to 1973, the growth of capital per hour worked was 2.8 percent per year, but from 1973 to 1981, this capital deepening slowed to a rate of 1.8 percent per year.
- From 1973 to 1981, the annual growth of labor productivity was the slowest of any decade since 1909–18, when there was no measured improvement in productivity, according to BLS.

The relevant facts also include how the United States compares to other countries in terms of postwar productivity. The evidence indicates that it compares poorly.

- Between 1963 and 1979, for example, Japan devoted 32 percent of its GNP to gross investment and experienced a 6.5 percent annual increase in labor productivity.
- Over the same period, only 17 percent of U.S. GNP was devoted to gross investment and annual productivity gains averaged only 1.2 percent.

The relevant facts are also unfavorable to the United States in terms of international comparisons of productivity in manufacturing.

- Between 1950 and 1983, output per hour in U.S. manufacturing increased by 120 percent.

- In West Germany, output per hour increased by over 500 percent during the same period.
- In Japan, output per hour increased by over 1,600 percent during the same period.

However, all is not negative in the relative U.S. performance. While other countries have been gaining on us, there is no indication that they are about to surpass us. Herbert Stein (1983, p. 204), former chairman of the Council of Economic Advisers, has put it this way: "Between 1960 and 1979 Japanese real per capita output rose from 31.5 percent of ours to 70.2 percent of ours. But the rate of gain on us fell sharply. If it continues to fall at the same pace, Japan's real per capita GNP would still be only 74 percent of ours in 2083."

What is true of Japan is also true of other countries: as they come closer to catching up with the United States, their growth rates tend to fall. What explains this? A popular explanation is that the industrialized countries started with major differences in the amounts of capital goods and output per person at the end of World War II. The countries that began with low capital per worker grew faster and invested larger fractions of their income. People in these countries were willing to sacrifice more and take advantage of high-return investment opportunities in their shattered economies.

Another, more plausible, explanation is that the growth rates are sensitive to government and trade union policies. For example, evidence is beginning to accumulate that the proportion of national income spent by government is a major depressant of economic growth. Consider the following (see Reynolds 1985b for references):

- Between 1967 and 1982, the percent of gross domestic product (GDP) spent by the Japanese government rose from 19 to 34 percent and Japan's rate of economic growth fell by 55 percent.
- Over the same period, the percent of GDP spent by the U.S. government rose from 32 to 38 percent and the U.S. growth rate of GDP fell by 30 percent.
- In Sweden, the share of GDP spent by government rose from 40 to 62 percent and Sweden's growth rate fell by 61 percent.
- A recent study of 104 countries covering the 1961–76 period finds a strong negative impact of government spending on the growth of per capita income.

Conclusion

The slowdown in the rate of productivity advance that has occurred in the United States over the past 15 years has been a major focus of recent research and policy debate. There is a consensus on the nature of the problem and its approximate magnitude, but there is little agreement about the probable importance of the various potential causes of the slowdown. Edward N. Wolff (1985), for example, has surveyed recent studies and found it difficult to form a summary judgment. He guardedly concluded that most economists attach much explanatory importance to the slowdown in the growth of the capital-labor ratio; they attach some importance to the decline in research and development investment, shifts in the composition of output, increased government regulation, and adverse cyclical factors; and they attach relatively little importance to the changing composition of the labor force or changes in labor relations.

There is no obvious association between the degree of unionism and aggregate productivity growth in the historical data. In the past 15 years, for example, labor productivity growth has slumped to less than half of the 1948–73 growth rate while union coverage of the work force also has slumped. It would be foolish, however, to infer cause and effect from this episode. The accelerating productivity advances of the 19th and early 20th centuries were not correlated with substantial or growing union power, and the poor economic performance of the 1930s was associated with growing union power. We must rely on a more refined analysis to disentangle the union-productivity connection from other productivity factors.

Appendix

The purpose of this appendix is to show precisely why there is a long-run tendency, as capital accumulates, for labor's share of the rising national income to grow.

National income in the business sector (NI) can be split into an accounting identity of labor hours (L) times labor's average physical product (AP_L):

$$NI = (NI/L) \times L = AP_L \times L. \tag{4.1}$$

Labor's share of national income (total labor compensation divided by national income) may be written as

Labor's share $= wL/NI$, (4.2)

where w is average labor compensation and L is labor hours.

If we substitute expression (4.1) in the denominator of (4.2), we have:

Labor's share $= wL/(AP_L \times L) = w/AP_L$. (4.3)

That is, labor's share of national income is simply the average price of labor (labor's marginal product) relative to labor's average product. The wage–average-product ratio fluctuates with supply and demand conditions for labor and capital, as the data in Figure 4.1 suggest. In production function theory, the wage-productivity ratio also is the output elasticity of labor.

If labor's share of national income rises, capital's share necessarily falls. If the real price of labor grows more rapidly than labor productivity, the real price of capital services falls relative to capital's average productivity. If the demand for capital services grows more slowly relative to the supply of capital than the demand for labor relative to its supply, the wage–labor-productivity ratio rises, as shown in Figure 4.1.

To establish that a rise in the wage-productivity ratio implies a decrease in the price-of-capital-services–capital-productivity ratio, we divide national income into labor and capital compensation:

$$NI = wL + rK,$$ (4.4)

where

r = price of capital services per hour,
K = number of capital hours,
w = average 1 hr. compensation, and
L = number of labor hours.

Dividing through by NI, we have:

$$1 = wL/NI + rK/NI.$$ (4.5)

This can be rewritten as

$$1 = wL/AP_L L + rK/AP_K K$$
$$= w/AP_L + r/AP_K.$$ (4.6)

Subtracting r/AP_K from both sides, we have:

$$w/AP_L = 1 - r/AP_K.$$ (4.7)

That is, any change in the wage-productivity ratio implies an equal, offsetting change in the capital-services-price–capital-productivity ratio.

In the late 1960s, the wage-productivity ratio (w/AP_L) began rising, implying a rise in labor's share. If we assume that the output-capital ratio did not fall during this period $(AP_K$ tends toward constancy over the long run; for example, U.S. Department of Labor 1983, p. 1), the real price of capital services must have fallen. The assumption of a constant output-capital ratio is plausible because although there was a small decrease in output per unit of capital services between 1973 and 1981, it represented a change from the peak of one cycle to the trough of another, rather than a long-term trend. Long-run output-capital constancy supports the view of most economists that capital is the vehicle of economic progress. It is difficult for output to expand faster than capital for an extended period of time. (For more on the theory of labor and capital shares, see Ferguson 1969, especially pages 239–41.)

Table 4.3 displays five estimates of labor's share. Although they are based on different definitions and procedures, all the estimates show a rise in labor's share since 1965 and only one fails to show a rise in labor's share since 1948. These data support the data in Figure 4.1 because if real wages rise more than productivity, it implies a rise in labor's share of income.

Table 4.3
ESTIMATES OF LABOR'S SHARE OF U.S. NATIONAL INCOME, 1948–85

Year	BLS	Edward F. Denison	Dale F. Jorgenson	John Kendrick	NIA
1948	62.2	78.3	61.9	63.9	64.2
1965	60.9	79.2	57.1	64.3	68.3
1981	64.6	83.2	60.7	68.8	74.0
1985	—	—	—	—	73.8

SOURCES: All data except NIA data are from U.S. Department of Labor (1983), p. 79; NIA is employee compensation divided by national income, as calculated from *Economic Report of the President* (1986), p. 278.

V. Union Wage Rates

> The monopolists, by keeping the market constantly under-
> stocked, by never fully supplying the effectual demand, sell
> their commodities much above the natural price, and raise
> their emoluments, whether they consist in wages or profit,
> greatly above their natural rate.
>
> —Adam Smith, *The Wealth of Nations*

> It can hardly be denied that raising wages by the use of
> coercion is today the main aim of unions.
>
> —F. A. Hayek, *The Constitution of Liberty*

Adversarial unions damage the social fabric in a variety of ways. The economic effects may be grouped into the wage and nonwage effects of unions. This chapter analyzes the impact of union wage premiums, a much-investigated topic among economists. Distortions in labor pricing cause suboptimal employment of resources, avoidable wage inequalities, and flatter lifetime wage profiles in the union sector, thereby depressing work effort and skill acquisition. The next chapter explores the inflexibility of union wage rates and its economic consequences. Subsequent chapters discuss the nonwage effects of unions: the cost of union work rules and the costs of union negotiating, strikes, grievances, and other forms of discoordination imposed by unionism.

Estimating the Union Wage Premium

Unions have the announced objective of obtaining higher wage rates and fringe benefits for their members, and they have already secured the privileges that allow them to aggressively pursue this objective. Two questions arise: (1) how successful have the unions been? and (2) what is the impact on national income and other economic variables?

In recent years, economists have continued to devote a great deal of effort to estimating the magnitude of the union impact on the wage rates of otherwise identical union and nonunion employees. Their findings have varied, depending on the method of estimation, data, time period, and other factors. The result is that it is difficult to give a single number that summarizes the relative wage impact of unions, although this is far from saying that nothing is known.

From a theoretical standpoint, the lack of a single number is not surprising. To assess the independent effect of unions on the hourly pay of union members, we must figure out what their pay would have been without a union. We must estimate what would have happened but did not; that is, we must construct a counterfactual. The closest that we can come is to compare the earnings of union employees with the earnings of nonunion employees who appear to be similar in other respects.

This procedure sets the stage for controversy, often technical, over whether a particular method or study adequately controls for the many potential differences among union and nonunion employees that may affect rates of pay. Indeed, there is controversy over whether unionization should be treated as an independent factor in statistical regression models. Economists can have different judgments about whether the true effect of unionization on wage rates has been isolated in a particular study or not.

The difficulties are highlighted by viewing the problem from an employer's point of view. Suppose a plant is unionized and, following union threats, strikes, and disruption, the employer agrees to raise pay by 25 percent. Now the employer faces the problem of getting unit costs back down and surviving in the marketplace. A number of adjustments become necessary that were not economical at lower labor costs.

First, the employer would use less labor, relying on normal turnover, layoffs, or other devices to cut back employment. He would substitute labor-saving machinery, apply tighter supervision, use more capital-intensive production techniques, and contract out work to economize on expensive labor.

Second, the employer would demand more effort per hour from employees because they are overpaid and more eager to retain their jobs. The union, naturally, fights management over control of any increases in monitoring, tightened work standards, work speedups, and related changes in working conditions. Surveys of on-the-job satisfaction report that union workers have lower levels of job satisfaction than do nonunion workers (Freeman and Medoff 1984, ch. 9; Reynolds 1987; and Toner 1985). The adversarial struggle between union and management over the reward-output structure is a major factor in explaining such dissatisfaction, in addition to the job rigidities and make-work practices of unions that increase monotony. Unionized workers have a poor opinion of supervisors and of their own relationship with supervisors; this is not surprising in the politicized environments of unionized establishments, where the concept of team cooperation disappears. Gregory J. Duncan and Frank P. Stafford (1980) have reported that about 40 percent of the union-nonunion wage differential for production workers was a compensating wage differential to compensate for a more structured work setting, inflexible hours, employer-controlled overtime, and a faster work pace. Gopa Chowdhury and Stephen Nickell (1985) have attributed the 14–24 percent wage boost they isolated as a union wage differential to compensation for the more rigorous work environment in unionized settings.

Third, because money wage rates are only part of the compensation package, the employer would reduce the nonmonetary rewards of employees. People are effectively paid in wages, pensions, bonuses, and such fringe benefits as employer-paid insurance, air conditioning, low noise levels, music, locational convenience, free parking, safety measures, courteous supervisors, company picnics, sports programs, on-the-job training, and schooling subsidies. In the absence of unions, employers try to adjust these forms of compensation to minimize their labor costs per unit of output; at the margin, an additional dollar spent on any form of compensation would yield the same gain in productivity and/or reduction in other labor expenses. In a free market for labor, employers must cater to the preferences of workers to maintain the quantity and quality of the labor services they want. Unionized wage schedules prevent this free-market adjustment in the mix of compensation in accord with employee preferences. Attempts by the employer to offset wage increases by fringe reductions are opposed by the union, of course. Recent studies show that unions impose a larger percentage increase in fringe-benefit spending than in wage rates, relative to competitive labor markets, suggesting that the mix of remuneration in union markets is out of alignment with employee preferences, contrary to the assertions of Freeman and Medoff (1984, ch. 4).

Fourth, because overall compensation in unionized settings is generally more attractive as a result of union pressure, the employer would hire higher-quality people from the queue of qualified applicants. More productive people gradually end up in unionized jobs because of so-called cream skimming by employers. Such employees also have lower rates of turnover, further reducing the labor costs associated with hiring, firing, quitting, and replacing. This is not likely to be efficient, however, because it is the result of union coercion rather than a voluntary decision on compensation and turnover policy intended to minimize production cost.

The net effect of an initial wage boost of 25 percent exacted by union pressures might be controlled to something like a 10 percent premium after all these adjustments by the employer. Outside observers might come to widely varying conclusions about the union effect on wage rates, especially since some enterprises would pay a 5–10 percent premium in the absence of a union.

Now consider the nonunion employees whose earnings might be used for comparison in assessing the union-nonunion wage gap. In general, the relative wage advantage of union members has two sources: (1) unions raise wage rates above competitive levels; and (2) nonunion wage rates are restrained (depressed) by the increased supply of people seeking work in the nonunion sector.

For every artificial scarcity, there is a corresponding artificial abundance. The resulting diversion of capital and labor from higher to less productive activities eradicates part of the real demand for labor, thereby lowering real wages overall. As Jean-Baptiste Say would have put it: In order to demand, you must supply (Say's Law); that is, to consume, you must produce in an exchange economy. And supply (production) is restricted by monopolies and barriers to entry, including those in labor markets.

Any statistical comparison is complicated by the fact that a nonunion employer in specific circumstances may pay unionized levels of compensation to reduce the chances that his employees will unionize. Only a minority of firms would find it profitable to concede part of their cost advantage this way, however, because it amounts to throwing in the towel without a fight. But this tactic can be used by enterprises that are at serious risk of unionization to avoid some of the nonwage costs of unionization, such as rigid work rules, belligerence on the job, strikes, costly negotiations and grievances, and walkouts. The scientific problem is that the so-called threat effect of unionism raises the wages of similarly situated nonunion employees (although threats continue to diminish the overall social wage flow by discouraging investment); therefore, statistical estimates of the wage-increasing effects of unions can be understated. An econometric solution is to make wider comparisons, but this means greater correction for differences among employees in such other productivity characteristics as schooling, sex, race, industry, occupation, experience, geography, cost of living, fringe benefits, and marital status.

To confuse matters further, a two-way dependency can occur between high wages and unionism. The common view is that unions get high wage rates for their members, but high-wage workers also are more likely to unionize. Unions with market power originated among printers, construction tradesmen, railroad workers, and other high-wage craftsmen. A contemporary example is the Air Line Pilots Association. In recent years, senior airline captains earned $150,000 per year for 45 hours of flying time per month, although since deregulation, competitive pressures by nonunion companies have moderated these prices and/or compelled wage cuts and two-tiered wage systems. The average annual earnings of ALPA members is still $85,000 per year for less than 80 hours' flying time per month. Two-way dependency between wages and unionism makes statistical disentanglement of the independent effect of unionism on wage differentials more difficult. Union officials direct their organizing efforts toward the compact, cohesive groups that promise to be relatively easy to organize. From an econometric point of view, these considerations imply models with two or more equations and two-stage least-squares estimation or more exotic techniques.

Estimates of the Premium

Theoretical considerations suggest that some statistical comparisons underestimate union impacts on relative wage rates, whereas others appear to overstate the union wage impact. The best available evidence on this issue has produced estimates of the relative wage advantage of union workers of − 10 to 100 percent, depending on the union, time period, nature of data, statistical techniques, and so on. The premier work in the field is *Union Relative Wage Effects*, a new book by H. Gregg Lewis (1986) that is the follow-up to his 1963 classic, *Unionism and Relative Wages in the United States*.

In his new work, Lewis finds that from 1967 to 1979 the mean, overall union-nonunion wage differential in the United States was 14–15 percent. There is a slight upward trend in the estimated wage gaps over the period but Lewis puts no confidence in this. He believes his figures are upper bounds on the true mean because of the omission of control variables correlated with union status. The new estimates do not stray from the range of 12–16 percent that he estimated for 1957–58 in his 1963 survey.

Lewis summarizes, refines, and extends nearly 200 empirical studies to reach his conclusion, versus only 20 studies in his 1963 book. In surveying the work up to 1963, much of it done at the University of Chicago, Lewis observes that most of the studies looked at situations in which a measurable union advantage was likely to exist. Nonetheless, a wage advantage of more than 25 percent was relatively rare. Among unions with comparatively large effects in certain periods were the mine workers, building trades, printing, entertainment, airline pilots, and seamen. Unions with negligible wage effects, according to Lewis's estimates, were garment workers, textile workers, shoe workers, and white-collar government workers.

Unions not only raise the wage rates of their members but also make these labor prices less flexible. The typical bargaining agreement is negotiated every three years. Although such an agreement may have cost-of-living adjustments and allow for wage reopeners or annual improvement factors, labor prices are relatively fixed for a definite interval. This means that the union wage advantage fluctuates relative to the nonunion sector, where adjustments to changing market conditions are more fluid. Lewis estimates that the general wage advantage of union members was 45 percent in the early 1930s, slipped to 22 percent by the late 1930s, fell further to 6 percent in the early 1940s, and then fell to zero in the late 1940s. The union premium rose to 12 percent in the early 1950s and to 16 percent in the late 1950s.

There is a plausible interpretation of these major fluctuations. The 45 percent figure for the early 1930s reflects the rigidity of union contracts relative to nonunion wage rates during the early years of the Great Depression. These early years were before people knew that they were going to be in the most serious depression in U.S. history, largely caused by government activism and disastrous monetary policies (Brunner 1981, Rothbard 1983, Alan Reynolds 1979, Morgan O. Reynolds 1982). The last free-market recession was in 1921. Between 1929 and 1933, as a result of union wage rigidity, union membership plunged and few members could secure full-time employment at union rates (25 percent were unemployed and another 25 percent worked part-time). Informal wage-cutting was common. The latter part of the Great Depression was a period of aggressive growth in union membership, especially in the mass-production industries, wherein initial wage contracts did not command the high premiums the craft union contracts did in the early 1930s. The negligible union-nonunion wage differentials in the 1940s can be accounted for by the wage-price controls of World War II, plus union and management underanticipation of the wartime and postwar price inflations.

Lewis's estimates of union wage differentials of 12–16 percent for the late 1950s, which Lewis views as normal or equilibrium wage gaps, were based on cross-sectional survey data gathered from households. In principle, these data are better than earlier data because of more detailed information about individual characteristics, permitting more accurate estimation of the union impact on wage rates, holding other factors constant.

Lewis's 1986 book surveys an enormous number of studies and methods based on macro equations, simultaneous equations, panel data, and ordinary least-squares models using cross-sectional data on individual earnings (see Reynolds 1987a). Lewis has much more confidence in his 1967–79 adjusted average of 0.14 than in the yearly figures, which range from 0.11 to 0.18. Lewis believes that 0.14 is an upper bound because of the omission of right-hand variables correlated with union status.

On its own terms, there is no question that Lewis's 1986 book is outstanding, a product of painstaking scholarship. Deficiencies center on omissions and the narrowness of the work. Lewis does not tell us why we should care about union-nonunion wage gaps, nor why there is such a huge number of estimates. Further, he apparently puts no stock in anecdotes, has no analysis of the ongoing deunionization of the U.S. economy, and says nothing about troubled unionized industries or the evidence—numerical and otherwise—that indicates a rising wage gap during the 1970s and early 1980s. His exclusive attention to the average ignores the potent unions (and the associated problems) that exist in construction, automobiles, steel, and the postal service.

Nor can we can be as certain as Lewis that omitted productivity variables associated with union status imply statistical overestimation of the union wage effect. Some high-quality workers (maybe productive people such as Lewis himself) do not like unionized situations because of the encumbrances that go along with the (average) union wage premium. If the union wage premium is less than 14 percent, as Lewis believes, then surely some high-productivity employees are better off in nonunion situations; they can reap their personal productivity premiums and reduce their exposure to strikes and the other costs of unionized working conditions. Such behavior diminishes the hypothesized strong correlation between union status and unmeasured productivity traits.

Lewis's two studies together provide a unifying view of the magnitude of the wage gap attributable to unionism, but there are different views of the size of the union impact in recent years. John H. Pencavel and Catherine Hartsog (1984) have reexamined Lewis's 1963 work with aggregate data and have duplicated Lewis's findings for his time periods. They found that the union impact on relative wage rates was larger than average in the early 1930s and smaller than average in the late 1940s. The unique part of the Pencavel-Hartsog results, however, was that the relative wage effect declined in the late 1970s in their time-series data (p. 216):

> The aggregate data imply a declining relative wage effect of unionism from the late 1960s to the late 1970s, whereas the evidence from microeconomic studies tends not to accord with this finding. . . . [W]e do not know why the implications from fitting the equations to the aggregate time-series data do not agree with those from fitting wage equations to individual cross-section data in different years.

Lewis believes that macroeconomic, time-series estimates of the wage effect of unions are so biased that they are useless. Most economists believe that the union wage impact grew tremendously in the 1970s and early 1980s, jeopardizing the competitiveness of unionized firms. George E. Johnson (1984) used aggregate data to reestimate Lewis's results, confirmed them, and found that during the 1970s, the union wage premium increased from 17 to 26 percent relative to equally productive nonunion employees. Robert J. Flanagan (1984) has presented convincing evidence that union wage increases consistently exceeded nonunion wage increases during the 1970s, raising the union-nonunion wage differential to historic post–World War II highs by the early 1980s (Table 5.1).

As Table 5.1 shows, overall union wage gains exceeded nonunion gains each year up to 1982, and in manufacturing, wage increases were greater for unionized than nonunionized workers every year from 1969 to 1982 (pre-1976 data not shown in table). As a result, Flanagan (1984) has calculated that the union-nonunion wage gap in manufacturing widened by 13.5 percentage points, which would imply boosting a traditional union wage gap of about 16 percent to 30 percent (assuming no change in union-nonunion worker quality).

This tremendous disparity between the wage costs of union and nonunion labor must be corrected or else unionized companies and unions are headed for extinction. The first hint of serious union adjustment was the concessions in labor costs granted to the Chrysler Corporation in 1979. By 1983, as Table 5.1 shows, the concessions began to show up in the overall data. For the first time since 1969, wage increases in manufacturing were lower for union workers (3.6 percent) than for nonunion workers (4.7 percent). The pattern continued in 1984 and 1985, as union members averaged annual increases of 3.5 percent and nonunion employees averaged increases of 4.2 percent. Between 1976 and 1982 in nonmanufacturing, a pattern similar to that in manufacturing prevailed, with union wage gains exceeding nonunion gains, although Table 5.1 does show that union increases did not dominate their nonunion counterparts as strongly as in manufacturing, partly because nonmanufacturing is a more heterogeneous group than manufacturing.

Virtually all observers agree that the recent reversal of the widening union-nonunion wage gap was attributable to "inconvenient" competition in the marketplace. Deregulation in air and surface transportation permitted the entry of efficient, nonunion competitors, while foreign producers and nonunion domestic companies hurt unionized firms in the so-called smokestack industries, construction, and mining. The deep recession of the early 1980s put additional, cyclical pressure on unions to bring their prices more

73

Table 5.1
UNION AND NONUNION WAGE CHANGES, 1976–85 (percent change)

	ECI Average 1976–79*	1980	1981	1982	1983	1984	1985
Private nonfarm sector							
Union	8.1	10.9	9.6	6.5	4.6	3.3	3.1
Nonunion	7.4	8.0	8.5	6.1	5.2	4.5	4.6
Manufacturing							
Union	8.7	11.0	8.9	5.8	3.6	3.9	3.2
Nonunion	7.8	7.9	8.3	5.6	4.7	4.3	4.1
Nonmanufacturing							
Union	7.5	10.8	10.2	7.1	5.5	2.5	3.1
Nonunion	7.3	8.1	8.6	6.2	5.5	4.6	4.9

SOURCES: 1976–83, Flanagan (1984), p. 186; 1984, *Monthly Labor Review* (February 1985), p. 101; 1985, *Monthly Labor Review* (August 1986), p. 80. All original data from the U.S. Department of Labor, Bureau of Labor Statistics.
*ECI = employment cost index.

closely into line with historic 15–20 percent monopoly wage premiums.

Despite givebacks and concessions in some collective contracts, however, the unions have a long way to go before reestablishing their competitiveness. It would take another decade of union and nonunion wage changes of the scale observed in the 1983–85 period to restore the wage gaps in smokestack industries to their pre-1970s levels. In the much-publicized steel and automobile industries, for example, hourly employment costs in 1969 were about 40 percent above all U.S. manufacturing employment costs; by 1982, however, they were 85 percent above the U.S. average in manufacturing. Concessions were limited to a few industries—rubber, airlines, railroads, trucking, meat packing, food retailing, and construction—in which competitive pressures increased the most. Unions have taken only the first steps toward realistic, competitive wage levels. If unions are to avoid complete self-immolation before the calendar turns to the 21st century, they must make more far-reaching adjustments.

Most scholars agree that the union-nonunion wage gap widened during the 1970s and early 1980s. Orley Ashenfelter (1978) has reported that the adjusted union wage gap increased from 12 percent in 1967 to 17 percent by 1975. William J. Moore and John Raisian (1983) found that real wages grew faster in the union than in the nonunion sector from 1967 to 1977 and that the overall union wage premium rose to 24 percent. Among special groups, however, Moore and Raisian found that the premium was only 16 percent for manufacturing workers and 4 percent for white-collar workers, but was 31 percent for nonwhite workers, 30 percent for Southern workers, 31 percent for all blue-collar workers, 46 percent for construction workers, and 40 percent for workers with less schooling than a high school diploma. Marvin H. Kosters (1984a) found that the union wage premium grew dramatically, compared to the 1960s, in automobiles, coal, and steel; Yale Brozen (1981) and Reynolds (1984a, 1986c) concurred with respect to automobiles and steel. Similarly, Freeman and Medoff (1984, p. 46) have asserted, "In the 1970s, the archetypal union wage effect was on the order of 20 to 30 percent," and in several major sectors, the union-nonunion differential reached levels inconsistent with the survival of many union jobs. Freeman and Medoff view the concessions of the 1980s as dramatic instances of a return to more normal union premiums. They express confidence about the survival of unions because a return to normal differentials after a period of rising premiums "occurred in the past when union differentials got out of line" (p. 56), although they urge unions to "use their economic power more judiciously in the future" (p. 250).

Ronald G. Ehrenberg, Lief Danziger, and Gee San (1983) have claimed that during the 1970s, the wage rates of employees in heavily unionized industries who were covered by cost-of-living adjustment clauses grew significantly relative to the wages of other employees in the economy. Daniel J. B. Mitchell (1980, 1982) has reached the same conclusion. Chris Robinson and Nigel Tomes (1984) have found large union wage differentials for hourly workers, and Richard B. Freeman (1984) has argued that the cross-sectional estimates are an upper bound on the true union impact and that the time-series estimates are a lower bound. Jacob Mincer (1983) found a union-nonunion differential of over 20 percent for the "standardized" worker in his data for 1968–78, half attributed to union monopoly rent and half to a quality adjustment in hiring.

Most recently, Peter Linneman and Michael L. Wachter (1986) have found large increases in union wage premiums triggering statistically significant declines in union employment over the period from 1973 to 1984. Over half of the employment decline in nondurable manufacturing, transportation, and wholesale trade is accounted for by growing wage premiums. The upward trend in union wage premiums continued through 1984, reaching 21 percent in government, 57 percent in construction, 62 percent in mining, 33 percent in durable manufacturing, 26 percent in nondurable manufacturing, 46 percent in transportation, 33 percent in wholesale trade, 12 percent in retail trade, 9 percent in finance, insurance, and real estate, and −1 percent in services.

In summary, technical studies have not completely restored the consensus that prevailed in the 1960s about the magnitude of the relative wage effect of unionism. Labor economist Albert Rees once ventured the guess that about one-third of unions had virtually no effect on wages, one-third had moderate effects of 10 to 15 percent, and one-third had a large effect of 25 percent. Subsequently, though, Rees (1977, p. 74) wrote:

> My own best guess of the average effects of all American unions on the wages of their members in recent years would lie some-

where between 15 and 20 percent. This is a somewhat higher range than I would have guessed a decade ago. The difference is more the result of the availability of new data than a belief that union power has been increasing.

A safe generalization is that few economists would quarrel with 15 percent as a lower limit on the average boost that unions give to relative wage rates, especially in view of recent events. H. Gregg Lewis continues to believe that the union wage premium, properly estimated, remains at a maximum of 15 percent, but most economists believe that it is higher. The issue remains empirically alive, especially given the long delays in the collection of data and the publication of econometric results.

Perhaps the best evidence that the union wage premium rose during the 1970s and early 1980s is the dramatic decline in union membership. Between 1980 and 1984, organized labor lost 2.7 million members among wage and salary workers, while wage and salary employment increased by nearly 4 million people (*Monthly Labor Review* 1985). The total number of employed union members fell from 20.1 million to 17.4 million during this four-year period. In the goods-producing sectors of mining, construction, and manufacturing—historically the largest source of union membership— total employment fell by 800,000, the net result of 1.1 million new jobs among nonunion workers and a 1.9 million decline among union workers. Between 1980 and 1984, employment in the service sector grew by 5 million and union membership fell by 700,000, with half the loss in the transportation sector and another one-third in wholesale and retail trade.

Flatter Age-Wage Profiles

Another consistent finding among economic studies of union wage effects is that unions compress the wage differentials between junior and senior employees. An early study by George E. Johnson and Kenwood C. Youmans (1971) found this compression of age-experience-skill wage differentials, and this result continues to be confirmed in studies by Freeman and Medoff (1984), Mincer (1983), Moore and Raisian (1983), Simpson (1985), and Lewis (1986, ch. 7). All studies of wage differentials by age or job tenure, to my knowledge, find this union effect. The union relative wage effect is greatest among the youngest, lowest-paid workers and least among the experienced, higher-paid workers. Another way to put it is that in comparison with free-market (nonunion) employment situations, unions flatten the wage profile in such human capital variables as schooling, age, experience, and seniority.

This leveling effect may sound very egalitarian but it does economic damage, as any forced compression of the price structure must. The damage occurs in three ways. First, the compression in union labor prices directly lowers productivity in the economy by pricing inexperienced workers out of employment in the high-productivity unionized sector. This forces young workers to seek employment in less productive areas (sweeping up at the Burger King, as Walter Mondale put it in 1984).

Second, wage compression reduces opportunities to find any beginners' jobs in the economy, denying youth the vehicle to acquire skills on the job. Accepting a low-paying job for its training component is no different in principle from paying to go to school. Both are devices to raise a person's productivity and subsequent value in the marketplace. Mincer (1962) estimated that more than half of the training in the United States occurred on the job rather than in school. More recently, the U.S. Department of Labor (1985c) found that only a slight majority of employees needed specific training to qualify for their jobs. By implication, 45 percent of employees did not need any specific training to begin their jobs. The study also confirmed that the most common source for obtaining and improving skills was on-the-job training (OJT). In 8 of 12 occupational groups, informal OJT was the source of qualifying training more frequently than school programs. In all occupational groups, OJT was the source of qualifying more often than formal company programs. Over the long run, any forced narrowing of wage differentials for skills in the union sector must reduce the supply of skilled workers in the economy.

Third, wage compression destroys the incentive to improve personal performance. Why work hard at improving skills and gaining promotions if these only mean another $0.50 an hour before taxes? Lazear and Moore (1984) found that the lifetime profiles of earnings for the self-employed are flatter than for similar wage and salary employees. The reason, they conclude, is that the upward slope of wages for employees is an incentive to exert sustained effort. The self-employed do not need this improvement in wages over time because they automatically reap the gains from any productivity improvement. The union standard "rate for the job" removes the personal incentives for productivity improvement among employees. By contrast, nonunion employers induce employees to work harder through the incentive of steeper lifetime wage paths, thereby raising employees' lifetime earnings and overall wealth in the economy. Unions thwart these favorable productivity effects by compressing the lifetime wage structure. The recent two-tier system of wage agreements in some unionized (and nonunion) firms directly lowers labor costs and also corrects some of the harm done by lifetime wage compression. The two-tier system in nonunion firms suggests that the wage structure had narrowed too far in some of the competitive sector too.

Industrial relations scholars view "wage uniformity" as one of collective bargaining's "greatest accomplishments" (*Industrial Relations* 1983). However, any wage uniformity that is not the result of market freedom and equal productivity among individuals must be counterproductive. Consider the limiting case: If everybody were paid the same amount, it would destroy all incentive for improvement in skill, effort, and acceptance of greater responsibility. Moreover, Leo Troy, C. Timothy Koeller, and Neil Sheflin (1980) have pointed out that even union members do not universally applaud the tendency for unions to compress the wage structure. Skilled workers in the United Automobile Workers (UAW), for example, have been on the verge of secession for many years because of the egalitarian wage policies of the UAW hierarchy. Nor have white-collar workers in unionized firms been pleased with the relative erosion of the difference between their earnings and those of skilled blue-collar workers, although this is partially the result of market supply and demand as well as unionism.

The union policy of the standard wage has a series of widespread effects on various individuals, effects that are in substantial measure unintended and arbitrary. For example, the union wage effect is greater for nonwhites than for whites, greater for males than for females, greater for blue-collar workers than for white-collar workers, greater for transport operatives and laborers, less for service workers and nontransport operatives, and greater in the relatively unorganized South and West than in other regions; further, the effects vary widely in terms of occupations and industries (Freeman and Medoff 1984, ch. 3). Union wage rates have discoordinating and allocative effects similar to the arbitrary wage-price controls periodically imposed by government. At the individual level, wage rates bear less relation to individual differences in effort, productivity, and skill in the unionized sector, with all the resulting perverse effects on efficiency. Nor are those efficiency losses offset by any substantial improvement in anyone's sense of equity in pay. Wage distortions are piled on top of one another, and some offset one another in a statistical sense, at the cost of lower output in the economy.

Impact on National Output

What do these monopoly wage effects imply for national output? Standard economic analysis emphasizes the misallocation and loss in efficiency due to the wage effects of unionism. Monopoly wage effects lower national output due to suboptimal employment of labor and capital. But what is the magnitude of the loss in efficiency? Economists such as Freeman and Medoff (1984), who are sympathetic to unions, do not deny the existence of these losses; they simply dismiss them as "minuscule" based on static estimates of the losses amounting to substantially less than 1 percent of GNP.

The first of these static estimates was made by Albert Rees (1963). Using conventional assumptions, Rees estimated that the efficiency loss due to union wage policies was 0.3 percent of GNP, or $12 billion in today's $4 trillion economy. The conventional model used by Rees implied that the loss of market output in the economy could be estimated as the gap between the displaced workers' output in the union and nonunion sectors and the number of workers displaced by union pricing. This is Arnold Harberger's "deadweight loss triangle"—that is, production value that is forever lost to the community, wealth that is not transferred to union workers but simply disappears. The people excluded from unionized employment are assumed to be fully reemployed in nonunion jobs. Following H. Gregg Lewis's estimates, Rees assumed that the relative wage effect of unions was a 15 percent markup over market wages and that the disemployment impact reduced employment by 15 percent—that is, the implied elasticity of demand for labor was −1 in the relevant range. The result was a national loss of production of 0.14 percent due to union wage distortions across industries.

Rees also considered wage distortions within industries, such as the artificial suppression of North-South wage differentials and wage differentials by skill. Based on sketchy arguments, he judged that their costs were probably smaller than the 0.14 percent estimate for interindustry impacts. Rees concluded, "This would suggest a combined cost of less than 0.3 percent of gross national product. If this estimate seems low, it is because the social costs of transferring resources to less productive uses are far less than those of wasting resources altogether" (p. 75).

Harry G. Johnson and Peter Mieszkowski (1970) followed the same Harberger-based procedure for estimating the excess burden of the union "wage tax," and they concurred that the burden was quite small. With an assumed average union wage differential of 15 percent, they deduced a national income loss of 0.33 percent and a loss of about 1 percent with a union wage differential of 25 percent.

To illustrate these calculations with today's numbers, suppose that the unionized sector employs 22 million people if market labor rates prevail and that a 20 percent wage differential imposed by unions reduces employment by 20 percent to the actual 17.6 million in 1984. The displaced 4.4 million people find employment in the lower-productivity nonunion sector. If an average union employee earns $20,000 per year (a lower bound of $10 per hour excluding fringe benefits), the cost in reduced output per year is $20,000 times 4.4 million displaced employees times one-half of the productivity (wage) differential of 20 percent, or $8.8 billion, which is only 0.22 percent of GNP. If we double this figure to account for within-industry and diminished age-skill premiums and incentives, it still only amounts to 0.44 percent of GNP.

In a recent version of this calculation, Robert H. DeFina (1983) has used a more complex, general-equilibrium approach to estimate the efficiency loss due to union wage differentials. He concluded that the loss is even smaller, less than 0.2 percent of GNP (about $8 billion) under his alternative scenarios. This cost in GNP cannot be viewed as large relative to total output, although $8 billion would keep the Department of Defense running for 10 days or raise the income of the average American household by $87 per year. DeFina's estimates allow for wide substitution effects in the economy; therefore, losses are smaller in magnitude than in earlier studies, reinforcing the consensus that the economic burden of unions is "minimal." Many observers would conclude that 0.2 percent is a modest overall price to pay for the (allegedly benign) noneconomic effects of unions.

These traditional measures of the efficiency loss due to unions underestimate the overall magnitude of losses that union policies impose on consumers, producers, investors, and the unemployed. Although the Harberger-inspired method of estimating the loss in efficiency due to monopoly is sound on its own terms, it is very restrictive. The calculations ignore seven wasteful effects associated with union policies:

1. The redistribution of income (rent) from the general community to union bureaucracies and their members.
2. The unemployment effects of unions.
3. The consequences of union wage inflexibilities over the business cycle.
4. The cost of union work rules.
5. The dynamic impact of unions in discouraging research and development, investment, and entrepreneurship.
6. The direct costs of strikes, strike threats, negotiating costs, labor consultants, National Labor Relations Board elections, bureaucratic costs, grievance costs, and related expenses.
7. The political role of unions in increasing inflation, international trade barriers, government spending, and related forms of discoordination sustained by political action.

Each of these effects rivals the static, deadweight costs of union wage policies as losses to society. The remainder of this book analyzes these costs in detail, but for now just consider the first item above. Public choice economists, who specialize in the analysis of how decisions are made in the public sector, refer to the transfers of income caused by government actions as rents. A similar analysis applies to unions, with unions being seen as pressure groups redistributing income from the rest of the community to themselves. The monopoly rents ("plunder," according to less bashful writers) that unions acquire are large, but economists do not treat rents as social costs, but merely as transfers. Implicitly, economists treat unionists and nonunionists as equally blameless members of the community. But union wage premiums are at the expense of the rest of the community (a zero-sum game, at best). To gauge the magnitude of union rents, note that in the public finance literature, the deadweight losses due to tax distortions are about 10–20 percent of the tax revenues collected (the analogue of union rents). A comparable numerical result holds in the union context.

If the 17.6 million union members earn an average of no less than $20,000 per year and the monopoly wage premium averages 20 percent, union rents are $70.4 billion, or nearly 2 percent of GNP—nine times as large as the social cost of union wage rates. These represent losses to the nonunion community—pensioners, nonunion employees, investors, the unemployed—just as much as the Harberger losses of $8 billion. The $8 billion social cost is merely the difference between the larger losses of consumers and nonunion factor suppliers and the smaller rents gained by unionists. The losers in the redistributive struggle do not care whether their losses are called transfers or social waste.

Since the nonunion community has more to gain from deregulation of labor markets than unions have to lose, why does government not deregulate labor markets? The answer, in a word, is politics. George J. Stigler (1971) and Sam Peltzman (1976) developed what has come to be the orthodox theory of regulation. The essence of the analysis is that politicians and regulators maximize their political support by trading off marginal support from the beneficiaries (usually producer groups) against the marginal opposition from regulatory victims (often consumers ignorant of their losses) by way of manipulations in price, entry, and other factors in wealth transfers. The best available explanation for the failure to deregulate is that well-placed beneficiaries outbid the dispersed political losers for legislative favor. The superior unrealized gains of nonunionists relative to unionists from deregulation are not large enough—at, say, a 10–20 percent differential—to offset organizational handicaps. In the politics of redistribution, tariffs, price supports, ad infinitum, it is evident that well-organized producer groups such as unions exert disproportionate influence.

Public choice economists, following Gordon Tullock's lead (1967), point out that political rents are not costless to extract from the rest of the economy. Resources are consumed daily to achieve, maintain, and subvert monopoly in labor markets. The costs range from expenditures to operate unions (over $5 billion per year) to the expenses of some 6,000 management consultants at $600 million per year to oppose unions. In the long run, the costs of redistributive struggle in the marketplace and in Washington, D.C., can easily exceed union rents because unionists are willing to spend up to $70 billion per year to preserve their rents while the victims are willing to spend up to $78 billion to recover their redistributive losses. This assertion must be discounted by the probability of success, although each deregulation benefits the community generally by making monopolies less durable and therefore of lower present value. Since the long-run benefits of resisting monopolies and deregulation are diffused social benefits rather than concentrated private benefits, there appears to be a need to restore the old constitutional constraints on intervention that once prevailed in the United States, in place of deterrence by costly piecemeal opposition.

Some portion of union rents is dissipated in resource costs, but public choice analysis does not provide a general method to estimate how much. Unfortunately, it is much easier to estimate the size of monopoly rents than the resource costs of acquiring, maintaining, and resisting them. It is unlikely that the entire $70 billion in union wage premiums is dissipated in costs, and it is equally implausible that the real costs are zero. Logic dictates that unionists spend $1 at the margin to retain or gain $1 in wage rents. Tentative estimates based on other work in this book suggest that as much as half of union rents represent real resource costs. The net result of monopoly wage rates is a loss of $80 billion (2 percent of GNP) borne by the nonunion community. About $8–10 billion of this money never reaches unionists, and probably half of the remaining $70 billion is used up in the social costs of redistribution.

VI. Wage Inflexibility and Unemployment

[Labor unions] are formed to prevent the lowering of wages even more than to further the raising of wages.

—*Organized Labor* (May 23, 1914)

Unemployment as a mass phenomenon is the outcome of allegedly "pro-labor" policies of the governments and of labor union pressure and compulsion.

—Ludwig von Mises, *Bureaucracy*

From the beginning of economics as a scientific discipline, there has been virtually unanimous agreement among economists that a price system performs important coordination and equilibrium functions. "Prices have work to do," in the words of Benjamin Anderson, whether in the market for soybeans, heating oil, or labor services. Prices—exchange ratios between money and other goods— silently convey signals and incentives to market participants around the world. The people who have seriously studied the behavior and coordinating effects of market prices usually prefer that prices be free to tell the truth about relative scarcities among goods and services. Few economists, not even such socialists as Oscar Lange and Abba Lerner, have shared John Kenneth Galbraith's confidence in the ability of politics to fix prices that are "better," in some sense, than those determined in the marketplace. Perhaps the best evidence for the shared skepticism among economists is how few of them favor a permanent system of wage and price controls to replace market pricing (Kearl et al. 1979).

The 1930s brought the Keynesian revolution to economics. This new theory about aggregate employment and output (really a set of fallacies from the economic underworld of Simonde de Sismondi, Thomas Malthus, Karl Marx, and Silvio Gesell) appeared quite independent from standard microeconomic theory. John Maynard

Keynes's theory was not explicitly connected to micro theory in any obvious way. Today, virtually all mainstream economists agree that aggregate behavior must be derived from microeconomic—or choice theoretic—foundations. Differences among economists arise as to how to incorporate wage-price decisions into models of the economy, not as to whether it is wise to do so.

Sustained Discoordination

Microeconomic thinking is the only basis for whatever understanding of economic phenomena we have today. The price system fundamentally is a coordinating process. If prices are not allowed to change in accord with market conditions, the coordinating process is impeded. If prices depart from equilibrium levels on a wide scale for sustained periods of time, the result is massive, sustained discoordination.

The Great Depression is a prime example. Any theory of business fluctuations—the semiregular ups and downs in total employment and output experienced by mixed economies—must be able to explain major depressions in business activity. The alleged inability of classical economic theory to explain the Great Depression led Keynes to his new theory of aggregate demand deficiency, which much of the economics profession embraced for three decades and which still rules the economic policies of Western governments. Recently, Thomas Sargent, a leading macrotheorist of the so-called rational expectations school, said, "I do not have a theory, nor do I know somebody else's theory that constitutes a satisfactory explanation of the Great Depression" (see Klamer 1984, p. 69).

Sargent apparently has failed to read the writings of Hutt, Rothbard, Hayek, and Mises, because he does not ask the proper questions. One such question is, What do we rely on to coordinate human actions in a complex world? Answer: the price system. Another question is, Why did the price system fail to promptly recoordinate economic activities during the 1930s—that is, what prevented prices from correcting the imbalances (gluts) across the markets for goods and services, especially for labor services? Likely answer: Government, businessmen, and labor unions did not permit prices to adjust enough (that is, market-selected price reductions) to bring supply and demand into equilibrium (to "clear" markets); political policies prevented market prices from restoring full employment and full output (for example, see Rothbard 1983 and Higgs 1985, 1987).

Contrary to common perception, the Hoover and Roosevelt administrations derailed the normal adjustment processes of the marketplace, exacerbating the tragedy of the Great Depression and steering the United States into the so-called mixed economy. Their efforts to boost wages and prices painfully confirmed the validity of the classical emphasis on the importance of prices, rather than falsifying economic theory. The failure of most observers, including many economists, to understand this point is illustrated by a statement of Nobel prize–winning economist James Tobin: "The main thing was that classical economics didn't explain the Great Depression and didn't give you any hope of solving it. Keynesian economics did" (quoted in Klamer 1984, p. 101).

Imperfect Price Flexibility

The reasons for imperfect price flexibility are many. Some of them are economic, particularly long-term commitments to mutually agreed upon prices for both capital and labor services. Other reasons are directly political (price setting or price regulation by government) or indirectly political (legal privileges for unions or business cartels). Labor unions interfere with the smooth adjustment of prices in accord with market conditions, and failure to adjust in timely ways normally makes the inevitable adjustments worse later on.

The key historical issue is price flexibility downward, especially wage rates. Flexibility upward is not as much of a problem, at least on a sustained scale, because although there are lags in price adjustments upward in accord with new market conditions, these lags are rarely long enough to present serious coordination problems. Sellers have few problems in recognizing the opportunities for price boosts, and if they are free of government price controls, they can act to boost prices promptly, especially in modern, inflationary economies. Cutting prices, however, is painful and creates longer delays.

The welfare state is an indispensable ingredient that allows producer groups, especially union members, to play the waiting game and resist market-selected price cuts. Recessions and depressions were shorter in the late 19th and early 20th centuries because prices had to adjust promptly to market conditions. Workers had to price themselves into work if they were to continue eating, and merchants had to adjust their prices in accord with demand conditions if they were to continue eating. Neither group could count on monetary inflation, business cartels like those sanctioned by the National Recovery Administration in the New Deal, or welfare benefits to insulate them from market pressures during business recessions.

A natural comparison to illustrate the importance of price flexibility in the coordination process is the last "free market recession" in 1920–21 and the Great Contraction of 1929–33 (see O'Brien 1985). The recession after World War I was sharp but brief. A painful, major reallocation of activities was necessary following demobilization and the winding down of the government contracts from World War I. In 1919, federal spending was $18.5 billion; it declined to $5.1 billion in 1920 and then to $3.2 billion in 1921, where it remained throughout the 1920s (tax receipts remained at $4 billion per year during that decade). Between 1920 and 1921, the money supply (M1) dropped 9.4 percent, as the monetarist explanation of the business cycle would suggest. Between 1920 and 1921, unemployment rose from 5.2 to 11.7 percent of the labor force, reaching 5 million at the peak. Total output—real gross national product (GNP)—declined by 8.7 percent. The consumer price index fell 10.7 percent, the wholesale price index fell a whopping 36.8 percent, and average hourly earnings in manufacturing fell 7.3 percent, suggesting the price flexibility once familiar to the American economy. After these sharp but brief corrections in response to market conditions, the justifiably famous prosperity of the 1920s ensued.

The wage flexibility of the 1920s is shown more dramatically in Table 6.1. Averages are not as important as changes in relative wages, and the astonishing flexibility that once characterized U.S. labor markets is illustrated by the wage changes during 1924 and 1925 in manufacturing employment. The consumer price level fell by a trivial −0.2 percent and then rose a modest 4 percent in 1924 and 1925, respectively, suggesting a relatively steady average level of prices. The table shows the wide array of changes in wage rates, ranging from deep cuts of more than 20 percent (affecting 2 percent of manufacturing workers in 1924) to increases of over 20 percent. A slight majority (56 percent) of manufacturing workers experienced cuts in 1924 and a majority (70 percent) experienced gains in

Table 6.1

DISTRIBUTION OF WAGE CHANGES IN U.S. MANUFACTURING,
1924 AND 1925

Percent Wage Change	Percent of Employment 1924	Percent of Employment 1925
Wage cuts		
12 or greater	7	3
8–12	37	18
4–8	8	6
0.1–4	4	3
Total	56	30
Wage increases		
0.1–4	4	11
4–8	21	26
8–12	14	25
12 or greater	5	8
Total	44	70

SOURCE: Calculated from Mitchell (1985), p. 37. Original data from the U.S. Department of Labor, Bureau of Labor Statistics.

1925, but even in 1925, 18 percent of employees had their wage rates cut by 8–12 percent. This dispersion in labor prices and the related flexibility of capital and labor moving to more efficient firms is remarkable by post–New Deal standards.

In the modern era, the evidence shows that nominal wage cuts are a rarity, even during periods of low price inflation. When cuts occur, they result from long, extended negotiation against a background of mass layoffs and threatened or actual plant closures. Since 1946, no matter how severe the recession, average hourly earnings have never declined. The lowest average wage gain was 0.4 percent in 1958. Economists agree that wage flexibility is far lower than it used to be (O'Brien 1985 and Sachs 1980).

By contrast, the forces of expansion, ever so resilient, seemingly failed in the 1930s; more accurately, they were not allowed to work or were seriously hampered in operation. Why? The price indexes suggest that the first year of the Great Contraction did not exhibit nearly the degree of downward price flexibility that the 1920s did. During the calendar year of 1929, the money supply (M1) actually rose slightly, and then it declined by a relatively modest 4.2 percent in 1930, only one-third of the percentage decline experienced in 1921. This lends doubt to the conventional monetarist explanation of the Great Depression because the initial reduction in M1 was not large by historical standards. Prices, however, fell only a small amount: the consumer price index was down 2.6 percent, the wholesale price index down 9.4 percent, and hourly wage rates down 1.8 percent. Output, however, fell a steep 8.9 percent. When prices are relatively rigid in the face of demand fluctuations, quantities necessarily fluctuate more sharply.

Hoover Activism

Why the difference in price flexibility during the two episodes? In 1921—the last free-market recession—the Harding administration followed federal tradition and stood by and did nothing; a recession was something that "ran its course, like measles" (Lyons 1964, p. 166). There was pressure to intervene, especially from the industrialists and academics who had recently experienced the heady power of running the economy during the halcyon days of World War I. Within the government, Secretary of Commerce Herbert Hoover was among the minority urging federal intervention to "help the economy." The argument that carried the day was the oft-repeated statement of earlier business crises: "Businessmen got themselves into this mess, so let them get themselves out of it."

Historians have called the 1920s the "new economic era" and "welfare capitalism" (Hawley 1981 and Burner 1979). Many prominent businessmen came to embrace the new doctrine of prosperity through payment of high wages, dispensing with the outmoded law-of-the-jungle and every-man-for-himself capitalism. Elevated talk of social responsibility and enlightenment was everywhere.

Herbert Hoover—the "Great Engineer," humanitarian relief administrator, and secretary of commerce in the Harding and Coolidge administrations between 1921 and 1928—played a leading role in the transformation of thinking about labor markets during the 1920s. Hoover praised unions, collective bargaining, unemployment insurance, the American Federation of Labor (AFL), and child labor laws, and he championed the naive theory that U.S. prosperity was based on enlightened employers generously paying high wage rates (for example, see Hoover 1951, 1952, ch. 15). *Time* magazine featured the secretary of commerce on its November 16, 1925, cover and saw him not only as the "brains" of the Coolidge administration, with his fingers in an amazing number of pies, but as an entirely new breed of public official capable of getting results without much political fuss and with very little legislation (Hawley 1981, p. 3).

In 1928, Hoover was elected president and was then in a position to apply his economic remedies when the crisis of 1929 came along. Although Hoover may be known as a conservative, he was never laissez-faire in his economic philosophy. After the stock market crash in late October 1929, he quickly sprang into action, armed with his new economic doctrines. His first labor-market actions were to call a series of White House conferences with leaders of industry, commerce, and organized labor. They pledged to carry out Hoover's program of maintaining wage rates, employment, and investment spending.

Although unions and federal regulations were modest factors in labor markets then, the evidence supports the hypothesis that the wage pledges were carried out. By March 1930, the AFL was hailing the fact that not one of the big corporations had thought of lowering wages as a means of reducing unit costs. Until April 1931, the wage arrangement was policed by Julius Barnes, chairman of the board of the U.S. Chamber of Commerce, through a 400-member National Business Survey. The wage promises Hoover had extracted seemed to hold firm for almost two years, at least among large firms, thereby becoming a prime engine of unemployment. At the AFL convention in October 1930, William Green introduced Hoover to the crowd by proclaiming that Hoover's "great influence served to maintain wage standards and prevent a general reduction of wages" (quoted in Rothbard 1983, p. 218).

In May 1931, Secretary of the Treasury Andrew W. Mellon summed up the administration's philosophy on labor prices: "In this country, there has been a concerted and determined effort on the part of both government and business not only to prevent any reduction in wages but to keep the maximum number of men employed, and thereby to increase consumption" (quoted in Rothbard 1983, p. 237).

Leo Wolman (1931, p. 2) wrote:

> So deeply embedded was this doctrine of high wages in our

national thinking, that the largest of our industries resisted wage cuts until the end of the second year of the depression. . . . It is indeed impossible to recall any past depression of similar intensity and duration in which the wages of prosperity were maintained as long as they have been during the depression of 1930–31.

Hoover forced a reversal of reductions in railroad pay as late as 1932 (Burner 1979, p. 252). Responding to falling product prices, mounting unemployment, and severe business losses, employers made wage cuts secretly for fear of disapproval by the Hoover administration. The U.S. Steel Corporation cut wage rates 10 percent in September 1931, over the opposition of its president, James A. Farrell, whereupon AFL president William Green promptly accused U.S. Steel of violating its 1929 pledge to President Hoover (Rothbard 1983, p. 239). By September 1931, farm wages, in contrast to wages in the more visible firms and industries, plunged to 64 percent of the August 1929 level and fell to less than 50 percent during 1932 (Beney 1936).

As employment and output continued to decline through 1931, the Hoover administration gradually substituted more ambitious compulsory measures. In 1930, Hoover had already signed the Hawley-Smoot Tariff Act over the petition of 1,000 economists; Hoover subsequently banned further immigration and accelerated deportation to keep wages up, signed the Davis-Bacon Act to impose a maximum eight-hour day and maintain wage rates on federally financed construction projects, enacted various public works projects, signed the Norris-LaGuardia Anti-Injunction Act to exempt unions from antitrust law and injunctions, revived the War Finance Corporation as the Reconstruction Finance Corporation, and imposed higher income tax rates. The result was an appalling disaster, never before known in U.S. history, which has haunted American politics ever since. Sen. George W. Norris did not realize how prophetic he was in 1922 when he commented on Hoover's activism: "We had better let God run [the economy] as in the past, and not take the power away from Him and give it to Hoover" (quoted in Burner 1979, p. 166).

Many people apparently believed that maintaining wage rates was a patriotic duty, rather like respecting union picket lines. These ideas (or "emerging social custom") can affect human action in labor markets, at least temporarily, as they can in public policy formation (Kalt and Zupan 1984). Hoover played a large role as "America's foremost public instructor in the new era" (Lloyd 1972, p. 108), and according to Mark Sullivan, Hoover's journalist-historian friend, Hoover regarded "our entire business structure as a single factory, conceiving himself, as it were, consulting engineer for the whole enterprise" (quoted in Lyons 1964, p. 160). The diminished wage flexibility of 1929–31 was due to a combination of misguided idealism and White House pressure, ending up in more formidable interventions.

Generating Price Inflexibilities

My argument is not that flexibility in prices degenerated from perfect flexibility to perfect rigidity in 10 years, but simply that the 1929–31 period shows less flexibility, on average, and set in motion a self-reinforcing downward spiral in employment and output. Every failure to adjust prices in the face of falling market demand implies that fewer people work, fewer goods are produced, and therefore real demand for other goods is lower. This deterioration in the ability of the market system to operate flexibly is a central characteristic of the welfare state, even with Hoover's "cooperationist" philosophy. The short of it is that union and government actions can more or less permanently price some resources out of full employment, after which private and public relief keeps them in subsidized idleness.

This tendency was taken to its height during Franklin D. Roosevelt's first New Deal, when the Agricultural Adjustment Act, the National Industrial Recovery Act, and other measures were used to try to boost prices in the mistaken belief that falling prices were causing the Depression. It is common for those of the Keynesian persuasion (and interventionist thinking generally) to mistakenly believe market pressures for coordination to be the cause of disorder. The result was that price-fixing measures never cured the Great Depression; in fact, they prevented recovery. By 1940, for example, the unemployment rate was still at 14 percent, four times the 1929 rate. Nevertheless, most of the policy measures that failed to get the country out of the Depression became permanent fixtures of government growth.

Labor unions are only one element, albeit a major one, in the mix of welfare state policies that reduce the efficiency of operation of the labor market. The other major elements are government policies that enshrine wage rigidities, subsidize idleness, and inflate the price level to crudely recoordinate an economy. The official if implicit ideology is that no wage rate can be permitted to fall. To allow reduced wages is to backslide in the struggle for economic progress.

Since the 1930s, unions have been the major element among the factors making wage rates unresponsive, and the increased rigidity is especially damaging during recessions, when nominal demand falls or grows less slowly than anticipated. Price flexibility is essential under these conditions if the economy is to sustain employment and output. The union mentality, in truth, is Marxist-inspired; it is based on an adversarial class theory that they—the union officials who claim to represent labor—win wage gains through struggle with capital, and ground won is not to be surrendered to the enemy.

To further complicate matters, government embraces the purchasing-power doctrine that wage rates should never be cut. If wage incomes fall, the argument goes, aggregate spending will fall. Based on this erroneous doctrine, maintaining or increasing wage rates, not cutting them, is the right policy for business downturns.

Business leaders have become imbued with this erroneous notion too. They believe that good employers do not cut wage rates, no matter how few people will be employed at high wage rates and how many people will be forced into unemployment. If powerful trade unions can reverse falling wage rates, the theory goes, fine. Purchasing power will then rise.

However, this theory ignores the fact that higher labor prices reduce employment and thereby reduce output (real income), which means deflating the real demand for goods. Properly understood, the aggregate output of goods is also the aggregate demand for goods (Say's law of markets).

The New Deal represented the high-water mark for the idea of the wage-underconsumption doctrine, a totally upside-down brand of economics. As any freshman in economic principles can describe, only a competitive price results in the maximum amount of a good or service being produced and exchanged in a market. If price is too high, demand limits the amount purchased (and therefore sold); if price is too low, supply constrains the amount sold (or produced and therefore purchased). The same truths hold in labor markets too. If labor prices are fixed above competitive levels, employment is not maximized and output is held below capacity too. Competitive prices maximize the volume of trade, production, and employment, and therefore they keep poverty at as low a level as possible. It all derives from the law of demand: If goods go unsold and workers unemployed, the only reason is that the prices asked are too high in view of the competing demands in the community.

Statistical Evidence

That unions reduce the downward flexibility of wage rates is disputed by few economists. Ronald G. Ehrenberg, Leif Danziger, and Gee San (1983), for example, have argued that the average rate of wage inflation has become less sensitive to unemployment; so has James Tobin (1980). Increases in the rate of unemployment now "buy" smaller reductions in wage inflation, according to these economists, than in the 1960s. Ehrenberg, Danziger, and San, however, admit that their econometric results did not provide strong support for their specific models, suggesting that there may be more market sensitivity than they hypothesized.

Robert J. Flanagan (1984) found that nonunion wage rates are much more sensitive to the business cycle than are union wages. Nonunion wage rates lead wage decelerations and display greater cyclical variation, whereas union wage rates—reflecting the influence of long-term contracts in which the wage provisions for later years are negotiated long before the economic environment can be known—lag behind the deceleration in nonunion wage rates and have less cyclical variation. Flanagan found that the union first-year negotiated wage changes are about as sensitive to unemployment rates (a crude indicator of labor demand conditions) as nonunion wages are. But the second- and third-year provisions of the typical collective contract (the average duration of union contracts was 32 months in 1983, down slightly from its 1979 peak of 33.4 months) introduce rigidities through fixed, deferred increases. The cost-of-living adjustment clauses (COLAs) in 60 percent of contracts since the 1970s accounted for less than 5 percent of wage changes in the late 1960s. However, by the late 1970s, COLAs accounted for one-third of wage changes for union workers, a trend not reversed until 1982–83. Although introducing sensitivity to price-level changes, the COLAs contribute—as do fixed, deferred wage increases and annual productivity improvement clauses (which deteriorated sharply after 1973 but were not reflected in union wage packages)—to rigidity relative to labor market conditions. The COLAs and annual improvement clauses have been the main way that union wages have resisted downward pressure in real terms, creating the wide union-nonunion differentials of the late 1970s and early 1980s. While a natural method to remedy this problem would be to negotiate more often, management and unions avoid this step because negotiating costs, especially the strike threat and actual costs of strikes, increase sharply with the frequency of negotiations.

In a study of the longitudinal evidence from seven industrialized countries, R. L. Thomas (1977) found that unions reduced wage-rate sensitivity to variations in demand conditions. William H. Branson and Julio J. Rotemberg (1980) found that the sensitivity of wage movements to fluctuations in demand was sharply reduced in the 1970s in five countries, including the United States. The United States was the only country that remained rigid in terms of nominal wage rates while the other four—Great Britain, Japan, Italy, and West Germany—were relatively rigid in terms of real wage rates. This is consistent with effective indexation in these countries as compared with the United States.

Robert J. Gordon (1982) has found that nominal wages in Great Britain and Japan are 5/10 times more responsive to changes in money GNP than in the United States. Gordon commented that the drastic decline in U.S. wage responsiveness in the post–World War II era compared to the 1892–1940 period is more than coincidental with the arrival of the three-year staggered wage contract in the U.S. unionized sector. American labor-market institutions are much further from optimal than are Japan's, according to Gordon.

Dennis Grubb, Richard Jackman, and Richard Layard (1983) have found that the United States has had the highest degree of nominal wage rigidity relative to other Organization for Economic Cooperation and Development (OECD) countries owing to its long lags, and also that the United States suffers about average rigidity in terms of inflation-adjusted wage rates. The countries that enjoy comparative flexibility in real wage rates include Switzerland, Japan, New Zealand, Sweden and Austria—all countries with small or zero increases in their unemployment rates in the 1970s and 1980s relative to earlier years. Otto Eckstein (1968) commented that the literature provides a uniform pattern of results: trade unions, among other institutions, introduce long lags into wage change. Unions also dampen the responsiveness of wage changes to excess spending, although they apparently escalate the overall wage reaction to price inflations.

One of the few exceptions to the finding that unions make wage rates sticky has been the work of John Raisian (1983). Raisian found that wage schedules are not as fixed during the course of demand disturbances as commonly believed. Surprisingly, unionized blue-collar employees had higher procyclical wage variation than their nonunion counterparts in Raisian's data, although the nonunion workers had more stable employment in terms of weeks worked. This fact suggests that the greater variation in union wages is still not sufficient to put their employment stability on a par with that of nonunion workers.

A curious intellectual sidelight to the question of wage and price flexibility is that many economists of the Chicago school are likely to argue that flexibility is very high despite the world having failed to meet the assumptions of the perfectly competitive model. In the extreme, the rational expectations school postulates continuous clearing in the markets for all goods. Keynesian-type economists, on the other hand, are more likely to argue that inflexibility characterizes wages and prices.

There is a good reason for downward inflexibility in prices. For over 40 years, wage and price setters have experienced accommodating, inflationary monetary policy. The institutional arrangements and decision makers in the marketplace adjust to their experience and the general environment. In a world with governments committed to full employment by any and all fiscal and monetary means, disinflation and moderate policies are not credible to market participants unless the policies are pursued for an extended period of time. This is especially true since the policies are subject to political determination, not constitutional rules—the rule of men, not laws.

The process of inflation is a genuine two-way street in which the labor-market institutions, especially labor unions, increase the willingness of the Federal Reserve Board to print money; this, in turn, increases the willingness of unions to set wage rates irresponsibly high. Under these circumstances, announcements of more responsible fiscal and monetary policies usually are not credible to market participants, and price and wage setters do not adjust their behavior. The recessions due to a deceleration in monetary inflation are comparatively long and severe because the announced change in political policies is not credible until the authorities follow through for an extended period of time. The welfare state, of course, encourages people directly and indirectly to hold off making the necessary adjustments. Tragically, this robs the community of the stimulus of the new output that the first price cuts create. Consistent with this view is Salih N. Neftci's (1984) statistical analysis, which shows that the unemployment series is characterized by sudden jumps followed by gradual drops.

Indexing Pay to Performance

Many economists have recently urged that some part of pay be linked to company performance to introduce more flexibility in labor costs. Their proposals include linking wages to output price, profit-sharing plans, employee stock ownership plans, and—the ultimate in such plans—employee ownership of the firm. These proposals are distinct from the codetermination or worker-participation plans required by law in much of Europe, but there is a connection: If remuneration is linked to the company's bottom line, then demands for employee decision-making power increase.

Advocates promise greater flexibility in pay and therefore better macroeconomic performance. They also argue that workers have an incentive to increase their effort, relax or abandon work rules, and generally contribute to the efficiency of the firm. But if these schemes are so virtuous, the obvious question is, Why haven't people adopted these arrangements voluntarily? One problem is that the link between the incentives and personal productivity depends on the size of the firm and the exact monitoring-compensation scheme of the firm. Many schemes would have such a diluted relationship between individual performance and company results that the personal reward for additional effort would be nil.

Scholars such as Martin L. Weitzman (1984) and Daniel J. B. Mitchell (1985) have urged companies and unions to adopt so-called gain sharing to restore flexibility in labor compensation. Such an approach is essentially a patch-up, that does not confront the fundamental problem, namely, the government policies and government-supported unions that are responsible for the major

98

rigidities in the first place. The authors of such reforms implicitly accept existing unions and government rigidities as politically impossible to modify. Once accepted as given, the rigidities become binding constraints that impede a well-behaved economy. It then is necessary to search for damage-minimizing changes, or second-best policies, to accommodate unions and related labor-market policies.

The recommendations for greater profit sharing attempt to emulate the greater sensitivity of nonunion wage rates to market conditions. In particular, nonunion compensation is adjusted more frequently and is implicitly tied to the success of the firm. The natural question is: What is so sacred about unions that public policy should protect them from the consequences of their own pricing rigidities? My answer is, nothing. Instead of searching for ingenious public policies to make union wages more flexible, we can repeal the National Labor Relations Act of 1935 (the Wagner Act) and all similar laws and regulations, thereby putting unions on the same footing as everyone else (see chapter 2). To gain flexibility in labor markets, we can deregulate and remove union privileges, just as we have done in such markets as air and surface transportation.

There have been a few signs—but only a few—in recent years that unions have become more flexible than in the past. Marvin H. Kosters (1984b) has pointed out that unions have increasingly renegotiated contracts before they were scheduled to expire, given up or deferred scheduled increases, been willing to adjust long-term wage and benefit formulas in mid-contract, deviated more frequently from industrywide provisions at the plant or company level, conceded two-tier wage systems, and modified work rules under the pressures of the marketplace. Kosters (1984b, p. 220) says, "I do see increased union wage flexibility resulting from more competition, and I expect the timing of adjustments in union wage trends—both up and down—to be affected by the cycle." Robert J. Flanagan (1984), on the other hand, believes that these measures are likely to have only modest impact on the flexibility of aggregate union wage rates. At a minimum, our recent history demonstrates how large an economic disaster labor unions and unionized industries must suffer before adjustments begin. And Peter Linneman and Michael L. Wachter (1986) show that union-nonunion wage differentials were at an all-time high in 1984.

Profit sharing as an economywide means of increasing flexibility is fundamentally flawed. Martin L. Weitzman (1984) wants to "encourage" (subsidize) profit sharing relative to other forms of labor remuneration through exhortation and tax privileges. Why should this be necessary if profit sharing is mutually agreeable to employers and employees relative to other payment mechanisms? That it has not been widely adopted in most manual jobs suggests serious disadvantages.

To some extent, the absence of profit sharing has been the result of historic opposition by labor unions, who see profit sharing and similar bonus schemes as anti-union tools of employers and devices to increase loyalty to the firm. The trade unions and the labor laws from the 1930s that make them effective have channeled personal policies of unionized and nonunion companies into a narrower framework than would otherwise exist. If we were to deregulate labor relations, much more diversity would quickly develop in labor relations as nonunion companies experiment with a wider array of personnel practices, much as in the 1920s. These revisions almost certainly would include the participatory forms of management demanded by an increasingly professional and well-educated labor force.

The defects of profit sharing extend further, however, than to their conflict with traditional union policies and the adversarial premises of U.S. labor codes. To be symmetric, profit sharing would also involve loss sharing. The returns to capital are always residual—that is, what is left of revenues after contractual costs, including interest payments on borrowed capital funds, have been paid. Workers, by and large, prefer to avoid the uncertainty of being residual claimants in favor of the greater security of regular pay. Firms that pay workers in the mix of wages, benefits, and profit sharing that workers like can attract and retain the quantity and quality of employees they want at lower average cost than firms that do not pay in this way. Competition for labor, in other words, tailors compensation to workers' tastes.

Another difficulty with profit sharing is that compensation that is solely in accord with company performance is ultimately in conflict with market efficiency. In the 1960s and 1970s, the problem was vividly illustrated in communist China, where communes that happened to be well-situated made their members rich, while equally capable workers in less-fortunate communes were impoverished. If profits rise in a firm or industry, consumers are signaling that they want more and the output should be expanded. High returns are the incentive for investors to respond to the signals. If labor in profitable firms takes substantial portions of increases in profit, the incentive to respond to consumer wishes diminishes. Meanwhile, equally competent employees in unprofitable firms would suffer pay reductions. This would be widely considered inequitable, and it would be inefficient too. Firms that perform poorly would have lower labor costs than successful ones, thereby rewarding inefficient firms and penalizing the expansion of efficient firms that serve their customers well. In the limit, investors, consumers, and unlucky workers would be the hostages of workers in successful firms.

In competitive labor markets, by contrast, all firms are compelled to pay the same prices for the services of equally productive inputs, thereby allowing only the relatively efficient firms to survive. Profit sharing, when imposed or subsidized by government, simply promotes an inefficient allocation of labor. The statistical evidence consistently shows that the wage gains of workers are not correlated with the productivity gains in their particular firms or industries, a result that supports the competitive labor-market theory.

If labor suppliers or their representatives really want to make the fundamental managerial decisions, as W. H. Hutt has argued (see Reynolds 1985a), they must become fundamental entrepreneurs. There are no legal impediments to labor borrowing the funds, using pension money, or using other forms of wealth to buy out the assets of a firm and then run the firm under its own direction. Labor would presumably seek to maximize the yield so that the employees receive at least the rate of interest on their money. This shows the absurdity of the idea that workers have no alternative to being corporate wage slaves in the marketplace. Workers have always had this option but have chosen not to exercise it, as Hutt has argued. Laissez faire is open to all organizational forms, but not all forms are viable or competitive. Although employee-owned enterprises can succeed, it is clear that many workers do not care to risk everything they own (pension included) at their place of employment. They simply do not wish to keep their wealth in such a narrow form.

From the point of view of incentives for employee productivity in the workplace, many profit-sharing plans would be ineffective because individual effort has a negligible impact on aggregate profit, which, in turn, would be shared by all employees. Piecework pay schemes, which once covered half of all U.S. production workers but now cover fewer than one-quarter (largely due to union opposition), link personal productivity and reward more closely. Even in piecework pay, though, there is a problem in adjusting to change, especially in the presence of a union. Suppose a piecework worker earns enough to exceed the earnings that he could get elsewhere. In the economist's terms, the firm is covering the worker's opportunity cost. Now the firm installs some new equipment that enables the worker to triple his hourly output without any more effort or discomfort. The worker or his union will insist on keeping the old price schedule, but the worker will make three times the wages as before, far in excess of his opportunity cost. Social efficiency considerations imply that the piecework rate should be reduced by two-thirds, ultimately benefiting consumers and all workers. But will the union allow it? Who will have to be bought out? The impediment to progress is obvious.

Most of the profit-sharing schemes have additional defects in terms of practical administration. For example, differentials in compensation tend to narrow under profit sharing because workers are paid on a per capita basis or number-of-hours-worked basis rather than in proportion to base wage rates. This is a serious handicap for employers trying to induce workers to acquire training for skilled jobs or to recruit skilled employees. Until now, the tax code has offered favorable treatment (relative to straight wages) only to profit-sharing plans that put their bonuses into retirement funds, and advocates such as Mitchell (1985) and Weitzman (1984) seek to widen the favorable tax treatment of profit sharing to nondeferred payments. But the actual operation of every-worker-a-capitalist schemes always depends on the specifics of the tax code passed by Congress, Internal Revenue Service decisions, and court rulings.

Unions and Profitability

An irony of the proposal to share profits with unions is that recent evidence shows that unionized firms earn substantially lower returns than similar nonunion firms. Unions already redistribute profits away from the owners of capital to unionized workers, so, in a sense, formal profit-sharing plans would merely validate an ongoing phenomenon. Michael A. Salinger (1984), for example, has found that unions capture 77 percent of monopoly profits (defined as the ratio of a firm's market value to the replacement cost of its physical assets). He also has found little long-run monopoly power in the U.S. economy, and his statistical results suggest that a combination of concentration and barriers to entry allows firms to raise price above cost but that the primary beneficiaries in such cases are unionized workers.

Kim B. Clark (1984) also has found clear evidence that unions seize investors' quasi-rents. This finding partially explains how unionized firms can operate over extended periods of time (unions take the returns from yesterday's long-lived investments, but it only pays the firm to operate until the assets need replacement). It also suggests why capital owners are strongly opposed to unionization. Ronald G. Ehrenberg (1979) found that the unionized wage rates of the employees of the New York Telephone Company were above those of equally qualified employees elsewhere in the economy, and that these costs were passed on to telephone customers through regulated prices. Richard B. Freeman (1983) also has found evidence that unionism quite substantially reduces profitability, although he argues that it is not harmful but even beneficial because it occurs in concentrated industries. Redistribution to unionized workers, he presumes, reduces the overall degree of inequality of income. There are many problems with this argument, not the least of which is that even if it were true in the short run, the possibility of extraordinary returns would be reduced in the economy, thereby discouraging investment. There is no better example of this effect than in Great Britain, which has been turned into an industrial museum (and museums are expensive to maintain) through the confiscatory policies of the unions and government.

When unions win a National Labor Relations Board representation election, according to Richard S. Ruback and Martin B. Zimmerman (1984), the equity value of the company declines an average of 3.8 percent. This decline occurs whether or not the union ever gains a contract. Even when unions lose an election, there is an average reduction of 1.3 percent in the equity value of the firm. This suggests that investors feel that the company's earnings are at increased risk of union exploitation even if a company continues to defeat unionization at positive cost to itself.

Paula B. Voos and Lawrence R. Mishel (1986) use a two-equation model to control for the potential two-way interdependence between the degree of unionization and profitability in manufacturing. They have found that the union impact on profits is even larger than with the single-equation approach.

The Cost of Wage Inflexibility

So how much does the wage inflexibility due to unions cost the U.S. population? We can make an educated guess at the order of magnitude. The cost primarily takes the form of higher unemployment in the union sector, which therefore reduces unionized output and consequently reduces the demand for the noncompeting outputs of the rest of the economy. My rough estimate is that inflexibility in union pricing costs nearly 1 percent of GNP when the economy is in the neighborhood of full employment and 2 percent of GNP when there is a deep recession (unemployment at 10 percent or higher). Over the course of the business cycle, then, the average loss would be in the neighborhood of a higher unemployment rate by about 1.3 percentage points and lower real output by about the same percentage, given that the productivity losses are concentrated in the high-productivity jobs.

Despite all the publicity about concessions and givebacks, union decision makers still price the services of their membership at rates that ensure the loss of large fractions of the membership and permanently shrink industries such as steel to one-half or less of their former sizes. Union leaders amazingly refuse to adjust to market conditions, thereby accelerating the downward spiral in their membership, dues income, and union staff. For example, the United Steelworkers of America claimed 1.3 million members in 1980 but only 589,000 by 1983. Unemployment rises to disastrous levels before union officials admit their error in gauging market demand for their members' services, partly because such an admission creates the wrong psychological aura if the officials acknowledge they are powerless to generate the customary or desired level of income for their members through tough or skillful bargaining. Another factor to explain this apparently suicidal policy is that workers with seniority and good pension plans prefer high-wage policies that result in layoffs of young workers—sometimes even letting the plant close so that they can draw benefits. This hardly benefits the

104

younger and potential workers, much less consumers and the economy generally.

Some union officials know they are in a dilemma but think they can hold out, that things will work out somehow, despite their failure to advocate or accept the necessary adjustments. They run to Washington seeking additional monopoly protections and subsidies so that their industry can survive the labor costs that they have imposed. But these interventions protect employment in a particular industry at the expense of greater employment elsewhere in the economy. In an interdependent system, employment arises from the sale of productive services in other sectors, which in turn demand productive services from another sector. Both labor and capital must be permitted to seek their highest yields in free markets if we are to maximize production and employment.

The examples of unresponsive overpricing of labor and its disastrous results can be multiplied indefinitely. In the state of Michigan, for example, half a million people were unemployed on a typical day in 1985, yet unions imposed labor costs of $22 an hour or higher on many manufacturers. Large numbers of qualified production people are available at lower prices, and U.S. automobile manufacturers continue to suffer a $1,500 cost disadvantage per car relative to foreign producers.

U.S. recessions and depressions were short-lived prior to the 1930s because sellers, including labor unions and workers, had to accommodate themselves to demand conditions if they wanted to continue working, producing, and eating. Prices and wage rates adjusted to market-clearing levels because there was not much choice. This flexibility allowed full employment output to revive more quickly. Although unions have played a central role in diminishing this flexibility, the income-support mechanisms of the modern welfare state are crucial complements too. Idleness must be subsidized if tranquility is to be preserved. Unions and taxpayer-funded transfers to the jobless go together.

Unemployment insurance is the most important element in keeping excess labor off the market, allowing postponement of wage adjustments. The U.S. Department of Labor implicitly admits this by proclaiming that unemployment insurance tends to prevent the "breakdown of labor standards." What are labor standards? This is the bureaucracy's phrase for wage and working conditions, so an accurate translation in economic terms is that paying people to remain idle allows wage rates to stay higher than they would otherwise be. Unfortunately, spending more than $20 billion per year on unemployment benefits, in addition to other programs, postpones wage adjustments. The reservation wages of the unemployed remain high, thereby impeding the restoration of full employment production and lower rates of inflation.

VII. Work Rules and Absenteeism

Portland, Ore.—A teenager who cleaned and repaired some bus shelters as a community service project . . . has found himself . . . in a labor-relations dispute. Kenneth Pulley, 16, led other Boy Scouts in sprucing up eight of 800 shelters owned by Tri-Met, the regional transit agency. . . . The Amalgamated Transit Union says that the project . . . violated a labor contract with Tri-Met. . . . The project, completed Feb. 17, 1985, helped Kenneth receive the Eagle [Scout] rank.

—Associated Press

The simple truth is that nothing in the world can increase employment which does not create in the minds of manufacturers and contractors the expectation of an improved margin of profit.

—John Maynard Keynes, *Essays in Persuasion*

In the 20th century, there have been many government programs to create jobs, and uncounted billions of tax dollars have been spent on them. Similarly, unions have spent a great deal of effort to preserve jobs, and they have generated a considerable amount of conflict in the process. Here today, here tomorrow is the implicit union slogan. Such devotion to the status quo, of course, condemns us to stagnation or, more likely, retrogression.

Both the government and union efforts to create or protect jobs are cut from the same intellectual cloth—the idea that opportunities to work and their associated income streams are scarce, if not nearly impossible to find. This notion can be labeled as the economics of abundance, a form of upside-down or Keynesian economics, a world in which the scarcity of productive resources, especially labor, buildings, and machinery, has disappeared. What remains is a glut of all goods and services and merely a distribution problem.

Job creation or protection is a wholly mistaken idea. In the world of scarcity in which we actually live, there is an infinite amount of work to do and, as a result, an infinite number of jobs. Our age is characterized by sloppy language and sloppy thinking, a claim nowhere better illustrated than in the lament that there are "not enough jobs." Properly speaking, people are not interested in jobs or in finding more work to do. What interests them is the payment associated with work. The employment problem always reduces itself to a question of price; we have a shortage of high-paying, "decent," "American" jobs, not a shortage of jobs.

In our world of unsatisfied demand for more consumer products and services, opportunities to serve our fellow man by working are unlimited. Nevertheless, Western economies have been plagued by lagging employment, lagging production, and more-or-less chronic bouts of mass unemployment with all its tragic consequences. Why? Despite all the government spending and union policies to make jobs, the problems persist. The answer, in a word, is pricing. Modern labor policies violate David Ricardo's 170-year-old dictum on a grand scale: "Like all other contracts, wages should be left to the fair and free competition of the market, and should never be controlled by interference of the legislature" (Ricardo 1821, p. 61). Governments and their offspring, the labor unions, prevent competitive pricing from coordinating the economy and restoring full employment of capital and labor.

If economists know anything at all, they know how to create surpluses of any product or service: simply keep prices above competitive, market-clearing prices. Labor services are no exception to this law. When labor is overpriced, as it is in most unionized employments, preserving employment under those circumstances is a chronic problem.

Work Preservation by Unions

From an economic point of view, work rules are a predictable consequence of monopoly wage rates. To preserve employment and thwart the strong tendency to economize on expensive union labor both in production by managers and in product markets by customers, unions try to preserve jobs for their members, as well as their bargaining clout, the political prestige of large membership, and high dues income for officers. The depression mentality of union men, the notion of saving some work for the next guy, is a direct result of the excess labor supply available at union wages.

The natural tendency of free labor markets to establish prices that bring the quantities of labor supplied and demanded into equality—thereby promoting the fullest possible use of resources, high levels of efficiency in allocation, and the highest possible community income—is thwarted by union price fixing. Work rules are just one of the ill effects caused by the initial distortion in prices. Political pricing dooms an economy to chronic discoordination, idle people and equipment, and more political problem solving in the form of job-creation programs and union featherbedding, despite the demonstrated failure of such measures. The measures fail because they are not directed at the cause of the problem; consequently, they are inappropriate palliatives that actually aggravate the problem.

The union practices in question are called work rules by the unions and frequently "restrictive work rules," "featherbedding," "overmanning," or "overstaffing" by managers and the general public. Albert Rees (1979) suggested three principal types of union restrictions on output at the work site: (1) crew-size rules requiring a minimum number of union people to perform a particular task or operate a piece of equipment; (2) rules requiring unnecessary work to be performed; and (3) jurisdictional rules requiring that specified work be performed only by members of specified unions. To these we should add a fourth: (4) opposition to new labor-saving techniques.

These wasteful practices—shirking on the job and overstaffing—can occur in nonunion employment too. People who do boring and repetitive work often are not interested in the work itself, only in the pay and companionship on the job. Some try to take as much leisure on the job as possible. This behavior and related forms of informal restrictions on output on the job ordinarily are kept within narrow bounds by managers, who monitor employee performance and set incentives to encourage productivity. As a limiting case, for example, managers of firms in competitive markets would never consciously retain employees on the payroll who did no work at all. Under work rules, however, some workers are paid for doing absolutely nothing.

Examples of the folly of work rules abound. Locals of the International Brotherhood of Electrical Workers (IBEW) have refused to install electrical switchboards unless factory wiring is torn out and rewired by IBEW members. Most freight trains still have four or five crewmen aboard, at least double what railroad managers claim is necessary. Each crewman earns a day's pay for every 100 miles traveled, although some freights can cover 400 miles in an eight-hour period. Other examples: the International Typographical Union has insisted on resetting existing plates of newspaper advertising; the stagehands' unions have required minimum crew size for theatrical performances; the musicians' union locals have insisted on standby orchestras; the motion picture projectors' union has compelled use of two operators per projection machine in some cities; and the operating engineers' union has required that one member operate each machine or engine on a construction site, even if only one switch must be turned on for an entire day's work.

Other examples: work rules often prohibit foremen or other supervisors from helping or working at the trade under any circumstance; restrictions demand that expensive craft union members perform unskilled work, such as operating automatic elevators or handling materials; other work rules prohibit drivers from assisting helpers who are members of the same union (Teamsters); and some longshoremen refuse to shift from ship to dock work, thereby compelling use of multiple crews.

In a rare, in-depth study of work-rule effects Paul T. Hartman (1969) studied the West Coast longshoring agreement of 1960 in which, in exchange for higher union pay, the union agreed to eliminate many of the work rules requiring multiple handling of goods, redundant crews, and other restrictions on productivity. Hartman found that productivity had dropped following unionization of the ports in the mid-1930s and then output per labor hour had remained fairly constant until 1960. Labor productivity increased by 40 percent in the five years after the 1960 agreement. Longshoremen earned higher pay, total employment of longshoremen was maintained, and the industry enjoyed higher volume at lower unit cost. ,

When Albert Rees (1979) was on the Construction Industry Stabilization Committee, he encountered a case in which a contractor hired union painters to paint a highway bridge across a river. Union rules required that a small boat patrol beneath the bridge to rescue any painter who fell, although the usual method of dealing with this hazard was to rig a net below the bridge. The boat, of course, was manned by a union painter. The boat had an outboard motor;

however, because the rules of the building trades did not permit a painter to operate an engine, a unionized operating engineer had to be added. The employer was obligated to pay skilled wage rates every day to both workers. The employer complained that he was not even offered any of the fish the two "workers" were catching.

The construction industry is blessed with many government-financed projects, providing a rich environment for featherbedding. For example, the *Houston Post* (1985) reported that George Morrison, an operating engineer supervisor in New York City, received $400,000 a year because the union contract specified he be paid overtime rates whether he was at work or not. Morrison, a supervisor at the Battery Park city housing development project in lower Manhattan, was entitled to receive unlimited overtime pay beyond his eight-hour workday if any union members worked overtime. Because a supervisor did not have to be on the site, Morrison was paid around the clock during times he was in Mexico, the Caribbean, Europe, and South Carolina. Without overtime, his earnings would normally have been a mere $60,000 per year. A state commission was shrewdly planning to hold hearings to determine if the work-rule provision was responsible for inflating construction costs in New York City.

Over the years, perhaps the railroad unions should be awarded the labor equivalent of an Oscar for Best Sustained Performance in Reducing Industrial Efficiency. Their maze of practices has run from requiring firemen on diesel locomotives to full-crew laws to train-limit laws. The industry's labor force is heavily unionized, with 90 percent of employees organized into 15 craft unions. On a division of the Norfolk & Western, crews get an extra day's pay every time they turn a locomotive around. Labor restrictions cost the railroad industry some $4 billion a year, according to some estimates (*Wall Street Journal* 1986a, p. 1). At the nation's largest railroad, the Burlington Northern, president Darius Gaskins, Jr., says internal studies show that his work force could be cut in half if work rules were abolished. In a dispute over work rules on the Guilford, the 16th-largest railroad, chairman David Fink says, "There's no better way to find what you need to run a railroad than to have a strike," and he claims to have restored 70 percent of service with 33 percent of the prestrike employment level (*Wall Street Journal* 1986a, p. 1).

Less well known is the fact that the Hollywood unions would run the railroad unions a close second in the efficiency-reduction category. Disputes over which union man should perform what task under which circumstances are common on television and movie sets. Propmen are allowed to carry in potted plants or firewood but not to frame a scenery flat with greenery, a job reserved for the greens man. Grips (equivalent to stagehands) handle certain kinds of tents but the drapery department handles others (Arabian-style, for instance). A prop maker or carpenter can build a set but cannot knock it down, a job reserved for grips if the set is to be used again. Makeup and hairdressing clash constantly, as do lighting specialists of every union variety, and on and on. Job protection is the name of the game, smothering productivity under rules written by depression mentalities and agreed to by compliant managers.

Unions consistently resist introduction of new technology and labor-saving equipment. For example, painters' locals have prohibited use of spray guns and restricted brush widths, hod carriers have fought ready-mixed concrete, plumbers have resisted plastic pipe, and print unions have opposed computer typesetting. In 1975, pressmen attacked computerized presses and left a million dollars' worth of damage at the *Washington Post*. The London *Times* was shut down for 50 weeks in 1978–79 because management wanted to introduce "new" print technology—equipment in common use in the United States and other parts of the world for 15 years—that would allow an average employee to increase output from 3,000 to 18,000 characters per hour.

In 1984, publisher Rupert Murdoch spent $93 million on a new computerized plant in London for his British newspapers, but Great Britain's powerful print unions, with a staggering 370,000 members, blocked him from using it. Salem Jihan "Eddie" Shah, a cousin of the Aga Khan, began publishing Britain's 10th national daily (*Today*) in the spring of 1986 at 75 percent below the usual cost in Great Britain by using state-of-the-art technology. Advertising rates are supposed to be 25 percent of those charged by established newspapers. If Shah succeeds, which is in doubt at this writing, he would confirm the proposition that obstructive print unions inflate costs a staggering fourfold over an efficient firm; other newspapers eventually will be forced to match Shah's and Murdoch's efficiencies. Shah claims that he is not anti-union and that if the unions want to run a newspaper, they should invest the money. Managers in the unhealthy British newspaper industry were not managers but industrial relations specialists. Rupert Murdoch and his managers finally broke the Fleet Street unions in 1986, the most historic upheaval in the British press and labor union structure in a century (Melvern 1986).

Both British and American unions assert exclusive jurisdiction (properly speaking, monopoly jurisdiction) over particular kinds of work and people, much as national governments claim suzerainty over people and territory. Interunion disputes break out at times, accompanied by strikes, picketing, boycotts, and violence. Two craft unions, for example, can claim the same work, especially if a new technique or material is introduced, and the employer is caught in the middle of a union battlefield.

As Woodruff Randolph, who ruled the International Typographical Union in the United States from 1944 to 1958, said, "The ITU is a craft union exercising jurisdiction over *all* composing room work. Our jobs are dependent on that work. The life of our trade is dependent upon that jurisdiction. Whatever weakens or destroys our jurisdiction destroys our union" (quoted in Leiserson 1959, p. 88). William L. Hutcheson's carpenters' union claimed to cover everything from the growing tree to the finished product: "Once wood, it is always the right of the carpenter to install it" (quoted in Mills 1948, p. 60). Ironically, unionists display little concern for the right of other unionists to work on terms that are mutually satisfactory on an employer's job site, despite all the cant about the labor movement, solidarity, and brotherhood. A little-known but important function of the AFL-CIO is to try to keep interunion conflict within bounds.

Absenteeism

Besides the output losses attributable to union work rules, unions also are associated with higher absenteeism. Absenteeism is costly because it disrupts production schedules and demands greater use of substitute workers, who are less efficient than regular workers. This cost is higher in work settings characterized by teamwork or by employees with specialized, firm-specific training. Absenteeism is likely to be correlated with other factors that reduce efficiency, such as low morale, job dissatisfaction, and poor motivation. This is nowhere more evident than in the coal fields, where unionized operators complain about excessive absenteeism. Miners do not deny this, saying, "Any day I don't work in that mine is one more day it isn't going to kill me," apparently a sufficient rationalization for many miners to avoid their chosen work (Miernyk 1980, p. 39).

The existing statistical studies—D. E. Taylor (1981), Steven G. Allen (1984a), J. Paul Leigh (1984)—find that unionism increases absenteeism, all else equal. In three data sets, Allen (1984a), for example, found that union members are 29–100 percent more likely to be absent than similar workers who do not belong to unions. The annual loss of work hours (and therefore production) attributable to unions was 1.3–1.5 percent in the Current Population Survey, 3.6–4.4 percent in the Quality of Employment Survey, and 3.1–4.2 percent in the Panel Survey of Income Dynamics. Judging from the nature of the data sets and the techniques applied, a loss of 3 percent in annual work hours appears to be a good estimate.

Unionized workers are more likely to be absent because of liberal sick-leave benefits, small penalties for absenteeism, an income effect from high union wages that encourages taking additional leisure, greater dissatisfaction in unionized jobs, inflexibility in unionized work assignments, and more labor conflicts and disputes. These findings, of course, are at odds with the theory advocated by Harvard economists of employee "voice" at union plants.

Quantitative Estimates of Cost

Anecdotes of union restrictions and case studies of work rules in industries could be multiplied indefinitely. Essential as these stories are, skeptics dismiss them as merely anecdotal and of little consequence. Skeptics also belittle the cost of work rules by arguing that most work rules originally were sensible policies instituted by management but that unions try to preserve the practices long after they have outlived their usefulness. Although it is true that management agrees to union work rules, few of the damaging practices—restrictions on paintbrush widths, resetting type, standby orchestras, and so forth—were instituted by management. Most union work rules never did bear a sensible relation to safety or efficiency considerations, but were and are simply work-preserving devices.

Nearly everyone condemns these union restrictions on output as

114

obviously wasteful, but what do they add up to? No one really knows, although most businessmen complain that work rules are more costly than the union wages they are forced to pay. As Daniel Luria, senior researcher at the Industrial Technology Institute in Ann Arbor, Michigan, says, "Work-rule savings are like a mythology at this point, you don't see a lot of numbers" (*Wall Street Journal* 1986b, p. 1). Company studies, however, continue to insist the savings are big.

Construction Studies

The most researched industry on the issue of work rules has been construction. One approach has been to examine union contracts for restrictive practices. The most comprehensive study of contract provisions is the examination by the Bureau of Labor Statistics (BLS) (U.S. Department of Labor 1974) of 769 contracts for 16 building-trades unions in the 66 largest metropolitan areas in 1972–73. Table 7.1 shows the proportion of workers covered by nine productivity-related clauses for each of the 10 major unions and for all 16 unions together. The most widespread restrictions are minimum crew-size provisions and requirements for a foreman after a given number of workers are employed. Crew-size restrictions cover one-third of all union workers and over two-thirds of bricklayers, ironworkers, electrical workers, and operating engineers. About 60 percent of contracts require foremen after a certain number of workers are hired, with over half of these requiring a foreman for only one to three workers. In addition, over one-quarter of the contracts specify foreman-to-journeyman ratios. Prefabrication limits cover 70 percent of plumbers and 77 percent of sheet metal workers. Limits on tools (mostly maximum brush size) cover 83 percent of painters. On the other hand, nearly half of the workers in the sample are covered by employer-initiated provisions that prohibit union limitations on the amount of work performed per day.

The Business Roundtable (1982, 1983) examined a large sample of agreements in effect in 1979 that covered almost half of the union work force. It found that 20 percent of its sample contracts contained crew-size restrictions resulting in an annual excess cost of $42 million. By contrast, the 1974 BLS study found much greater use of restrictions. The Business Roundtable cited exclusive jurisdiction as the greatest handicap faced by union contractors because it pre-

Table 7.1

ESTIMATED REDUCTIONS IN PRIVATE OUTPUT DUE TO UNION WORK RULES AND ABSENTEEISM, 1984
(percent)

Industrial Sector	Total Employment Share	Union Share	Effect of Work Rules and Absenteeism	Reduction in Private GNP
Mining	1.2	17.9	−10	−0.021
Construction	5.9	24.3	−10	−0.143
Manufacturing	27.1	26.5	−5	−0.359
Transportation, communications, public utilities	7.3	39.6	−10	−0.289
Trade	25.2	8.2	−5	−0.103
Finance, insurance, real estate	7.8	2.7	−2.5	−0.005
Services	25.5	7.2	−2.5	−0.005
Total	100.0	15.6*		−0.925

SOURCES: Data for total employment and union shares from Adams 1985, p. 26; estimates for effect of work rules and absenteeism and for reduction in private GNP prepared by author.
*Weighted average.

116

vents use of the most efficient mix of inputs and causes disputes among unions.

William Haber and Harold M. Levinson (1956) interviewed 268 representatives of labor, management, and government in 16 cities to determine how much effect union work rules had on costs. They concluded that work rules raise costs by 3–8 percent, which, they argued, was "much less than has been widely alleged" (p. 189). They attributed three-fourths of their cost estimate to restrictions on the employment of different types of labor (especially unskilled), and the remainder to restrictions on technique.

In a more recent survey of union and nonunion contractors in eight cities in 1976, Clinton C. Bourdon and Raymond E. Levitt (1980) found relatively few restrictive work practices in the union sector. No work-rule restrictions were reported by 55 percent of the contractors interviewed. Operating engineers and ironworkers set strict limits on the number of workers for a given job, and the mechanical trades were very restrictive on work performed off-site. According to the union contractors, the major restriction imposed by work rules was that they rarely allowed workers to cross trade lines. Only 27 percent of the union contractors—compared to 82 percent of nonunion contractors—said that their workers crossed occupational lines anywhere from occasionally to often.

Steven G. Allen (1986) argues that effective work rules imply that managers have less flexibility to select least-cost combinations of inputs. As a result, union contractors should be less responsive to changes in relative labor prices and have lower ability to substitute among types of labor (in technical terms, lower demand elasticities and labor–labor substitution elasticities). Estimating a translog cost system in two sets of construction data, Allen finds that price responsiveness and substitution flexibility are much lower for union contractors, supporting the hypothesis that they are effectively constrained by work rules. To estimate the added expense, Allen assumes that average union wage rates would fall to average nonunion wage rates; the result would be a decrease in total labor costs of about 25 percent to produce a given amount of construction. The lower cost would be mostly attributable to lower wages. Removal of work rules reduces labor costs by about 5 percent, or 20 percent of the cost impact.

Railroad Studies

Albert Rees (1963) is the only academic economist, to my knowledge, who has ventured a quantitative guess at the magnitude of the economywide cost of work rules. He concluded in 1963 that the deadweight losses from work practices exceeded the losses owing to wage distributions. Managers in a single industry—railroads—claimed in 1959 that obsolete work rules were costing $500 million a year, or over 0.1 percent of national output. That would amount to nearly $4 billion today, or nearly half the social cost due to union wage differentials.

The railroads are a much smaller share of the economy today than in 1959. Between 1959 and 1985, railroad employment fell from 900,000 to 301,000, suggesting that the railroad unions were not very successful in preserving work for their members, despite all the work rules. There is some evidence that railroad work rules have been relaxed over the years. By 1973, only two states still had so-called full-crew laws on the books. More important, work rules were relaxed because of the sharp competition from deregulated truckers. Output per employee-hour in rail transportation, for example, jumped 23 percent in 1983 alone. From an accounting point of view, the 1983 jump in productivity was separable into one-third deriving from higher output and two-thirds deriving from continuing shrinkage in employment. This rise in productivity partially reflects the cyclical recovery in output, but also reflects measures, such as the recommendations of the Task Force on Rail Transportation during the 1970s, to improve the operation of the railroads to head off bankruptcy and government takeover of the companies. Still, the railroads have a long way to go in becoming efficient.

The only certain consequence of work rules is that they increase the costs per unit of output. This implies that the unionized companies and the industry are less efficient and prone to eventual retirement from competitive activity. Virtually all union attempts to retard progress must fail eventually, although at substantial social cost in the interim. If we accept the 1959 estimate of 0.1 percent of GNP, the smaller employment on the railroads today and the subsequent relaxation of restrictive practices imply that their work rules cost society less than 0.1 percent of GNP in waste today. In 1986 the largest railroad union, the United Transportation Union, approved a national contract that eliminates some unnecessary crew members, extends crew runs to 108 miles per day (up from 100 miles per day), and permits lower pay for new employees. A few railroads have won the right to operate some freight trains with two men instead of four or five. With the relative decline of railroads and the ongoing upheaval in the industry, we must search for another means to estimate the social loss from work rules over the entire economy other than Rees's extrapolation based on work rules in the railroad industry.

Overall Losses

The losses attributable to union work rules and union-induced absenteeism cannot be uniform across industries. They are widely believed to be worse in industries organized by craft unions—industries in which jurisdictional disputes, manning requirements, and opposition to new technology are a familiar and natural consequence of unionism. Industrial unions, however, are certainly not free of restrictive work practices. Industrial unions often have specified staffing for certain equipment. The longer that companies have been in existence and unionized, the longer is the list of work rules. Plants long unionized by, say, the United Steelworkers of America have work-rule books as thick as the Sears catalog. When his plant was a union plant, David Houck, chief executive officer of the new McDonald Steel Corporation in Youngstown, Ohio, said, "Each man knew all of the things that he didn't have to do. . . . Now, when you need to move something, anybody—maybe a guy from packaging—just goes up and runs the crane" (Waters 1984, p. 62).

Another example of restrictive practices by industrial unions is the revival of the former Kaiser mill in Fontana, California, now reopened as a nonunion facility called California Steel. The high labor costs imposed on Kaiser by the steelworkers' union were a major cause of the shutdown of the plant in the fall of 1983; it was not so much the union wage rates as the work rules. The plant, which once employed 6,000 workers, now employs only 600, all handpicked former Kaiser employees. They are paid about the same as they earned with Kaiser—$25,000 to $40,000 per year—but few rules limit what an employee is asked or permitted to do. One worker says, "The difference is morale. . . . Now we're being treated like grown men. It's a good feeling" (*Wall Street Journal* 1985b, p. 18).

In 1985, Cablec Corporation, a closely held cable maker, bought a Marion, Indiana, cable plant that ran by work rules adopted as long ago as the 1930s. Job categories were so rigid that when somebody classified as a millwright—essentially a mechanic—was told to repair a lift truck, first he had to call someone classified as an electrician to disconnect the battery cables. As a condition of buying the plant, Cablec got the plant's two unions to agree to reduce job classifications from 217 to 69 and weaken seniority rights. Plant demands for different skills are now as important as seniority in rehiring. Now a millwright can disconnect battery cables. Cablec vice president Richard Lusk credits the relaxed work rules with initially cutting the work force by 6 percent, reducing scrap costs by 30 percent, saving $3 million a year, and turning losses to profits (*Wall Street Journal* 1986b, p. 1). Despite the costliness of union practices in smokestack industries, the restrictions remain somewhat less burdensome than in craft-organized industries, partly because the rules are subject to negotiation at the plant level rather than being fixed at national levels.

Industries that have suffered from work rules have been transportation (air, rail, truck, and water, including longshoring), entertainment, construction, and printing. In the port of Houston, for example, newly formed nonunion stevedore companies load and unload ships with as few as half the workers required by the International Longshoremen's Association (ILA) (*Houston Chronicle* 1985b, p. 1). A conservative estimate is that nonunion firms use 25–50 percent fewer laborers than ILA companies to accomplish similar loading and unloading jobs. Nonunion stevedore companies bid for jobs at rates at least 25 percent lower than ILA-organized firms. In response to such nonunion competition, ILA unionists have threatened violence against nonunion workers. On a more constructive note, ILA steel gangs have been cut from 12 to 10 people, ore gangs from 4 to 2, and further negotiations are under way to meet the competition.

A crude way to estimate the overall reduction in private GNP attributable to work rules and union-induced absenteeism is to start with the fact that unions organized 15.6 percent of private wage and salary employees in September 1984. If it is assumed that private GNP per employee is the same in union and nonunion sectors (it is actually higher in the union sector, biasing the estimate downward) and that work rules and absenteeism make productivity 10 percent lower than what it would be otherwise, private GNP would be 1.5 percent lower (that is, 15.6% × − 10.0%). A figure of 10 percent seems a reasonable magnitude because the case studies cited above suggest that work rules alone increase labor costs 5 percent or more, whereas union-induced absenteeism reduces output another 3–4 percent in unionized employments.

At the upper end, the railroads claim a 50 percent boost in labor costs due to work rules. Alvin Toffler (1986), in a generally sympathetic treatment of unions, argues that the "drastic elimination of union-imposed jurisdictional restrictions, demarcation lines, work rules, narrow job descriptions and other rigidities" would allow the work week to be reduced to 25 hours—a dramatic (if unintentional) acknowledgment of the cost of union work rules. In addition, case studies such as Paul T. Hartman's (1969) suggest that the losses imposed by work rules are at least 10 percent. Although most academic studies downplay the losses attributable to work rules, many businessmen claim that work rules cost them more than union wage premiums. Since economists put the average union wage differential at 15 percent or more, 10 percent does not seem an overestimate of the true loss due to union work rules and absenteeism.

Another approach to estimating these losses is a sector-by-sector version of this estimating procedure, as depicted in Table 7.1. Based on anecdotal evidence, productivity-reducing impacts in terms of lower output per hour are assigned to various unionized industry and service categories as follows: mining and construction, 10 percent; manufacturing, 10 percent; transportation (including communications and public utilities), 10 percent; trade, 5 percent; and finance, insurance, real estate, and services, 2.5 percent each. The net result is an estimated overall drop of 0.9 percent in GNP, slightly lower than the crude 1.56 percent loss estimated above without a sectoral breakdown. These estimated losses in GNP make no allowance for the added value of the leisure time consumed by union members on and off the job due to work rules and absenteeism. These gains to union members partially offset the lost GNP, thereby reducing the social loss from inefficient union work practices and absenteeism.

Compared to Rees's quantitative estimate of the loss in productivity due to work rules, 0.9 to 1.5 percent of private GNP is high. Rees, however, believed that the railroads alone suffered a loss of 0.1 percent of GNP due to restrictive practices. Ironically, some recent industry estimates still put the railroad loss at 0.1 percent of GNP, despite the two-thirds decline in rail employment from 900,000 to 301,000. Table 7.1 estimates that union work restrictions and absenteeism in the transportation, communications, and public utilities sector reduce GNP by 0.28 percent, the second highest of any industry (manufacturing is first with 0.36 percent). Construction is third with 0.14 percent, and the remaining industries contribute little to the loss of output either because of the small size of the industry (mining) or because unions have organized few employees and are assumed to have trivial productivity-reducing effects (trade and services).

These calculations ignore the impact of union work rules on the second most highly unionized industry—government—because there is relatively little productivity there to worry about. In certain obvious instances, such as in the U.S. Postal Service and in situations where unions prevent the contracting out of public services to private firms, unions hamper productivity in the public sector too. The situation is probably worse in the public sector simply because there is virtually no competitive pressure on public employee unions and government managers to abandon inefficient practices. Mass transit is a perfect example of the gross inefficiency and redistribution of income from taxpayers to highly paid union members (Sowell 1980, p. 202).

Conclusion

Most observers agree that union work rules impede productivity, but there is a surprising dearth of quantitative information about the extent of the losses. Predictably, studies show that unionized workplaces are also associated with high rates of absenteeism. The case studies and other information issued by journalists, industry associations, government, and academics suggest that union-induced work rules and absenteeism reduce private-sector output by about 1 percent.

VIII. Strikes, Union Negotiations, and Administration

> The main losses caused by union power or worker unruliness flow not from strikes but from managements' fear of strikes . . . the sapping of will and decision caused by union power itself.
>
> —Arthur Shenfield,
> "The Rise of Trade Union Power in Britain"

> Our whole civilization rests on the fact that men have always succeeded in beating off the attack of the redistributors.
>
> —Ludwig von Mises, *Socialism*

Strikes are newsworthy. The media and the public apparently believe that strikes are costly and infantile ways to settle labor differences. Most labor scholars and economists, on the other hand, contend that strikes are not costly to the economy and may even be a sign of adversarial relationships that are "healthy." Richard B. Freeman and James L. Medoff (1984, p. 218), for example, argue that in the 1980s, only 11 percent of unionized workers went on strike in a typical year, reducing work time by an average of 0.9 percent in the economy. A similar view tends to prevail among free-market and Chicago-style economists, who hold no brief for monopoly unions but believe that plentiful substitution possibilities sharply limit unionists' ability to inflict social damage through strikes, thereby preserving a predominantly competitive economy. Strikes in manufacturing, for example, may have little direct impact on industrial output because struck firms draw on built-up inventories, some plants operate during strikes, and nonstruck firms expand their outputs during strikes.

Another issue closely related to evaluating the costliness of strikes is estimating the cost of the corporate, union, and government resources used to negotiate, review contract language, sit at the bargaining table, retain legal counsel and labor consultants, orga-

123

nize workers, process grievances, engage in arbitration, participate in NLRB elections, and incur other expenses. Little research has been done on this issue, probably because researchers in industrial relations believe that these costs are minor. But a substantial number of people directly earn their livelihood from the conflicts generated year after year in the labor-conflict industry (including the industrial relations scholars who act as mediators, arbitrators, fact finders, and labor consultants). The American Arbitration Association, for example, has more than 25,000 people listed on its labor roster, and the American Bar Association (ABA) has over 10,000 members in its labor relations section (out of 327,000 ABA members and 693,000 lawyers in the nation).

The Nature of Strikes

Strikes and the other direct costs of union activity must be of consequence. Informal evidence is abundant. First, unions gain substantial wage premiums almost solely as a result of strike threats. Strikes can impose enormous costs relative to a firm's main objective—profits—because profit margins average less than 5 percent of sales revenues (in 1985, an average business year, the net income of the 500 largest U.S. industrial corporations was 3.8 percent of their sales). Rational profit-seeking enterprises would not pay millions of dollars more than necessary for labor to avoid strikes if these private costs were trivial. Managers must believe that the corporate costs of a strike often outweigh the added expenses of higher wages and work rules. This calculation clearly depends on subjective estimates of the probable damage that a strike can inflict and the size of the union wage demands in light of product and labor-market conditions. Melvin E. Reder (1984), for example, has found some statistical support for the proposition that the larger the threatened strike costs, the higher the union wage premium.

Another piece of informal evidence that strikes can be costly is that many managers believe that employees fear strikes; companies strongly emphasize union strikes during NLRB election campaigns in an effort to discourage voters from casting their ballots for union representation. Also, some scholars claim that the near elimination of strikes over grievances and contract interpretation through use of arbitration procedures has been a major advance in labor relations.

124

It is essential to distinguish between the realized costs of strikes, which can be relatively small, and the potential costs of strikes, which can be substantial and therefore usually worth avoiding. Strike threats are similar to the threat of war, an ever-present possibility in a world of aggressive and well-armed governments. The only real difference between war and labor relations is that the unions consistently rely on confrontational tactics whereas the management literature just as persistently is filled with techniques to avoid and diffuse confrontation.

Why don't firms just treat strikes as mass resignations and hire new workers at open-market prices? This is not literally prohibited by U.S. labor law. However, labor laws and their enforcement generally are intended to give advantage to the underdogs (the unions) and raise labor prices. A strike is not simply a withdrawal of services to protest what the union declares are substandard conditions. Free men have always had the unqualified right to withdraw their labor services. Instead, unions work to see that if some of their members do not work, no one replaces them. Unions are not simply inefficient but peaceful cartels of the business variety. If they were, picket lines (another military term) would not be necessary to enforce labor solidarity during strikes. While coercion usually is kept in the background for obvious reasons, the question of so-called labor peace is always present in labor negotiations. Occasionally, union leaders threaten disorder quite openly. Union pickets at plant gates not only discourage interlopers (called "scabs") but identify any union members who return to work. "Coventry" is the state of ostracism or exclusion that the strikers intend to use after settlement. Arthur Shenfield (1986, p. 11) has described the behavior of strikers as follows:

> The jobs from which they have withdrawn performance belong to them, they maintain. Their labour is present and available for those jobs, and woe betide any other workers ('scabs', 'blacklegs', etc) who may seek to offer their labour in place of that of the striker. Woe betide also any employer who seeks to hire the labour of such 'interlopers'.

Managers must cope with the daily results of misguided labor policies, but the business community cannot escape some measure of responsibility for the situation. A lack of courage and the desire for popular approval are part of the general problem of defending private ownership of the means of production. Many businessmen do not understand this point. Instead, they follow what they believe are enlightened wage policies and embrace their so-called social responsibilities. Such behavior was permitted in many large corporations by the cartelized product markets that prevailed through the late 1960s and early 1970s.

Joseph Schumpeter (1962) thought that capitalism could not survive because businessmen lack the intellectual capacity, as well as the will, to defend economic freedom. Corporate executives succeed the self-made entrepreneurs of early capitalism, and these corporate climbers are not steeped in rugged individualism, have no strong sense of private property, and are indifferent to anonymous shareholders. More important, Schumpeter (1962, p. 161) said, "the bourgeoisie . . . absorbs the slogans of current radicalism and seems quite willing to undergo a process of conversion to a creed hostile to its very existence." Some modern businessmen respond to the encroachments of labor unions as the native girl did to Lord Jim's advances, described by Joseph Conrad this way: "He would have ravished her, but for her timely compliance" (quoted in Rogge, p. 34).

A Tale of Two Strikes

Economic troubles almost always can be traced to weak competition in the product and labor markets. Strikes can dramatically illustrate this proposition. The best-known strike of the early 1980s—that of the air traffic controllers—and the largest strike since 1946—that of AT&T workers in 1983—exposed the inefficiencies of unionized companies with sweet clarity.

The PATCO Strike

The famous strike by the Professional Air Traffic Controllers' Organization (PATCO) began on August 3, 1981. The result—replacement of the striking controllers and dissolution of the union—set a new tone in government labor relations during the 1980s and probably a new attitude in the private sector as well.

To understand the strike and its aftermath, it is useful to review the situation prior to 1981. The air traffic control system is a complex assemblage of people, equipment, facilities, and procedures owned and operated by a government agency, the Federal Aviation

126

Administration (FAA). The behavior of the FAA provides ample evidence of the drawbacks of government operation of the air traffic control system. The agency operates as a monopoly without competition, its costs are covered by taxes imposed on users and the general public, it runs on civil service rules, and it is handicapped by substantial amounts of political control and interference. According to the FAA's numerous critics, the agency is a technological laggard, is unresponsive to its customers (insulated from market pressures), lacks controls for cost-effectiveness, has a large and unwieldy bureaucracy, fails to plan long-range, and is managed by administrators who are short-term political appointees. There have been various proposals to privatize the air traffic control system (Poole 1982 and Poole 1986), including a modest one urged by the Air Transport Association (ATA), the trade group of the scheduled airlines.

The FAA had a quasi-military history, and its civil service managers—who, effectively, cannot be fired—have been labeled "autocratic" and "impersonal." Although it has been common to view the PATCO strike as a case of union militants exploiting their monopoly position, that is only part of the story. After the strike, an independent task force—the so-called Jones Commission—appointed by the secretary of transportation, Drew Lewis, found that the FAA's labor relations were dismal for 15 years (Jones et al. 1982). Judging by news accounts, they remain so today.

New York City controllers formed PATCO in January 1968 (Northrup 1984). There were six serious disruptions in service prior to the 1981 strike. In July 1968, there was a month-long slowdown. In 1969, a three-day slowdown triggered the suspension of 80 controllers for periods of up to 15 days. The Corson Report that year criticized both management and PATCO (U.S. Department of Transportation 1970). In March 1970, a "sick-out" of 20 days involving 2,200 controllers occurred. The ATA won court orders to end the sick-out after its members lost millions of dollars. PATCO ignored the orders; it was found in contempt of court and ordered to pay steep daily fines. The ATA sought collective damages in excess of $50 million. In exchange for dropping the damage claims, PATCO agreed to a permanent injunction against a PATCO strike or slowdown. The injunction specified a daily fine of $25,000 payable to the ATA in the event of a PATCO violation.

127

The FAA discharged 67 controllers in the sick-out, but 27 of them were reinstated on appeal and the secretary of transportation, John A. Volpe, ordered rehiring of the remaining ones in the election year of 1972.

In March 1973, PATCO and the FAA signed their first agreement, although Congress still held the power to set salaries. In July 1976, PATCO engineered a five-day slowdown at the busiest airports after the Civil Service Commission refused to reclassify controllers to higher salary grades. In January 1977, the Civil Service Commission reversed its initial ruling and increased most controllers' wages after PATCO threatened another stoppage. In May and June of 1978, there was a "spontaneous" slowdown at major airports, and the ATA won a contempt citation pursuant to the permanent injunction that the ATA and PATCO had agreed to in 1970. The court ordered PATCO to pay the ATA $100,000 and reprimanded the Department of Justice for doing nothing. On August 15, 1980, O'Hare International Airport controllers engaged in a slowdown that delayed 616 flights by 30 minutes or more and cost the airlines more than $1 million. The controllers demanded a tax-free bonus of $7,500 per year for the additional stress at O'Hare. The FAA refused and immediately sought a court order.

PATCO's leaders aimed to free themselves of civil service constraints and turn the FAA into a monopoly corporation like the U.S. Postal Service. In 1977, PATCO began a thinly disguised strike fund. The FAA filed a complaint but the Federal Labor Relations Authority dismissed it, reasoning that "preparing for a strike was a legal activity, provided that no strike ever occurred." By August 1981, the fund had $3 million. By that time, PATCO had won average pay of $33,000, superior fringe benefits such as retirement at age 50 with 20 years' service, and lucrative disability benefits that induced dramatic rises in "system errors" as controllers sought evidence for disability (Staten and Umbeck 1982). After quietly winning control of the PATCO executive board, militant Robert Poli suddenly replaced John Leyden as PATCO president in June 1980. Poli placed his own supporters in key positions and began preparations for the "definitive strike," to use his words, to induce Congress to establish an independent FAA. The plan was to paralyze air traffic after FAA rejection of PATCO demands of a $10,000 per year raise, a 32-hour work week, higher pension and disability benefits, and a liberal number of so-called familiarization flights (free airline trips). There were repeated warnings from President Reagan (whose candidacy PATCO had endorsed in 1980 because of PATCO's dissatisfaction with the Carter administration's FAA policies), Congress, the FAA, and others that there would be no amnesty for strikers and no negotiations with PATCO during an illegal strike.

PATCO strikes plainly violate the Civil Service Reform Act of 1979, which prohibits strikes by federal bureaucrats. They also violate individual contract terms signed by controllers upon hire and other federal laws, such as the U.S. Code, which states that "an individual may not accept or hold a position in the Government of the United States . . . if he participates in a strike . . . against the Government of the United States" (5 U.S.C. 73). When the controllers broke the law and their contracts by initiating their long-planned strike at 7:00 a.m. on August 3, 1981, the FAA was well prepared. The president announced at 11:00 a.m. that the controllers who did not return to work within 48 hours had voluntarily terminated their contracts and employment. Flights were controlled by a central flow operation. Fifty percent of the flights were maintained in the first few days, and that level was raised to 70 percent within 10 days. Initially, 4,199 controllers—about one-fourth of the total—continued working, and another 875 joined them before the president's deadline expired. That left 11,301 on strike and discharged. The controllers who continued to work were joined by military personnel loaned by the Department of Defense, retirees called back, and supervisors. The administration, joined by the ATA, moved quickly to punish PATCO, its officials, and strikers through use of an avalanche of injunctions, criminal actions, and contempt actions.

It soon became obvious that the strike would fail. Poli and his PATCO associates had totally miscalculated. Airline executives and the general public were not panic-stricken; nor was there much sympathy for the strikers. The constant PATCO claims that air travel was no longer safe were quickly discredited, especially by the statements and actions of the Air Line Pilots Association. Other U.S. unions offered only perfunctory support to PATCO, and the threat posed by the Canadian controllers' boycott quickly fizzled.

The airlines lost millions of dollars in the strike, but PATCO lost everything. PATCO's strike fund was immediately sequestered to pay fines of several million dollars per day. As provided by law, PATCO was decertified as the bargaining agent for the controllers. PATCO's top leaders all resigned. In 1982, PATCO tried to reorganize under the bankruptcy laws but was hopelessly bankrupt beneath the weight of fines. By May 1983, former strikers had filed 12,000 appeals seeking reinstatement to their high-paying jobs. Fewer than 5 percent of them ever succeeded. The fired controllers suffered drastic drops in pay and prestige, and many said they would return to their jobs if they could (*Wall Street Journal* 1986d, p. 15).

We can learn several lessons from the strike. First, President Reagan showed it was possible for an elected politician to uphold the law and the terms of a contract freely signed by two parties without loss of political popularity. Previously, President Nixon had tolerated an illegal strike by postal workers in 1970; the government had reacted equivocally, at best, to PATCO's pressures over the years; and countless mayors, governors, and school boards had tolerated illegal strikes by public employees. Instead of getting fired, these government employees usually got higher wages. No wonder the controllers were shocked when the president had the resolve to do what he had pledged to do: uphold the law.

Second, it always shocks us to see how replaceable we are. In economics, this is described as a high price-elasticity of demand. The controllers were confident that planes could not fly without them, yet flight clearance was 50 percent initially and over 70 percent within 10 days. The system was staffed by nonstrikers (20 percent of the controllers), military controllers on loan, recalled retirees, supervisors, and reallocations away from small airports. If presidents can be replaced—and they are constantly—what is so magical about assembling cars, mining coal, or guiding planes that only the elect can do it? (See Macaulay 1982.) Nothing. What generally prevents replacement is not the lack of qualified people but laws that raise the cost of trying to replace strikers, the disguised threats and violence that government allows unions to wield to thwart replacement, and spineless managers, especially those with little competition in their product markets.

Third, the overstaffing in the air traffic control system quickly became transparent. Counting supervisors, employment suddenly fell from about 19,000 to 9,000 people. Nevertheless, the smaller

130

numbers handled 75 percent of the previous traffic within a few weeks. This was a boost in labor productivity of nearly 60 percent with no decrease in safety (McKenzie and Shughart 1986). In fact, pilots praised the controllers as being far more cooperative and efficient than PATCO members. The system gradually moved to full capacity; by 1986, it was handling 20 percent more traffic than in 1981—with 20 percent fewer employees. The last of the military controllers left the system in June 1983; it is worth noting that they were high school graduates earning $15,500 per year who had replaced civilian high school graduates earning $33,000 plus lavish fringes.

Fourth, the arguments about stress are largely irrelevant in determining proper compensation for controllers. The PATCO controllers argued that they were often under stress and because their work was so important in keeping the planes flying, they deserved more pay, better working conditions, and other perquisites. These arguments seem powerful but are irrelevant. As Hugh Macaulay (1982) pointed out, Adam Smith's diamonds-water paradox helps to explain the value not only of diamonds and water but of different types of labor services too. Why are diamonds so expensive when we can easily live without them? Why is water so cheap when it is vital for survival? The answer is that the market price of anything depends on how much there is relative to how much people want. Diamonds are scarce relative to human desires and so they are expensive; water is abundant and therefore cheap.

We can restate the question: Who are more valuable and who should receive higher wages, farmers or rock singers? The world needs farmers vitally, but their wages are relatively low because people seem to like rural living. Meanwhile, few can sing like Mick Jagger and many long to hear him, so he makes millions of dollars. The same principles apply to controllers. The job may have some unpleasant characteristics and may be important, but if many people find the job an interesting challenge and can do it successfully, market pay will be far less than "sky high."

To decide whether pay is adequate, the main information we require is whether there is a large number of qualified applicants waiting to do the job at current compensation. If so, pay probably is higher than efficient operation requires. Such overpayment in the public sector is common (Reynolds 1984a, ch. 8). When the

PATCO controllers struck, there was a waiting list of 7,500 people who had already applied, been tested, and been approved for training as controllers. Since there were only 1,500 openings each year due to quits, retirements, or deaths, there was a five-year supply of qualified workers standing by for jobs. The FAA quickly received over 120,000 new applications once the 11,500 strikers left their jobs. If the pay for controllers was going to be changed, it should have been cut. (The FAA actually offered an 11 percent increase before the strike, so PATCO threw away another big pay boost and the precedent of negotiating its own terms with the federal government.) A long line of qualified applicants speaks far more eloquently than a million studies of stress on the job to determine what is fair compensation. After the politicians, union leaders, and experts read their lines, we should look at the line of applicants who want to improve their own lives and their families' lives.

The AT&T Strike

On August 7, 1983, some 675,000 telephone workers across the United States struck the Bell system of the American Telephone & Telegraph Company (AT&T). This was the largest number of workers involved in a strike since the steel strike in 1946, which had involved 750,000 workers. However, hardly any customers noticed the AT&T strike; the system continued to handle 500 million calls per day, with heavy users agreeing that service held up very well. The highly automated system functioned in the hands of some non-striking workers plus some 300,000 managerial and technical employees who worked overtime. The system was manned by about one-third of the normal complement, implying a twofold or threefold increase in short-run productivity. Direct-dial calls went through as usual, and delays were confined to four areas: operator assistance, directory assistance, repairs, and new installations. Maintenance being the most labor-intensive part of the system, repairs that normally took one day took four days during the strike.

Although the United States has the best telephone system in the world, AT&T's insulation from competition in the product and labor markets had spawned massive overpayment and overmanning in the system over the years. The 1983 strike occurred in anticipation of the January 1, 1984, breakup of the system. AT&T wanted to begin the task of creating a leaner and more efficient company; it even feared that the divested phone companies might seek redress in the courts if the union contracts were too rich. The company offered no pay increase in the lowest pay bracket, a 3.5 percent boost in the upper bracket in the first year, cost-of-living adjustments for all brackets in the last two years of the contract, proportionate increases in fringe benefits, and creation of a new job classification called "service assistant" to gradually replace $30,000-a-year employees (plus their fringes) who installed telephones and other equipment. Service assistants would be paid only 70 percent of technicians' wages. The company argued that it was far too costly to pay virtually unskilled workers $30,000 a year to string phone cable in an office building.

The Communications Workers of America (CWA) was vague about its demands but appeared to want a 28 percent wage and benefit gain over three years (emulating a California telephone settlement), would concede the service assistant job in principle but wanted it confined to a few employees, and insisted on more training and other job protection against impending restructuring. Its fallback position was to double the pay increase the company offered.

The 1983 strike was attended by the usual theatrics of negotiations, traditional strike vandalism, and picket-line confrontations. During the strike, telephone cables happened to be cut around the country and switching equipment happened to get splashed with gasoline and ignited. These incidents led the courts to enjoin certain union locals from vandalizing telephone lines and to limit their picketing. Many of the crimes, which violated federal as well as state and local law, required special knowledge. Some telephone companies posted rewards of $5,000 or $10,000 for information that would lead to the arrest of vandals damaging company equipment. Illinois Bell, for example, offered $10,000 for the arrest of vandals who attacked phone equipment in 43 incidents, and New Jersey Bell did the same for 25 incidents. Such vandalism also is a federal crime. While union officials were careful to avoid public endorsement of sabotage and other violence, they explained that it "could be expected in situations when workers come to believe they had been rendered powerless" and that "sometimes cables are cut accidently [sic]." The unions were bitter about the company rewards posted for the arrest of vandals, calling them "bounties"; they insisted that continued inquiries would impede improved relations between labor and management and that any disciplining should be left to the unions (*New York Times* 1983, sect. 11, p. 17). AT&T always declined to estimate the cost of these incidents, merely saying that it repaired them "at company expense." Translation: at consumer expense.

On the first day of the strike in New York City, picketers at 1,353 lines around the city would shake their fists and shout "scab" at nonstriking workers. There were 424 extra police officers on hand—at extra cost to the taxpayers of $100,000. Minor incidents included three strikers arrested for throwing eggs at employees crossing picket lines and two officers treated for minor injuries in picket-line scuffles. And so strikes go.

Following a 22-day strike, newspaper accounts claimed that the settlement provided for a 16.4 percent gain over three years, including cost-of-living allowances, and protection of existing union jobs. This boost was on top of average pay of $373 per week for operators and $535 per week for technicians at a time when the average employee in the private sector earned $280 per week. Ronald G. Ehrenberg (1979) offers a systematic study of the degree of overpayment of phone workers in New York State and the consequent cost to consumers in the 1970s.

In 1986, there was yet another strike, this time a much smaller affair at the dismembered AT&T. It proved to be a decisive defeat for the major union, the CWA. On June 1, 1986, the CWA, led by new president Morton Bahr and representing 155,000 members at AT&T rather than the previous 525,000, rejected the company's offer and went on strike. However, 26 days later, the union accepted the original AT&T offer. The settlement provided for a 2 percent raise the first year and 3 percent gains in the second and third years, elimination of cost-of-living adjustments, and creation of the service assistant's job at $240–$360 per week to replace many technicians at $646 per week. Technicians with 15 years of service whose jobs were downgraded would have their salaries phased down to the new salaries over four years. AT&T reported an 8.5 percent dip in earnings, mostly owing to the costs of the strike (*Wall Street Journal* 1986c, p. 2). In the past, monopoly earnings from the local phone service had disguised the impact. The downsized AT&T only returned 11 percent on stockholders' equity in 1985, and it still has much improvement to make in cutting its bloated labor costs. As one market analyst has commented, "They've got two big office towers in Morristown [New Jersey] filled with people they don't need" (*Fortune* 1986, p. 125). In 1984, the company hired Robert Allen, who reduced employment by 24,000, and in 1985, it named him president. In December 1986, AT&T announced another reduction in employment of 40,000; local telephone companies have reduced employment 40,000 since deregulation.

The Question of Violence

Any honest analyst cannot ignore the violence that often attends strikes. There is a long history of violence associated with labor disputes in the United States. Although there have been some pieces written on union violence and the whole question of labor peace, there has been a curious lacuna about the purpose and consequences of the violence and vandalism. For example, the two leading academic journals in the labor relations field—*Industrial Relations* and *Industrial and Labor Relations Review*—have never published an article that analyzes violence in labor disputes. They have used silence to deal with this issue. But a strike by longshoremen or Teamsters is not going to be the same as one by secretaries or librarians. Labor unions are not uniformly peaceful cartels of the simple business variety. If they were, such terms as strikes, picket lines, rank and file, solidarity, and other military terms would not be so abundantly used for union activities.

No one has ventured to estimate the overall cost of union-related violence or the direct costs of strikes, but sketchy evidence suggests they are not likely to be trivial. From 1977 to 1979, according to a report by the U.S. Bureau of Alcohol, Tobacco, and Firearms (1979), incidents of labor violence by bombing alone caused $3.8 million in property damage. Between 1975 and 1983, there were 3,157 violent union incidents reported in the popular press, according to unpublished data gathered by the National Right to Work Legal Defense Foundation. Although there may be biases in the data, they are the only systematic records available on labor violence. Thomas R. Haggard and Armand J. Thieblot (1983) analyzed the data on the 2,598 incidents for 1975–81 in a much-needed and well-researched book. They found 49 deaths attributable to labor violence; $15.2 million in damage to company plant and equipment; 2,732 instances of damage to automobiles; 133 cases of managers' and nonstrikers'

135

homes being firebombed, shot at, or vandalized; hundreds of cases of sabotage and vandalism; and thousands of shots having been fired. Based on the evidence, the authors' conclusions seemed warranted: labor violence is substantial, systematically applied, and not diminishing, and much of the law enforcement community tacitly allows unions wide latitude to use intimidation and coercive techniques (Reynolds 1984b). This is not to suggest that each strike is violence-ridden, but that it is routine enough to warrant concern. (Even the air traffic controllers had their group of enforcers for the 1981 strike, but the FAA's extensive preparations kept strike violence minimal; see Northrup 1984b, p. 175.)

If each strike had only $100,000 in damages associated with it, the cost would exceed half a billion dollars annually at the strike rate of the 1970s (5,300 strikes per year). In the 1980s, the pace fell to half that of the 1970s, although this still implies 10 new strikes initiated every business day.

Unions that have engaged in substantial sabotage and violence over the years include the United Mine Workers of America (UMW), the Teamsters, the United Automobile Workers (UAW), the National Union of Hospital and Health Care Employees, the International Association of Fire Fighters, the Fraternal Association of Steel Haulers (FASH), and the Oil, Chemical and Atomic Workers International Union (OCAW). Haggard and Thieblot (1983) found that in terms of violent incidents per 10,000 members, the UMW led with 7.36, followed by the hospital and health care workers with 5.70, the fire fighters with 4.48, the steel haulers with 3.20, and the Oil, Chemical and Atomic Workers International Union with 2.88.

Strikes have been familiar in coal mining for many years. C. L. Christenson (1953), for example, found that from 1933 to 1950, there was not a single month without some working time lost to labor disputes in the coal industry. Frequent wildcat strikes still occur, in addition to major contract strikes. Christenson argued, however, that strikes had relatively little overall impact on coal production because of inventory buildups before contract expirations and expansions by nonstruck mines during strikes.

The persistence of UMW violence is confirmed by the lengthy Massey Coal strike, which involved extensive violence and vandalism, including a coal truck driver being killed by a sniper (*Wall Street Journal* 1985a, p. 6). In another incident, picketing UMW

136

strikers, some carrying baseball bats, repulsed a bus carrying company "reinforcements" (as the news wire account put it) at a Massey mine. The strikers threw rocks, set a company truck ablaze, and injured two people (*Houston Chronicle* 1985a, sect. 1, p. 3). Rich Trumka, the 35-year-old UMW president, blamed the company for encouraging violence, saying, "I never brought any armed guards into that community. I don't have paramilitary mercenaries who carry weapons" (*Wall Street Journal* 1985a, p. 6). Ordinary profit-seeking companies, however, do not incur security expenses unless the shareholders' assets are endangered. The unenthusiastic enforcement of law during labor disputes, especially in heavily unionized areas of the country, sometimes makes it prudent to pay for private security. Shareholders have sued management in a few instances for failure to protect company assets in labor disputes. Nobel laureate F. A. Hayek (1960, p. 267) put it this way:

> From a state in which little the unions could do was legal if they were not prohibited altogether, we have now reached a state where they have become uniquely privileged institutions to which the general rules of law do not apply. They have become the only important instance in which governments signally fail in their prime function—the prevention of coercion and violence.

Estimating the Costs of Strikes

The costs of strikes remain difficult to quantify. George R. Neumann (1980) found that equity prices respond negatively to the beginning of a strike and positively to the termination of a strike, but he did not estimate the cost (average, marginal, or total) of strike activity. Myron Lieberman (1981) put the total cost of a nine-day strike by the teachers' union in Modesto, California, at $924,000 and other reimbursable bargaining costs over a 17-month period (1979–80) at $440,000. California law specifies that the state government reimburse lower-level governments for documented expenses incurred due to a state law such as mandatory collective bargaining. The largest items in Lieberman's figures were the loss of state funds based on average daily attendance and the loss of teacher salaries.

J. Curtis Rose (1980) estimated the cost of Pennsylvania's Act 195 mandating collective bargaining in schools at $458 million in tangible costs from 1970 to 1980, with expenses ranging from $12 million in printing costs for the collective contracts to $110 million in dues paid to operate unions. Although Pennsylvania teachers' salaries showed no advance relative to national teacher salaries and Pennsylvania students did not advance relative to national norms, the taxpayer expense per pupil had risen sharply due to smaller class sizes and various work-rule restrictions. The decline in teacher prestige and the preoccupation with strikes and collective-bargaining procedures embittered the atmosphere. Furthermore, student achievement scores and attendance rates are negatively related to teachers' strikes; dropouts are positively related to teachers' strikes (Caldwell and Moskalski 1982; Caldwell, Moskalski, and Jeffreys 1983).

Among cities, there is evidence that a reputation for labor strife discourages investment and growth. Louisville, Kentucky, led cities in the nation from 1971 to 1980 in average annual days lost per worker at 9.5 days, or four times the rate in high-growth-rate cities such as Houston and Atlanta; further, local business recruiters and businesses in Louisville said they suffered from having a reputation as "the strike capital of the world" (*Wall Street Journal* 1982, p. 15). High labor costs, unionization, and frequent strikes made Louisville appear unattractive as a place to do business. The General Electric Company (GE), a major employer in Louisville, found out that liberal contracts do not help either. GE allowed employees to strike over grievances, and for a while workers walked off their jobs almost weekly over dress codes, job assignments, and other conditions.

George R. Neumann and Melvin W. Reder (1984) have found that although the private costs of strikes to companies in lost quasi-rents and to employees in lost wages can be sizable, the world is flexible enough in manufacturing that the social losses (defined as lost output) associated with strikes are insignificant in most industries. Neumann and Reder determined that an average strike resulted in a loss of output of $511,000 at most, or less than 0.25 percent of annual industry output. If all strikes were as low in cost to the nation as this estimate for manufacturing, the national total would be less than $3 billion per year at the strike rate of the 1970s and less than $1.5 billion per year during the 1980s. Even the highest strike-loss manufacturing industry—ordnance and accessories—lost only 1.5 percent of output per year.

The largest strike experienced in U.S. history was the 1959 steel strike, a loss of 41.9 million workdays—a greater total than the whole U.S. loss in all but eight years since World War II. Since some companies operated during the strike, customers stockpiled in advance, imports provided alternative suppliers, and production could be stepped up following the injunction that ended the strike in November 1959, only 0.6 percent of steel output was lost, or an output loss of only $30 million for the largest strike in U.S. history. If we accept Neumann and Reder's figures, the steel strike cost less than $1 per workday lost. The cost of this huge strike apparently was trivial in terms of GNP.

The 1959 steel strike, however, had indirect results that are still surfacing today in the demise of a once-great industry. By 1973, the major integrated steel producers signed the Extended Negotiating Agreement (ENA) because they found that resisting the USW gained them nothing. Each time the union was about to lose a strike, government officials would pressure the industry to give the union what it wanted in order to end the strike. It made no economic sense to suffer through strikes that industry (and therefore consumers) could not win. The ENA effectively ended the use of strikes in steel in 1973, and steel labor costs then increased greatly, with predictable consequences for the competitiveness of the industry. In 1959, steel workers earned 30 percent more than the average in all U.S. manufacturing. But the premium was 46 percent by 1973 and 88 percent by 1980. The quit rate in the steel industry fell to one-sixth that in U.S. manufacturing and less than one-half that in the high-wage automobile industry, although quit rates had been comparable in steel and automobiles in the late 1950s and early 1960s. Modernization, trigger prices, and other political interventions to save major steel producers were doomed in the face of horrendous labor expenses, especially when domestic minimills can buy scrap steel for $75 a ton.

An alternative way to measure the losses from strikes is to look at court-assessed damages. If a strike is illegal (usually in the public sector), then on economic grounds the courts should award damages equal to the social costs of the strike divided by the probability of detection and successful prosecution. Since strikes are public events, the probability of apprehension and prosecution can be taken as one, so court-assigned damages presumably reflect a judgment about the social losses suffered by strike victims. If the gains to strikers exceed these losses, the union can persist in the effort, which would be an efficient social outcome (Posner 1973). In the case of the 1981 PATCO strike, which ended with the union bankrupted, the court fines were several million dollars per day, or a billion dollars on an annual basis (Northrup 1984b). Although the gross revenues of the airlines exceed $30 billion per year, profits are about $1 billion. The substitution possibilities for services are more limited than for manufactured goods, so the social costs of strikes are potentially higher. But the steep price that strikes can cause means that they do not occur very often. The apparently low realized cost of strikes, ironically, is evidence for the potency of these threatened costs.

From the point of view of a free society, strikes should not be outlawed by legislation, even in so-called vital activities such as fire and police protection. Instead, if an employer wants a prohibition on strikes, he can specify this condition in individual labor contracts, enforceable at law, and pay the employees willing to surrender this option a market premium for their services.

Brian E. Becker and Craig A. Olson (1986) found that the average strike involving 1,000 or more employees depressed shareholder equity 4.1 percent. These losses varied widely across industries. Although the capital markets usually anticipated whether an impending decline would result in a strike or settlement, the market consistently underestimated the cost of a strike to shareholders, as evidenced by the fact that nearly two-thirds of the decline occurred after the strike was announced.

Ultimately, the costs of strikes are not so much a question of economic damages suffered in terms of reduced output—clearly less than 1 percent of annual output—as they are a question of power exerted by private, usually well-paid minorities. The public realized this after World War II when it grew tired of John L. Lewis and his mine workers and other belligerent unions holding the community ransom (Lewis: "You need men and I have all the men and they are here in the palm of my hand; and now I ask, 'What am I bid?'" [quoted in Reynolds 1984a, p. 215]). The result was a Republican congressional majority, which passed the Taft-Hartley Labor Act over Harry Truman's veto in a vain attempt to amend fatally flawed legislation.

In Great Britain, the issue is posed more dramatically than in the United States. The British trade unions control almost 50 percent

140

of the labor force, own the Labour party outright, and can bring the nation to its knees through a coordinated shutdown of the ports, railways, and power facilities—or at least they can do so without a severe government response. In 1971, for example, Britain had a two-week food supply on hand at the beginning of a nationwide port strike, and as one politician put it, the nation stood on the edge of an abyss (Burton 1979). In 1976, public opinion pollsters found that 54 percent thought that Jack Jones, the general secretary of the Transport and General Workers, was the most powerful and influential man in Britain, while only 25 percent named James Callaghan, then the prime minister. A democratic country cannot tolerate such minority power indefinitely, and the failure of Arthur Scargill's miners' strike in 1985 may mark a substantial decline in British trade union power. As Arthur Shenfield (1977, pp. 88–89) wrote:

> The situation in which Britain finds itself is not new. Centuries ago there were powerful barons who, with their private forces of retainers and liegemen, were able to make or break the weak kings who formally ruled the country. But this did not last. Strong kings arose who broke the power of these unruly barons. The modern baron is the union leader, and his liegemen are the workers who are dragooned into the union system. But this cannot last. It is a prescription for tyranny and poverty.

Administering the Collective-Bargaining System

Little effort has been put into estimating the administrative cost of operating the collective-bargaining system. Although there are only fragmentary bases for estimation, the rules of the current labor relations game ensure that an enormous daily waste of time and effort make it artificially expensive to conduct business. To suggest a minimum order of magnitude in the costs of operation, we can discuss the resources used in the process by unions, managements, and so-called neutral parties. Neutral parties, of course, have a financial interest in perpetuating the present system of labor conflict.

Union Outlays

Virtually all union expenditures can be described as a cost of operating the collectivized labor system. The LM-2 financial statements filed annually with the U.S. Department of Labor under the

Labor-Management Reporting and Disclosure Act (Landrum-Griffin Act) show that the national headquarters of 58 national unions alone spent $3.9 billion in 1983, a 44 percent increase over the $2.7 billion spent in 1979, despite a 25 percent slide in claimed membership from 20.9 million to 15.7 million members over the same period (Reynolds and Edwards 1985). Similarly, the employment of union directors, officials, and staff declined only 2 percent, from 14,268 to 13,997, over the same four years. Under continuing financial pressure, however, many unions have no doubt reduced their employment since 1983.

There is no official total for annual union spending, but it easily exceeds $5 billion. Nor is there an estimate of total employment in the union bureaucracy, but it easily exceeds 30,000. There are more than 50,000 union locals ranging in size from 5 to 40,000 members; although not all locals have a full-time union employee, many do (Reynolds 1984a, p. 118; Troy and Sheflin 1985, pp. 5-1 to 5-4).

Employer Costs

The personnel function is crucial to the success of any enterprise, as all management books recognize. An unknown portion of the personnel function is directed at dealing with unions and/or maintaining nonunion status. Another substantial portion of personnel administration is preoccupied with responding to Occupational Safety and Health Administration (OSHA), equal employment opportunity, pension, and other government directives. The labor relations component, therefore, is extraordinarily difficult to quantify. Myron Leiberman (1981) has claimed that the public school districts of California incur expenses of $150 million per year in collective-bargaining negotiations. These expenses are well-documented because they are reimbursable under California state law, which requires reimbursement of expenses imposed on lower-level governments by state law.

A 1986 survey of personnel executives finds that U.S. employers will spend $593 per employee on personnel activities, or 2.4 percent of company payrolls (*Personnel Management* 1986, p. 35). For 1986, this amounts to $60 billion because wage and salary employment is just over 100 million while total employee compensation in the national income accounts is $2,500 billion. The statistic we lack is the fraction of personnel resources devoted to union relations. A

142

reasonable guess would be 8–9 percent of personnel administration costs for negotiating teams, daily grievance processing, arbitration cases, and so on. Since union relations are a preoccupation in unionized firms, these figures suggest that firms match the more than $5 billion spent by unions. This may be an underestimate because it ignores the fact that firms usually pay the salaries of the unpaid local union officials on official union business in their plants.

The quantitative information on labor consultants is slightly better. As the *Wall Street Journal* has emphasized, keeping unions out has become a big business. The subscription list for the AFL-CIO's periodic *Report on Union-Busters* ("RUB") grew from 500 in 1979 to 11,000 in 1984. The AFL-CIO estimates that as many as 1,000 consulting firms are in operation, with total annual fees exceeding $500 million. Anthony F. McKenna, president of Modern Management, Inc., estimates that the legal fees added together would approach $200 million (*Labor Relations Reporter* 1985, p. 6). The so-called union-avoidance consultants are involved in two-thirds of all organizing campaigns. Nor is there any evidence that the organizing expenditures of unions have declined over time (Voos 1984).

Neutrals

There are some reliable data available on expenditures and personnel in the mediation, conciliation, fact-finding, and arbitration industry. According to the FY 1986 budget of the U.S. government, six federal agencies directly concerned with administering the system of unionized labor markets spent $413 million and employed 8,756 people in FY 1986, as shown in Table 8.1.

The Employment Standards Administration might be disputed as a direct component of the unionized system, but it does administer the wage and hour laws, such as the Davis-Bacon Act and minimum wage laws, which directly benefit unions. It could even be argued that the U.S. Department of Labor (sometimes irreverently referred to as the Department of Organized Labor), which spent an estimated $27.2 billion in FY 1986, and the department's 18,000 employees, are in business either to support unions or to offset their harmful effects (for example, unemployment insurance). In addition to federal spending, there are uncounted expenditures by state and local labor relations agencies and departments of labor, as well as court expenses in labor litigation generated by the strike-threat system.

Table 8.1

FEDERAL SPENDING AND EMPLOYMENT IN ADMINISTERING THE
COLLECTIVE-BARGAINING SYSTEM, FY 1986

Agency	Expenditures ($ millions)	Employment
National Labor Relations Board	130.9	3,000
National Mediation Board (Railway Labor Act of 1926)	6.3	58
Federal Labor Relations Authority	17.5	289
Federal Mediation and Conciliation Service	22.8	348
Labor Management Standards Administration*	56.0	1,040
Employment Standards Administration*	180.7	4,021
Total	413.5	8,756

SOURCE: Office of Management and Budget 1985.
*U.S. Department of Labor.

Murray L. Weidenbaum (1979) has argued that each dollar of federal regulatory outlay creates another $19 in compliance cost in the private sector. Using the same multiplier of 20:1 to convert federal regulatory expenditures into estimates of the social cost of labor relations regulation yields a total of $8.26 billion.

This is a substantial underestimate for several reasons. First, unions alone spend over $5 billion per year, outlays matched by corporate and government managers coping with unions. Second, membership figures for labor relations organizations show 5,000 in the Industrial Relations Research Association, over 25,000 on the labor roster of the American Arbitration Association, more than 10,000 members of the American Bar Association's Labor Relations Section, plus other organizations such as the Society of Professionals in Dispute Resolution. Although some overlap in these membership figures exists, a reasonable estimate would be that these resources alone cost society an estimated $1.4 billion annually. (This estimate assumes the full-time equivalent of 35,000 people-years, including support staff, at an average cost of $40,000 annually, or $20 an hour including all fringe benefits.)

Third, Rutgers–The State University processed 70 grievance cases between 1970 and 1975, and the estimated cost ranged from $20,000 to $50,000 per case depending on whether negotiating time was included, which it clearly should be (Reynolds 1984a, p. 192). Fourth, Federal Mediation and Conciliation Service data show that the cost of arbitrators' fees alone in 1981 was over $1,000 per case. Since there are an estimated 200,000 collective labor contracts, only one arbitrated grievance case per year per contract at a cost of $50,000 per case yields an economywide cost of $10 billion per year.

Regardless of how calculated, the direct cost of administering our adversarial labor system adds up to at least $10 billion each year. What are the social benefits of all this activity? None really. It is just another drag on economic progress.

Conclusion

We conclude that strike costs are modest, less than one-half of 1 percent of GNP, in terms of realized, direct impact on the economy in most years. Jack Barbash (1980, p. 554) has observed that collective bargaining is concerned with price and power. The expenses incurred in strikes are a periodic display of power. These expenses are kept relatively small chiefly because it is in the interest of the parties to avoid them under most circumstances. As economist Henry C. Simons (1944, p. 22) wrote, "Where the power [of coercion and intimidation] is small or insecurely possessed, it must be exercised overtly and extensively; large and unchallenged, it becomes like the power of strong government, confidently held, respectfully regarded, and rarely displayed conspicuously."

The basis of union power is the threat of the strike, not the strike itself, and hence the strike threat is the ultimate source of the general damage done by unionism to national productivity. The highly visible but limited damage of strikes is less important than the less-visible long-run damage to national output and investment.

The additional staff and related expenses required to pressure, resist, negotiate, and administer collective contracts are a continuing drain on U.S. prosperity. These costs exceed $10 billion a year, or about 0.3 percent of GNP. We can conclude that the direct cost of strikes and the administrative costs of the strike-threat system together amount to about 0.5 percent of GNP annually.

IX. The Impact of Unions on Investment and Entrepreneurship

> If we want to preserve the market economy our aim must be to restore the effectiveness of the price mechanism. The chief obstacle to its functioning is trade union monopoly.
>
> —F. A. Hayek, *A Tiger by the Tail*

> The whole history of unionism has been . . . in determining how industries in decline are accelerated toward their extinction.
>
> —Paul A. Samuelson (Jackman 1984)

Economic growth is the sustained expansion of output per capita. If we gaze over the course of human history, we find there has been remarkably little of such growth. The lot of the masses has been mostly grinding poverty and tyranny. Short, brutish lives still are the rule in much of the world today.

The most prominent exception has been the last 200-odd years in limited areas of the globe, mostly in Europe and North America and more recently along the western rim of the Pacific—Japan, Taiwan, South Korea, Hong Kong, Malaysia, and Singapore. Why has growth occurred in these places?

The reasons for economic growth or lack of it are disputed among learned men. Formal economics, as Mancur Olson (1982) has observed, says more about resource allocation and output fluctuations in the short and medium term than in the long run, in which changes in technology, tastes, and economic organization matter. Each country and time period is unique, adding to the difficulty of deciding which factors may have raised or lowered saving and investment, what directed investment into high- or low-yielding projects, and why more innovation and capital accumulation have occurred in one society or period than in another.

Various reasons for economic growth have been proposed. Good fortune has been attributed, for example, to an extraordinary advantage in natural resources or climate, to racial superiority, or to farsighted politicians and bureaucrats whose planning directs populations into the best use of resources.

None of these reasons hold up. The crucial difference between rich and poor societies is the degree to which they rely upon private property and free markets. The poor nations of the world have always had natural resources, climates, and human resources that rival those of the West. And poor nations certainly have had plentiful amounts of government direction and bureaucracy relative to the available resources. Further, many of their planners have been educated at the best Western universities.

Wealth is generated through free enterprise, otherwise known as capitalism—the private-property system of free markets that coordinates the activities of millions of people without central direction. The evidence is overwhelming that free, competitive markets are the only route to mass prosperity (for example, see Rosenberg and Birdzell 1986). For evidence, we can compare the development of North America with that of South America, the former with a British legacy of private property and relatively mild government intervention and the latter under a Spanish tradition of weak private rights and heavier central control. Or we can compare the success of the Chinese in the relatively free-enterprise nations of Hong Kong, Taiwan, and Singapore with the experience in mainland China. Or we can compare West Germany with East Germany. To be sure, socialist governments can force higher savings, as the USSR has done, but this does not guarantee that the savings will be invested in high-yielding projects. Only when the domination of economic decisions by the state is eased can the price system peacefully channel the inventive and productive power of the population into enormous expansions of output.

What does this have to do with labor unions? Expressed in blunt terms, U.S.-style unions are government-supported worker cartels that interfere with the price mechanism and therefore impede the advance of prosperity. A prime objection to unions is that they reduce the level of real wages, despite all the ostentatious struggle to raise the prices of union labor.

If the population has an economic orientation and a commercial spirit, sustained growth is possible because private-property rights and free markets ("free" means reasonably free of government

148

control) are the key factors in economic growth. Private property secures the incentive to invest and accumulate capital because investors realize the profits or losses from their decisions; a free-market system allows people to do the rest. In the free market, the determination of all prices is democratic because the uses of all resources are controlled, directly or indirectly, by consumers on the one hand and natural scarcities on the other. By contrast, under socialism or under collectivist organizations such as unions, decisions are made by the small groups of private men and women who wield coercive power. Commands originate not with the great bulk of the people as under market capitalism but with the officials, whom it is difficult or impossible to subject to a discipline similar to the marketplace.

The Debate over Unions and Static Productivity

Various economists have estimated the static efficiency costs of union monopoly at less than 0.33 percent of GNP (see chapter 4). A major defect of this approach is that it ignores the long-run impact of unions on investment and economic growth. Economists take it as axiomatic that economic growth is retarded by anything that reduces the incentives to save, reduces the flow of saving into investment, distorts investment decisions, or causes capital to be used inefficiently. In the dynamic context, the question is not whether labor union policies are harmful to economic growth but to what degree these policies have been harmful.

The primary dissenters from this conventional view have been Richard B. Freeman and James L. Medoff (1984), who have argued in their controversial book on the collective-voice/institutional-response theory of unions that "unionism on net probably raises social efficiency, and that if it lowers it, it does so by minuscule amounts except in rare circumstances" (p. 247). Their conclusion rests primarily on a summary of eight Harvard-based empirical studies of the impact of unions on productivity. These eight studies relied on a production-function approach and cross-sectional data; the estimates generally indicate that unionized establishments are more productive than their nonunion counterparts. There were two exceptions among these eight studies: a study by Kim B. Clark (1984) of 902 product-line businesses, which found a small negative union impact, and a study by Margaret B. Connerton, Richard B.

149

Freeman, and James L. Medoff (1983), which reported a major reversal of what was originally a large positive union productivity differential in underground bituminous coal.

These eight studies and the Freeman and Medoff book (1984) are controversial, and the criticisms by economists hit the mark. Economists remain skeptical of the pro-union productivity studies, finding them weak on both theoretical and empirical grounds (for examples, see Review Symposium 1985; Addison 1985; Addison and Burton 1984; Reynolds 1984a, pp. 83–88; Reynolds 1986b; and Reynolds 1987b).

Three theoretical objections stand out. First, the Freeman-Medoff rationale for the positive impact of unions on productivity is unconvincing on its own terms. No rigorous theory integrated with orthodox theory describes exactly how unions raise productivity. Freeman and Medoff posit unions as the collective voice of the median (inframarginal) worker in resolving problems of imperfect monitoring, problems on the job, and the associated public goods and externalities problems. Productivity is supposed to be enhanced by lower quit rates, grievance procedures, seniority systems, work rules, and the like. Further, unionization is supposed to shock managements into reducing non-profit-maximizing organizational slack (so-called X-inefficiency). Although unionism does reduce quits (mostly because of the union wage premium), the remaining arguments are a "black box" because Freeman and Medoff offer no coherent theory, integrated with general economic theory, to displace the standard theory. There is no reason to accept their conjectures about raising productivity on balance, especially because the wage gains made by unions lead to an inefficient factor mix, unions introduce inefficient work rules, and unions limit compensation based on personal productivity. Even unions are anti-union, resisting unionization of their own staff employees. If Freeman and Medoff are right about the pro-productivity impact of unions, perhaps they should recommend that unions drop their resistance to unionization and thereby reap the gains of new vigor and new productivity in organizing the unorganized. Ralph Nader's enterprises also are anti-union, claiming that unionization is not appropriate for "cause" organizations (*Washington Post* 1984).

Second, and more damaging, is that the production-function approach initiated by Charles Brown and James L. Medoff (1978)

150

and still used by others (Allen 1984b, Hirsch and Link 1984, and Warren 1985) is fundamentally flawed, rendering the researchers' estimates incapable of resolving the question of what impact unions may have on productivity. Because firms try to maximize profits (avoid losses) and unions raise wage rates in organized firms, surviving firms must employ labor in amounts such that the marginal productivity of labor is higher than that in nonunion firms. No amount of statistical control over the quality of workers or capital-labor ratios can avoid this difficulty. Even when capital and labor quality are fixed, firms burdened by union pricing must have higher marginal products of labor because managers must employ appropriately smaller amounts (see Reynolds 1986b for details). Econometric estimates can show a favorable union productivity effect even if unionization shifts marginal productivity schedules downward; firms must always establish the equality of labor's marginal product and the higher union wage cost.

Confirmation of this proposition is that most cross-sectional studies find that the union wage differential and the union productivity differential are nearly identical; for example, they are both 22 percent in the Brown and Medoff study (1978). This result must hold in sound econometric work if firms behave in accord with profit maximization in their input decisions. As Orley Ashenfelter (Review Symposium 1985) pointed out, the Freeman and Medoff generalization about the favorable impact of unions on productivity rests on only one broad-based study: Brown and Medoff (1978). This study analyzed data on manufacturing industries aggregated by state, and if the authors did not assume that capital-labor ratios are the same in union and nonunion plants within state-industry groups, their estimated productivity impact of unions is zero. Looking over the many empirical studies, Barry T. Hirsch (Review Symposium 1985) also observed that union productivity effects are largest in those industries in which union wage effects are largest and competitive pressures are most intense. For example, large union wage and productivity effects are found in construction (Allen 1984b, Allen 1986, and Mandelstamm 1965), especially in the Southwest, where nonunion competition is most extensive (Clark 1980b); small effects are found in cement (Clark 1980a and Clark 1980b); and industries with negligible union wage effects tend to have zero productivity effects (see Ehrenberg, Sherman, and Schwarz 1983

151

for public libraries, Pencavel 1977 for British coal fields, Sloan and Adamache 1984 for hospitals, and Noam 1983 for public regulators), even in the presence of positive union wage impacts in the public sector. This evidence supports the contention that any positive union productivity effects reflect the monopoly wage effect rather than a benefit attributable to unionization.

Third, some firms—the least efficient ones and those with little or no quasi-rents to be seized—cannot survive union pricing and work rules. The data, by and large, are limited to firms that survive the obstacles erected by unions, so the observed distribution of firms is truncated. Therefore, a comparison of union and nonunion sectors is likely to show that the unionized firms, on average, are more productive than the nonunion firms. Surviving union firms are necessarily more efficient than nonunion firms selling similar products at similar prices in open markets. Although such fortuitous results do occur, it would be a mistake to attribute these situations to the productivity effects of unions per se, particularly in view of the fact that unionized firms generally have a difficult time competing in open markets and are dependent instead on favorable protections, regulations, and subsidies bestowed by government (Reynolds 1984a). The problem of the nonsurvival of inefficient union firms is statistically known as sample selectivity bias. Legal scholar Richard A. Epstein (1983, p. 1439) has put it effectively:

> It is probable that certain firms have been unable to survive either the threat or the fact of unionization. The loss of these firms must be reflected in any total picture, but it will not be captured in any study that mistakenly confines its attention to the wage and productivity profiles of those firms able to survive unionization.

These objections do not exhaust the list of problems with the contention that unions have positive productivity effects, but they suffice for present purposes (for more, see Reynolds 1984a, pp. 83–88; Reynolds 1986b; and Reynolds 1987b).

Unions and Dynamic Change

Another branch of the productivity literature asks whether unionized labor inhibits the growth of total-factor productivity and technical change in industry. This literature looks at the dynamics of technical change (shifts in production functions) rather than trying to ascertain outcomes under static technology with cross-sectional data.

There is good evidence that unions do retard technical change. John W. Kendrick (1983), for example, has analyzed the wide dispersion in productivity advance among industries, which provides data useful for econometric exploration of the correlates of productivity advance across industries. Multiple-regression analyses strongly support the positive importance of investments—in physical equipment, human capital, and research and development—and the negative impact of unionized labor and product market concentration on productivity improvements. Both the amount of unionization and increases in its extent have negative impacts on productivity gains, and unionization also is positively correlated with another negative factor in productivity: man-days idle. Kendrick's numerical summary is that for every 10 percentage point increase in the unionization ratio, total-factor productivity growth falls by 10 percent.

Similar time-series regressions by Barry T. Hirsch and Albert N. Link (1984) also show that productivity growth is slower in industries with a greater degree of union coverage of employees. Using total-factor productivity indexes for 1957–73 calculated independently by John W. Kendrick and Elliot S. Grossman (1980) and Frank M. Gollop and Dale W. Jorgenson (1980)—the indexes are only correlated 0.56, indicating substantial differences—Hirsch and Link found that both the level of unionization and changes in it had significant negative impacts on total-factor productivity growth, no matter which productivity measure was used.

Many other studies have looked at the correlates of total-factor productivity without focusing on unionization per se, but they have tried to identify the effect of research and development expenditures on productivity growth. These studies, however, consistently introduce unionization as a control variable. Studies by Nestor E. Terlecky (1974 and 1980), Kendrick and Grossman (1980), Edwin Mansfield (1980), Link (1981 and 1982), and Catherine Defina Sveikauskas and Leo Sveikauskas (1982), for example, consistently report that total-factor productivity growth is negatively associated with the level of unionism. Unionism, however, is not statistically significant in all regressions.

Dennis R. Maki (1983) focused on both the short-run and long-run impact of unions and strikes on productivity growth in manufacturing in Canada from 1927 to 1978. He argued that in the short run, unions "shock" managements into stricter efficiency but that the long-run impact of unions is likely to be deleterious. His regressions used the level of unionization as a short-run impact proxy and the changes in percentage unionized as a long-run impact proxy. His regressions reported that the short-run impact of unions is to raise total-factor productivity by 6 percent but that the long-run impact is to lower total-factor productivity by at least 40 percent. The drag on productivity imposed by unions was even greater in the 1970s because union density and strikes were at historic highs in Canada.

For the last two decades the South and Southwest have been the fastest-growing regions in the United States, reflecting a historic shift in the location of economic activity. A study by Robert J. Newman (1983) explains why. States with stronger employment growth have lower corporate tax rates and a lower degree of unionization in the labor force; they also have right-to-work laws. Newman's employment regressions show that capital-intensive firms are especially sensitive to changes in corporate tax rates and that labor-intensive firms are especially sensitive to the degree of unionization and existence of right-to-work laws. Tax rates, degree of unionization, and right-to-work laws affect not only movement to the South but also movement within the South.

Dwight R. Lee (1984) has put these results in their proper theoretical perspective by suggesting that unions are myopic organizations that undervalue future gains relative to present gains. The time horizon of union decision-makers is short because the distant consequences of their decisions are not properly weighted. The property rights (ownership) structure of trade unions impedes proper consideration of the present-value consequences of union actions. Anything that increases union control over corporate decisions, for example, only shortens the time horizon of business decisions. Unions live for today, then lobby tomorrow to secure the privileges to insulate them from the consequences of their own policies. As integrated steel companies have gone bankrupt and half a million jobs have been lost in steel since 1979, the United Steelworkers of America have continued to believe that these events have nothing to do with their wage- and productivity-reducing practices.

Union myopia and its results show up in two prominent ways. First, in anticipation of the negative impact of unions on the return to capital, the equity value of newly unionized or threatened firms falls (Ruback and Zimmerman 1984). Second, union wage demands in older industries, in which union power has been exercised the longest, eventually reduce the competitiveness of each industry, pushing it into serious decline. Unions effectively confiscate part of the return to capital, thereby retarding capital formation and concentrating the regional damage in the Northeast and upper Midwest, where union monopoly control over the labor supply traditionally has been strongest. The plant-closing legislation (which imposes severe costs on firms that wish to close uneconomical operations) supported by unions is another kind of Berlin Wall—an attempt to lock investors and their capital in, to stop them from escaping the grip of myopic, exploitive unions (McKenzie 1984b).

Strong support for this interpretation of union behavior is given by the empirical studies that find a negative impact of unions on profits (Salinger 1984, Clark 1984, Ruback and Zimmerman 1984, Freeman 1983, and Voos and Mishel 1986) and by the obvious difficulties of unionized firms in manufacturing, construction, trucking, mining, and other industries. Freeman and Medoff (1984, p. 186) view the union confiscation of capital returns for union members as acceptable because it allegedly "reduce[s] the exceedingly high levels of profitability in highly concentrated industries toward normal competitive levels. In these calculations, the union profit effect appears to take the form of a reduction of monopoly profits." Supposedly, unions redistribute income from high-income capital owners to lower-income workers.

Freeman and Medoff's view is deficient in virtually every respect. First, it is highly doubtful that unions confine their monopoly gains so precisely to concentrated industries. The high degree of unionization in transportation, mining, and construction—decentralized industries populated by numerous firms—belies the Freeman-Medoff characterization. Second, even if unionization is concentrated in regulated or concentrated industries, it aggravates the distortion of the allocation of resources by raising their marginal cost of production. The underproduction of products in monopolistic industries is aggravated, not offset, by trade unions. Of course, many economists would quarrel with the idea that manufacturing firms, even in concentrated industries, have substantial monopoly power, rendering the Freeman-Medoff justification moot (Brozen 1982). Third, to blithely assume that capital recipients are rich and workers are poor ignores the fact that capital income is concentrated among the elderly and that at least one-third of corporate equity and bond wealth is in workers' pension funds. Fourth, Freeman and Medoff appear unconcerned over the long-run impact of the union exploitation of investors' returns. Productivity growth and technical change, however, are directly linked to investment (Hirsch and Connolly 1984). Finally, Freeman and Medoff find no ethical objection to the means that unions use to confiscate stockholder wealth, as long as they believe the wealth is being redistributed from the rich to the poor. For some of us, however, the use of legitimate means is more important than immediate results (also see Reynolds 1987b).

W. H. Hutt (1930) has been a lonely voice for many years in emphasizing that most talk about the exploitation of immobile labor by rapacious owners of capital is 180 degrees from the truth. Unionization has far more to do with exploiting the investors who commit their capital to relatively long-lived, immobile form. Investors abstain from immediate consumption of income and, in the hopes of personal gain, supply the complementary capital that multiplies the output of human effort. Once installed, much of the equipment, buildings, mines, ports, transportation facilities, public utilities, and other productive assets is immobile and relatively fixed by nature. The opportunities and legal privileges to exploit complementary input owners are far more abundant among unionists than among the investors (capitalists) who commit their resources to long-term uses and contract with wage and salary earners to cooperate with specific assets that entrepreneurs predict will best satisfy consumers. In terms of discouraging investors and entrepreneurs, the cost is incalculable.

The process of union seizure of shareholder wealth has been labeled "opportunistic behavior." However, in the truly long run, especially with international markets for capital funds, neither investors nor wage employees can really exploit each other on a sustained basis in a predominantly market economy because all parties adjust their expectations and behavior to these possibilities. In particular, investors protect themselves from exploitation by unionists; unfortunately, we are all poorer as a result because otherwise profitable, productive investments are not exploited due to fear of union opportunism. Unionists can exploit yesterday's investment but not tomorrow's. A stark example is Great Britain, once second in per capita standard of living but now the poor man of northern Europe, ruined largely by adversarial unions.

Plant-Closing Laws

In the 1980s unions branched out to a new form of industry regulation at both the state and national levels: to control business closing and reinvestment decisions (Bluestone and Harrison 1982, McKenzie 1984a, McKenzie 1984b, and Rothstein 1985). The conservative nature of unions—due to their intent in maintaining the status quo—is evident in their daily opposition to production changes, but union constraints on entrepreneurial decisions traditionally were confined to controlling the conditions of work and the physical environment. Although unions claim to be the main source of economic progress for workers, unions ironically acknowledge the importance of physical capital and entrepreneurship by their demands for restrictions on capital mobility. Their support for legislation that imposes additional notice requirements, taxes, and other restrictions on companies implicitly admits that economic progress comes from productive plant and equipment, technical advances, and managerial efficiency rather than from union struggle. Why else hold capital hostage?

Free markets direct capital and labor to those places where they can earn their highest returns. When markets are allowed to operate freely, resources are continually reallocated to their most productive uses. Efficiency and growth are the results. Unions have impeded this process by restricting the mobility of labor, but they have been comparatively unsuccessful in directly hampering capital reinvestment in the past.

Proponents of state penalties on capital mobility concentrate on the employment losses due to plant shutdowns. Television and newspapers find newly idled resources easy to understand, but as Richard B. McKenzie (1981) has pointed out, this brand of myopia is on a par with studying banking by looking only at withdrawals. Such an analysis would naturally conclude that banking is doomed. But restrictions on closing plants are equivalent to prohibitions on

157

opening plants because a firm forced to continue operating uneconomic plants cannot invest in new facilities. Labor and capital remain tied up in inefficient activities because they cannot seek their highest yields. The political appeal of capital-mobility restrictions is that the worker-victims of the failure of new plants to open are invisible and cannot know that their economic circumstances have worsened due to union-supported legislation.

Communities with eroding industrial bases have an alternative to federal or state coercion if they want to retain growing industries. They can compete with successful communities by reducing oppressive taxation, burdensome regulation, and support of artificially high wage costs and adversarial labor unions, and by efficiently providing public services. Unionists, however, are not much interested in this proposal because they want to escape competition, not engage in it. Some unionists even declare that shutting down a (union) plant is a criminal action and should be treated as such.

Unionists want protection from the economic consequences of their own behavior. As McKenzie (1981, p. 130) has said, plant-closing legislation "hands over to unions the power to price labor out of the market—to turn a profitable concern into a losing proposition—and then gives them access to the coffers of the federal government for a 'bailout' or 'buyout.'" In a free society, people should have the right to decide what they do with their investment funds, how they live, and where they invest their labor and capital. The human rights to move, invest, buy, and sell, however, seem to play little role in discussions of federal policy in contemporary America. As someone said, the last move in politics is always to pick up a gun.

In recent rulings, though, the courts have stalled union ambitions by holding that companies need not bargain with unions over plant closings. Further, the courts have held that in Chapter 11 bankruptcies, union contracts do not hold a privileged position among a firm's obligations.

Conclusion

Union leaders and most governments fail to understand (or cannot act on a correct understanding because they want to stay in office) that people accumulate capital and invest it based on the expectation that government or unions will not expropriate it. If this expectation is absent, people prefer either to invest elsewhere or to consume their capital instead of safeguarding it for the expropriators. Rolls-Royces on the streets of London, ironically, are a consequence of high British taxes, which lower the returns to investing and make immediate consumption cheaper compared to future consumption.

Prosperity is built on capital formation and entrepreneurship. After all, the world is filled with masses of unskilled labor producing very little output. Union-supported measures that retard capital accumulation, restrict its mobility or ability to flow into the highest-yielding allocations, and harm entrepreneurial innovation must impoverish working people. The harassment that the disadvantaged suffer in crossing picket lines may be proof enough of the friends the poor have in labor unions.

X. Unionism across Industries and Countries

My central interest, and the criterion in terms of which I
wish to argue, is a maximizing of aggregate labor income
and a minimizing of inequality. If unionism were good for
labor as a whole, that would be the end of the issue for me,
since the community whose welfare concerns us is composed overwhelmingly of laborers.

—Henry C. Simons, "Some Reflections on Syndicalism"

The preoccupation of economists, after all, is with making
scarce resources go as far as possible in catering for the
unlimited demands upon them.

—Ralph Harris, *Job 'Creation'—Or Destruction?*

Preceding chapters examine the effect of unions on U.S. productivity in terms of various wage and nonwage effects. Now we turn
to a case-by-case examination—by industry and country—to see if
the previous conclusions are supported from comparative industrial
and national vantage points. Traditionally, the economy is divided
into nine broad industries—agriculture (including forestry and fish-
eries); mining; construction; manufacturing; transportation and
utilities; wholesale and retail trade; finance, insurance, and real
estate; services; and government—and it is useful to look at the
labor situation in each industry of the private sector.

Industries rise and fall, expand and contract, come and go. The
reasons are diverse, but ordinarily change is benign and in accord
with evolving consumer preferences, income, and technical advance.
To prohibit change is to condemn ourselves to stagnation and
regression. The role that unions, labor costs, and work rules play
in the process of industrial decline has not received enough attention.

There is an impressive association between unionism and sick
industries. Great Britain is a case unto itself, an industrial museum

161

with the usual high maintenance expenses for institutions that try to conserve the past. In the United States, naming a sick industry or enterprise usually coincides with naming an industry or firm with above-average unionization, whereas the reverse is true for a healthy industry. Whether the industry is automobiles, rubber, steel, construction, postal service, railroads, airlines, coal mining, telephone service, or many others, unionization means competitive problems. In these same industries, by contrast, nonunion firms generally have an edge and do better, and nonunion industries such as electronics, computers, finance, agriculture, professional services, and retail trade are dynamic and productive. Leading firms such as International Business Machines Corporation (IBM), McDonald's Corporation, Michelin, Digital Equipment Corporation, and Sears, Roebuck & Company remain nonunion.

Agriculture, Forestry, and Fisheries

Agriculture employs 3.7 million people—2.3 million family members and 1.4 million hired employees. Total employment has remained relatively stable in recent years, with family employment slowly declining and being offset by a gradual rise in the number of hired hands. The industry has experienced rapid productivity advances, with farm output per labor hour increasing 250 percent since 1960. Aside from extensive government intervention in agricultural markets, the industry is inherently competitive and decentralized, and it rapidly adopts any new technology and equipment that promise to reduce production costs. This is not to claim that the industry is a picture of economic health (it rarely has been), only that it serves consumers well.

Unionization has been minimal in agriculture, although many organizing efforts have been made over the years (Koziara 1980). Without pro-union collective-bargaining laws, the obstacles to unionization are virtually insurmountable: high turnover among workers who are relatively young, disproportionately unskilled, often minority or illegal immigrants, geographically dispersed employers who have a strong sense of private-property ownership and actively resist unionization, and so on. In 1978, only nine unions had any members in agriculture, yielding a 2.6 percent ratio of union members to employees in agriculture. Two unions have the bulk of members: Cesar Chavez's United Farm Workers (UFW)

162

with 22,900 members as of 1983, and Local 142 of the International Longshoremen's and Warehousemen's Union (ILWU), which organized virtually all of Hawaii's field workers in the late 1940s and had some 12,000 members at the end of the 1970s.

The low degree of unionization in agriculture and the correspondingly small threat of unionization imply that unions have done relatively little direct harm in this industry. Even in California, the UFW has organized only 10 percent of hired hands in agriculture. But millions of dollars have been lost in certain sectors such as table grapes and lettuce. There have been millions of dollars spent by growers in attorneys' fees in the California labor struggle alone, and the union has ruined some growers. Sun Harvest, once the largest lettuce producer in the world, succumbed to UFW labor management and quickly went bankrupt because it could not control quality, could not be a reliable supplier, and could not get its labor force to work efficiently. Both California and Hawaii have pro-union collective-bargaining laws, a necessary but not sufficient condition for organizing agricultural labor into worker cartels (P. Newman 1983; Cottle, Macaulay, and Yandle 1982). Growers fear destructive strikes at harvest time, especially in perishable, labor-intensive crops such as fruits and vegetables that have been unionized.

The negative impact of unions on productivity is sharply exposed in agriculture. The UFW and California's Agricultural Labor Relations Board, which it dominated for many years, illustrate how unions expand their power over managerial decisions without accepting the corresponding responsibility. The 1982 case of Paul Bertuccio tells the tale. Bertuccio had a 40-acre garlic crop that was stained by rain. To salvage something, he had the crop picked by machine to sell for seed rather than by hand for the fresh market. The UFW complained that this took work away from union people, even though Bertuccio's permanent farm employees already had other work to do. The ALRB found in favor of the union, ruling that the farm must negotiate with the UFW over such decisions. It is through cases such as this and by piecemeal advances that the union gains control over what crops to put in, what pesticides to use, which operations to discontinue, and so on. The UFW also opposes further research in land grant universities on new technology or equipment that could improve labor productivity in farming (Martin and Olmstead 1984). Nationally, productivity growth in fruits and vegetables has been less than half the rate for total agricultural output, although this lag cannot be wholly attributed to the UFW.

Although agriculture is a relatively low wage industry, this is partly explained by the presence of unions in other sectors of the economy, which forces unskilled workers to crowd into the open-employment sectors. In 1983, the average wage rate for hired workers in agriculture was $4.12 an hour and average full-time wages were $11,000 (U.S. Department of Agriculture 1984, p. 389). Although agricultural work is mostly unskilled, there are skilled jobs and there is good money to be made, especially in the highest-paying state, California. In 1984, for example, Bruce Church, Inc., a leading lettuce producer in the Salinas Valley, paid an average of $10.01 an hour, as documented by M. T. Payne, vice president, from W-2 tax forms. Bruce Church, Inc. guaranteed workers $7.01 an hour in 1985.

In 1983, forestry and logging employed 126,000 people and fishing, hunting, and trapping employed 53,000. These industries are lightly unionized, although logging once was the battleground for the Wobblies—the leftist Industrial Workers of the World (IWW)—and the Loyal Legion of Loggers and Lumbermen, a union created by the federal government during World War I. Trade rings of fishermen have periodically formed to try to force up the prices of their catches, claiming exemption from antitrust law as labor unions. The courts have struck down their claims, however, ruling that these groups, much like painters and steel haulers who attempt to fix their prices, violate antitrust law because they try to fix product prices rather than wage rates.

Mining

Mining employs 800,000 people, the majority of whom are in oil and gas extraction, which has negligible unionization. Coal mining employs 19 percent, metal mining (iron and copper) employs 5 percent, and nonmetallic mining and quarrying (stone, gravel, sand, and chemical minerals) employs the remaining 11 percent. The 1984 Current Population Survey data show 162,000 union members in mining, or only 16 percent of mining employees unionized (Adams

164

1985). Unions are concentrated in special sectors and regions, especially Eastern coal mining and Western copper mining.

Whether union or nonunion, mining is a high-wage industry, contrary to media impressions. In 1983, total wages and salaries in mining were $29,800 per full-time equivalent employee, the highest of any industry (public utilities were second at $28,570). Data for 1986 show that miners were second to public utility employees in pay. Nonunion miners earn more than unionized miners, although their fringe benefits are lower, a very old phenomenon (see references in Reynolds 1984a, p. 98). Nonunion mines and miners are also more productive than union mines and miners.

The strife and damage created by the United Mine Workers of America need no retelling, but the once-powerful union is fading fast, falling to only 86,600 members in 1983, down from 300,000 as recently as the mid-1970s. Productivity gains since World War II have been below average in mining, with the 1970s proving disastrous. Union mines simply are not competitive with nonunion mines, thereby shrinking UMW membership. From 1973 to 1979, labor productivity in the mining industry declined at an average annual rate of 5.2 percent, while capital in the industry declined at an average annual rate of 3 percent. Some of the productivity decline could be attributed to diminished capacity of active mines; health, safety, and environmental regulations; and strikes by bituminous coal miners. Among the measures reducing output were the 1960 Coal Mine Health and Safety Act, state reclamation laws, and the Federal Surface Mine Control and Reclamation Act of 1977 (Zeisel 1983).

Construction

In 1986, construction employed 4.9 million people. Traditionally, this has been a unionized industry in commercial and government building, but unions have fallen on hard times in recent years. Unionized construction employment was only 31 percent in 1980 and was down to 24 percent by 1984. Some 28 labor unions have members in the construction industry but the major building-trades unions have all suffered serious membership losses. Between 1978 and 1983, for example, the carpenters' membership fell from 769,000 to 589,000, the laborers' membership fell from 610,000 to 405,000, and the bricklayers' membership fell from 135,000 to 87,000. The

165

changes are even more dramatic in certain locations, such as the Washington, D.C., area, which was 67 percent unionized a decade ago and now is only about 10 percent unionized.

The central reason for this transformation of the construction industry is that organized labor has become increasingly uncompetitive with its growing wage differentials and restrictive work rules. The unions have granted substantial concessions in recent years, but these have not stemmed the tide of decline. The wage differentials between union and nonunion workers generally increase with the percentage of construction employment unionized in urbanized areas, hitting a peak differential at about two-thirds unionized (Welch 1980). With the deunionization of construction has come a fall in the relative wage. In 1970, construction workers earned the same full-time equivalent wage as workers in mining; by 1983, though, average earnings in construction had fallen slightly below manufacturing wages and 26 percent below mining wages. The last bastion of the construction unions—large industrial and government construction projects—has been breached because now there are many large, efficient nonunion contractors to choose from, even in the Northeast, a traditional union stronghold. Nonunion contractors have the advantage of paying wage rates as low as 60 percent of union rates, paying lower fringe benefit packages, and having flexible work teams unhampered by union rules.

The construction industry has been one of the worst performers in terms of productivity improvements. Between 1973 and 1979, for example, labor productivity declined at an annual rate of 3.1 percent, increasing the declines experienced since the mid-1960s (Kendrick 1983). Recently, the decline has moderated to 1 percent per year, and there are now signs of a reversal to positive productivity growth. Capital per hour of labor also declined at an annual rate of 0.8 percent from 1973 to 1979. This poor performance has sharply boosted the price tags of houses, factories, offices, and power plants. The declines in productivity are partly due to the erratic, inflationary monetary policies that government followed, thereby sending interest rates up and down in unpredictable fashion. However, a report by the Business Roundtable (1983), which includes the construction industry's biggest customers, pointed at organized labor as the principal culprit. Exclusive jurisdiction of the unions, including their associated work stoppages, was cited as the biggest obstacle,

166

but other problems were also identified, including double-time pay for overtime, excessive crew sizes, short 7.5-hour workdays, excessively lengthy apprenticeships, and severe restrictions on the numbers allowed to enter the trade.

Steven G. Allen (1984b) and Allan B. Mandelstamm (1965) have claimed that unionized construction workers are more productive, all else equal, than nonunion workers. However, these studies are of dubious value because they fail to recognize that the marginal productivity of unionized workers is necessarily higher due to the monopoly wage effect (Reynolds 1986b). Mandelstamm (1965) compared two Michigan cities, one heavily unionized and the other not, and he found that the cost of building a standard house was no higher with union labor; he concluded that union labor was more productive. Ironically, unionized contractors have not been competitive anywhere in the country in residential building. Open-shop firms produce 95 percent of residential homes and 85 percent of high-rise residential units. Open shop was 65 percent of office and commercial construction in 1984 and rising (Northrup 1984a). Eventually, construction unions will be confined to federally financed construction, where union inefficiencies are protected by the Davis-Bacon Act. In open competition, the building-trades unions—with their exorbitant wages, inefficient work practices, and strikes—cannot survive.

Manufacturing

In 1986, U.S. manufacturing enterprises employed 19.2 million wage and salary employees. Total employment in manufacturing has fluctuated with the business cycle since 1966 but shows no trend: Employment was 19.2 million in 1966, hit a low of 18.3 million in the recession of 1974–75, and reached a peak of 21 million in 1979. While manufacturing was nearly 33 percent of employment in 1950, it now is 19 percent.

Three out of four manufacturing jobs are nonunion today, and this proportion continues to increase. Unionization is more extensive in durable than in nondurable goods, but all unions in manufacturing have suffered sharp membership declines. Between 1978 and 1983, the United Automobile Workers (UAW) went from 1.5 million to 900,000 members, the United Steelworkers of America (USW) went from just under 1.3 million to 589,000, the International

Association of Machinists and Aerospace Workers went from 921,000 to 475,000, and the International Woodworkers of America (IWA) went from 118,000 to 33,000. In nondurable manufacturing, a similar story occurred: the Amalgamated Clothing and Textile Workers Union (ACTWU) went from 501,000 to 221,000; the International Ladies Garment Workers Union (ILGWU) slipped from 348,000 to 283,000; the United Paperworkers International Union (IPIU) went from 284,000 to 230,000; the Oil, Chemical and Atomic Workers International Union went from 180,000 to 116,000; and the United Rubber, Cork, Linoleum and Plastic Workers of America went from 200,000 to 113,000.

In the post–World War II period, productivity advances in manufacturing barely exceeded those for the U.S. business economy overall, although manufacturing gains were better than in the rest of the economy during the stagnant 1970s. U.S. manufacturing productivity gains have been poor by international standards, as Figure 10.1 shows. The chart suggests why so many domestic manufacturers face serious foreign competition in terms of price, quantity, and quality of goods. Between 1950 and 1983, output per hour in U.S. manufacturing little more than doubled—increasing by 126 percent—while in West Germany productivity increased by more than 500 percent and in Japan by more than 1,600 percent. The huge advantage that the United States once enjoyed in mass-production methods and capital per worker used to make it easy to offset union hindrances and excel in manufacturing by world standards, but U.S. manufacturers no longer enjoy such advantages. As a result, unions are a bigger obstacle than ever to U.S. competitiveness.

The difficulties in manufacturing, of course, vary from industry to industry and fluctuate from year to year. Despite all the talk of decline in U.S. industrial competitiveness and managerial vigor, many nonunion firms remain formidable competitors because hourly labor costs are only somewhat higher than those in Japan, West Germany, most of northern Europe, and Canada (depending on exchange-rate fluctuations), and U.S. labor's output per hour tends to be high. Between 1973 and 1981, for example, U.S. exports as a percentage of the value of U.S. manufactured goods rose from 6.6 to 9.9 percent, outdistancing the rise, from 6.4 to 8.4 percent, in the value of imported manufactured goods. Unfortunately, the 1981

Figure 10.1

OUTPUT PER EMPLOYEE HOUR IN MANUFACTURING, SELECTED COUNTRIES, 1950–83

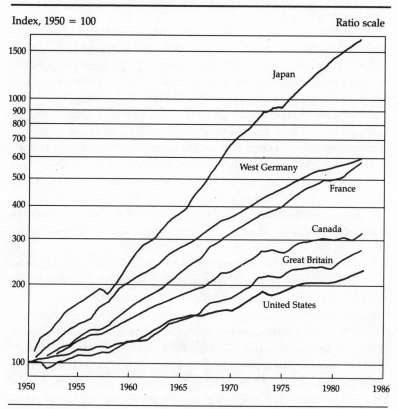

Index, 1950 = 100   Ratio scale

SOURCE: U.S. Department of Labor (1985a).

figures are the latest data available at this writing. More recent data suggest a deterioration in these rates, primarily because of the higher international value of the dollar (Lawrence 1984). When the dollar is relatively expensive, U.S. labor costs are high in international terms (monetary instability in a world of fiat paper monies suggests a central virtue of a gold standard for major currencies). Reasonable labor cost per unit of output continues to be a major factor attracting large amounts of foreign investment, including Japanese, to the United States. Political stability and a persistent (if

169

always threatened) free-enterprise ethic are also major reasons for the attractiveness of the United States for foreign investors. Fortunately, this inflow has augmented a low rate· of domestic capital formation in recent years. Investors, not labor monopolies, remain the worker's best friend.

The automobile and steel industries, despite all the publicity over their difficulties, are more exceptions than the rule in U.S. manufacturing decline. Their contraction basically has been the product of major increases in the obstacles to their success placed in their way by unions, government, and OPEC (energy costs). The major automobile and steel companies are saddled with union monopolies, and labor costs rose steeply in the 1970s and show little sign of changing now, despite all the talk about concessions. Aggravating the problem further is the fact that the UAW and the USW have monopolized labor costs for many suppliers to these two giant industries. Another factor in the demise of these once-great industries is that Washington forced them to spend millions in precious capital to comply with safety, energy, and environmental regulations.

The recent financial success of the automobile industry has temporarily concealed its long-run problems. Despite all the protections from foreign competition jointly won by unions and managers (at the expense of consumers), the competitive positions of domestic automobiles and steel have not improved. The safety and emissions standards imposed in the 1970s raised the price of cars a minimum of $1,000 per car, thereby cutting the number purchased, especially since fuel economy and performance also suffered. The quality of Detroit's products suffered relative to Japanese and European products that were already fuel-efficient. But the real problem in the long run is labor costs, not quality of fit and finish or product design. The U.S. plants of Honda and Nissan show that U.S. quality can equal or exceed Japanese quality and that U.S. product design is among the best in the world. Japanese producers, for example, rely on Southern California designers as a central element in their sensitivity to U.S. tastes.

In the 1950s, U.S. automobile manufacturers paid labor only 15 percent more than the average in U.S. manufacturing. Those were the days when many Americans bought a new car every two or three years. Then the premium paid to automobile workers began to rise steadily, reaching the current 50 percent in hourly wage costs and 80 percent in employment costs (Figure 10.2). The result has been a production cost disadvantage variously estimated at $1,300 to $2,500 per car and the export of some 250,000 high-paying jobs

---

Figure 10.2
RELATIONSHIP BETWEEN MOTOR VEHICLE JOBS AND PERCENT PAY PREMIUM, 1950–85

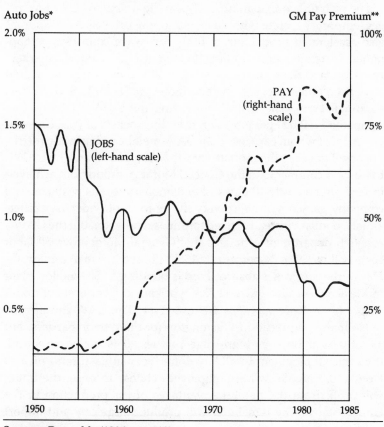

SOURCE: Reynolds (1986c, p. 113).
*Production employees in motor vehicle and parts manufacturing as a percentage of all wage and salary employment.
**Percentage by which the hourly employment costs of General Motors exceed the corresponding figures for all manufacturing.

171

(Reynolds 1986c). This is especially devastating in small cars; the natural cost advantage of the United States as a place for automobile production preserves U.S. competitiveness in larger and heavier cars. Ford, for example, never made money on the Escort, despite production of 430,000 units in 1983, which was 6.3 percent of total domestic output. Nor can Volkswagen make money under UAW wages and work rules, even at peak production of 200,000 units per year. In Japan, by contrast, the automobile makers pay a premium of only 23 percent over the average manufacturing wage there, rather like U.S. producers in the 1950s.

The restraints on Japanese cars gave the unionized U.S. producers temporary respite with quasi-monopoly privileges. The quotas also accelerated production in other low-wage countries, as happened in textiles and clothing following U.S. "orderly market" restrictions. U.S. car prices rose at least $800 above what they would have been otherwise, earning enormous profits for U.S. producers (Crandall 1985). The cost of preserving these UAW jobs was an estimated $160,000 per job taken from the pockets of U.S. consumers, most of whom earn less than UAW members. The trade restrictions will not save the industry or the UAW, however. The UAW's three-year contract with the General Motors Corporation, achieved in 1984 after a costly 10-day strike, demonstrates the problem. The company gained some flexibility in the form of wider pay differentials, bonuses instead of fixed formulas, and so on, but the UAW's research department estimates that General Motors' overall labor costs will increase 21 percent by 1987. Producing small cars profitably at these prices is absurd. Ford is building a $500 million plant in Mexico to produce Mazda 323–type cars at labor costs of under $3 per hour. Korean wages are lower yet. The UAW can oppose outsourcing and plead in Washington for more trade barriers, but as long as it pursues high-wage policies, it is voting to shrink domestic employment too. Only domestic manufacturers, such as Honda and Nissan, whose employees choose to reject the union will profit from the natural advantages of car production in the United States. The remainder will produce large cars and import small cars.

The 1983–85 profits ($24 billion) of the U.S. automobile makers temporarily concealed their long-run problem. The market value of Chrysler remains 4 times earnings, Ford 5 times earnings, and

172

General Motors 6 times earnings in a stock market averaging 14 times earnings and cyclical stocks 9–10 times earnings. The stock market is not especially impressed by the prospects of the U.S. automobile makers and it will remain so until the firms get control of their labor costs. Nor will technology and robotics, as Saturn Corporation proposes, save them (Reynolds 1986c).

The decline in steel is even more dramatic. The major integrated producers have gone from nearly 100 percent of the domestic market in the late 1960s (imports were less than 5 percent and U.S. firms had equal exports) to 60 percent and falling in 1985 in a market with falling total revenues—a shrinking market in real terms—with 20 percent shares each going to imports and nonunion minimills. The prospect of further decline, bankruptcies, and union shrinkage is certain. The USW leadership shows no willingness to make the necessary adjustments to allow the unionized sector of the industry to survive. Between 1960 and 1973, productivity advances of 2.4 percent per year helped to offset the USW wage premium, which barely rose during this period, nor did import protection increase significantly. After the 1973 Extended Negotiating Agreement and increasing import protections, the wage premium doubled and the productivity advance fell to 0.4 percent per year. All the modernization, trigger-price mechanisms, and dumping suits in the world cannot offset such numbers. Despite all the suffering in steel, the union makes virtually no concessions. Indeed, as the Bunker Hill (Idaho) mine situation in 1982 demonstrated, the USW national leadership vetoes even those concessions that local union members view as vital to maintain their jobs.

The minimills illustrate how efficient U.S. companies can expand output and employment in a troubled industry. About 60 firms use cheap (about $75 per ton) and abundant scrap steel, produce relatively simple (though increasingly sophisticated) products for predominantly local markets, and avoid the high labor and energy costs that plague the integrated giants. Small firms do not need enormous blast furnaces to melt iron ore or the complex pollution equipment required today. Minimills, which have quadrupled their shipments in the last 15 years, pay wages nearly equal to those in the basic steel agreement but pay lower fringe benefits. Unionization efforts have failed because the USW cannot match the combination of wage and job security. Nucor Corporation, for example, based in Charlotte, North Carolina, pays annual wages only 10 percent lower than those received by those unionized workers lucky enough still to have a job, and Nucor has yet to lay off a worker. Rewards depend on productivity—workers are not paid handsomely just to show up—and the company is unburdened by union work rules and strike threats.

Firms making nondurable goods are less unionized and have enjoyed more rapid productivity advances. Between 1950 and 1983, labor productivity advanced 2.2 percent per year in durable goods and 2.9 percent in nondurable goods. The differential was more dramatic from 1950 to 1973, in accord with the greater unionization differential. A good example is the meat-packing industry, which employed 117,000 people in 1986, down from 149,000 as recently as 1984. Between 1973 and 1981, productivity increased at an average rate of 4 percent per year and the price of meat products predictably declined relative to other manufactured goods. Once a highly unionized industry, it was depressed and plagued by overcapacity. The industry was revolutionized by newcomers such as IBF (formerly called Iowa Beef Processors). Many old-line packers such as Wilson Foods, saddled with wage and benefit costs of $17 to $19 per hour by the United Food and Commercial Workers International Union, have filed for bankruptcy, have cut wages 40 to 50 percent, and still can attract and retain qualified workers. Any firm saddled with high union wage costs and union work rules cannot compete for long in an industry experiencing rapid productivity advance and falling relative prices for output. Employee-run companies are no answer either, as demonstrated by the bankruptcy of Rath Packing in Iowa. Open markets are intolerant of privilege and inefficiency. Newly competitive markets punish the guilty and reward the innocent.

In 1986, the chemical industry employed slightly over 1 million people. Between 1948 and 1973, chemicals averaged 4.3 percent productivity advances per year, well above the 2.5 percent average for the private business economy. Although it is a high-wage industry, the chemical industry has generally remained nonunion; it is only about one-quarter unionized. Major companies such as E. I. du Pont de Nemours & Company, the Allied Corporation, and the Monsanto Company have largely avoided national unions through a variety of tactics such as the use of company unions, responsive

174

personnel policies, and aggressive resistance to organization drives by unions. Their success has meant a more productivity and open economy, more employment opportunities for nonunion people, including the unemployed, and more competitive pressure on unionized companies, thereby benefiting consumers, the ultimate beneficiaries of productivity advance.

In 1986, the rubber tire industry, formerly centered in Akron, Ohio, employed 89,000 people. The industry's major union, a spin-off of the UAW, has been the United Rubber, Cork, Linoleum and Plastic Workers of America, which once had a monopoly on labor supply to the industry. Between 1978 and 1983, claimed total membership of the union fell from 200,000 to 113,500. Productivity performance has been poor to average. The Big Five tire makers—the Goodyear Tire & Rubber Company, Firestone Tire & Rubber Company, B. F. Goodrich Company, General Tire & Rubber Company, and Uniroyal, Inc.—pay wages and benefits of about $22 per hour under union contracts. In 1982, the industry settled master contracts without a strike for the first time since 1962. Because of the big switch to radial tires in the industry, Michelin, a French company with nonunion plants in North America, gained a share of the market. The industry had severe difficulty with the transition from bias-ply tires to radial tires because radials last twice as long, lowering the demand for replacement tires and rendering bias-ply plants redundant and obsolete. The industry also was hurt by the switch to foreign cars shod with foreign rubber, as well as by the drop in miles driven by the U.S. public. Imported tires, some made in less-developed countries, are now an emerging factor. New domestic plants have been located in the Sunbelt, where the union finds it difficult to win elections, although it finally won in Oklahoma City after a 12-year effort.

Transportation and Utilities

In 1986, the transportation and utilities sector employed 5.2 million people, and it traditionally has been the most regulated, most unionized, and highest-paying sector of the economy. However, both the amount of regulation and the degree of unionization have been decreasing, thereby producing dramatic shifts in these industries accompanied by sharp revisions in compensation. Between

175

1980 and 1984, union membership in these industries fell from 2.5 to 2.1 million, or from 48.4 percent to 39.6 percent of employment.

Transportation, at 3 million people, accounts for most of the 5.2 million employees. There are 1.4 million in trucking and warehousing, 540,000 in air transportation, 301,000 in railroads, 290,000 in local and intercity passenger transportation, 289,000 in such transportation services as freight forwarding, 177,000 in water transportation, and 18,000 in pipelines (excluding natural gas). Following deregulation and greater competition, the major transportation unions have suffered sizable membership losses since 1978: the Teamsters are down from 1.9 million to 1.5 million, the railway clerks' union is down from 200,000 to 103,000, and the Transport Workers Union of America is down from 130,000 to 81,900. Nevertheless, a few unions, such as the National Maritime Union of America and the International Longshoremen's & Warehousemen's Union, have managed to maintain membership.

In most years since World War II, the railroads, despite their high degree of unionization and regulation, have managed to achieve greater productivity gains than the rest of the private economy. But productivity gains on the railroads have accelerated in the deregulated environment, jumping 33 percent between 1980 and 1983, following the 1980 Staggers Rail Act, which increased the freedom of railroads to change rates and routes. The gains mostly reflect relatively constant total output and a one-third reduction in employee hours. Rail rates have declined relative to the price level, and company earnings rose sharply from an anemic 2.4 percent rate of return on equity in the 1970s to more than 7 percent. As suggested in chapter 7, however, the railroads have a considerable distance to go in eliminating the inefficiencies of unions.

Nonrail transportation has performed worse than the general economy in terms of productivity gains since World War II. But this situation has changed with deregulation. For the airlines, where nonunion competitors in a deregulated environment have brought enormous productivity gains, productivity jumped 20 percent between 1981 and 1983. Airline employment increased by 100,000 between October 1983 and October 1985, by far the largest two-year gain in airline history.

Few people—other than the grossly overpaid members of the pilots', flight attendants', and mechanics' unions—any longer question the benefits to consumers and the economy of a competitive airline industry. However, the days of flight attendants receiving $40,000 a year and captains $150,000 a year for 45 hours of flying a month are over. The economists and their theory of markets have been vindicated again, whereas the forecasts of economic chaos by the opponents of airline deregulation have been falsified. Despite the predictable success of deregulation, people are not likely to listen to economists' ideas on the similar issue of international trade barriers and related policies because of the airline deregulation experience. Instead, we will continue to hear about how economists do not agree on anything, how there is no such thing as economics, and how it is important for government to save jobs in industry X. The most serious problem for the newly streamlined and cost-efficient airlines is the inefficient government-run air traffic control system.

In trucking, a similar deregulation tale prevails. Trucking jobs increased 200,000 in the past two years, an industry record. New nonunion companies and "double breasting" (operating both union and nonunion companies) by formerly unionized carriers have brought new freedom to routes, new types of service, lower prices, lower (market) wages, more efficient work practices, and higher unemployment and lower membership to the Teamsters. Thomas Gale Moore (1978), for example, estimated that the Teamsters had raised labor costs about 50 percent. Deregulation is reversing the situation. Sen. Edward M. Kennedy, an important supporter of trucking deregulation, did more to reduce Teamster power and corruption than all the criminal prosecutions once pursued by his brothers John F. Kennedy and Robert F. Kennedy.

Within cities, mass-transit subsidies have primarily benefited highly paid, union workers. In 1946, mass transit supplied 23 billion rides. By 1984, it was down to 7 billion rides and falling. In 1984, mass-transit expenses were $8.3 billion and fares were only $3.3 billion, the $5 billion deficit being made up by government subsidies. Transit workers' wages have risen 25 percent faster than the average employee's over the past 10 years. Even if market wages were paid and companies were privately operated, fixed-route mass transit is uneconomical in most circumstances. Cities are more dispersed, cheap personal transportation is widely available, incomes are higher, and time is more expensive. People increasingly make lateral trips around cities rather than commuter trips between suburb and city center. Municipal deregulation of taxicabs and vans and contracting out to private bidders does much more for intra-urban transportation than brand-new rail or bus systems. Private businesses are staging a comeback in urban transit (*Wall Street Journal* 1984, p. 33), but the power politics of the public transit agencies, their unionized employees, and middle-class riders make change difficult.

The communications industry—basically telephone and radio and television broadcasting—employed 1.4 million people in 1986. The telephone industry has been heavily unionized, and radio and television have been moderately unionized. Although communications is a highly regulated industry, a rapid rate of technical advance has made it the industry with the highest rate of productivity growth. The major story in terms of unions and productivity has been the breakup of the American Telephone and Telegraph Company (AT&T) and the deregulation of the telephone industry. The Communications Workers of America (CWA)—at 577,800 members in 1983, or more than 60 percent of the nation's phone workers—has begun to suffer membership declines, and nonunion competitors in the telephone equipment and service industry have begun to put serious pressure on the once-secure monopoly of AT&T and the CWA.

The booming communications and information industries are increasingly nonunion. The seven regional Bell companies have staffed their equipment subsidiaries with nonunion people. Management personnel and subcontracting work previously done by union people are increasing. Much more change is yet to come on all issues—wage rates, work rules, cooperation, and so on. The periodic strikes in the telephone industry, in which service is essentially maintained by management and supervisory personnel, suggest how overstaffed the industry is and what productivity improvements are yet to come. Previous studies by economists show that the high monopoly prices in the industry essentially went to pay for union wages and inefficiency (Ehrenberg 1979), as they have in the U.S. Postal Service (Perloff and Wachter 1984).

The highly regulated or government-owned and -operated electric, gas, and sanitary services industries have enjoyed rapid productivity advances over the years, on a par with agriculture's, primarily because of massive capital investments and technical improvements. Making up a very high wage sector that uses relatively skilled occupations, these industries also have been relatively highly unionized. The possibilities for deregulation, privatization, and competitive bidding to operate these services are still largely unexplored; their realization could one day usher in more dramatic productivity gains in a less-regulated environment (Poole 1982). The unions would then be forced to adjust their pricing, work rules, and strike threats.

Other Services

The remainder of the economy has two-thirds of all wage and salary employees—nearly 24 million in wholesale and retail trade; 6.2 million in finance, insurance, and real estate; 23.1 million in such services as hotels, business services, repair, and professional services; and 17.1 million civilians in government employment.

In the service sector, only government employment is heavily unionized. Public-sector unions grew rapidly from a membership of 900,000 in 1960 to almost 6 million by 1976, concealing organized labor's growing overall weakness from public perception. The unionized share of government employees rose from 11 to 40 percent, but by 1982 the union share had slumped back to 35 percent and 5.5 million members (Troy and Sheflin 1985). Nearly 30 percent of all union members are now in the public sector.

Union penetration in the private service sector is trivial: 8 percent in trade; less than 3 percent in finance, insurance, and real estate; and 7 percent in services. Major unions in these industries stagnate or suffer declining memberships. The Hotel and Restaurant Employees International Union has fallen from 404,000 to 312,000 members in recent years, while the musicians' union has slumped in membership from 330,000 to 185,000. The hopes for growth in white-collar occupations by unions such as the Office and Professional Employees International Union have gone unfulfilled. The prospects are virtually nil too.

The unions try to refine their image by soft-sell approaches, television advertising, and using young black women as organizers, but the negatives for unions in contemporary America are overwhelming. In a review of various public opinion surveys between 1966 and 1981, Lipset and Schneider (1983, p. 199) found that unions "are the least trusted major institution in American life, despite the fact that they have the largest mass membership of any organization in this country. . . . Americans [show] approval of their function accompanied by condemnation of their behavior." The shift of activity toward the Sunbelt, greater individualism among young workers, the fading memory of the Great Depression, and an increasingly white-collar, technical, female, and professional work force that identifies with management make it increasingly difficult for unions to gain voluntary adherents.

The rise of large unions both in the private sector and in government work owes relatively little to employee demand through private choices. Instead, it is due to collective choice through pro-union legislation and rulings by the state. Membership in unions never grew steadily but in leaps following specific changes in public policy. Without major changes to promote unions and collective bargaining in private services, unions are not likely to make major gains in white-collar work. It is wishful thinking by union leaders to believe otherwise.

The rise of unions in government work illustrates this proposition in almost laboratory-type conditions. The National Labor Relations Act of 1935 (Wagner Act) specifically exempted government employment from coverage, and government remained basically nonunion without the necessary (but insufficient) condition of mandatory bargaining with unions. The highly unionized postal service, covered by other legislation, was the major exception. John F. Kennedy, supported by the unions in his narrow election victory of 1960, signed Executive Order 10988 in January 1962 to promote unions in the federal bureaucracy. The order was modeled on the Wagner Act, although less generous to unions. The order stimulated a series of public-sector bargaining laws in states such as Michigan, New York, Washington, and Pennsylvania, where unions traditionally were politically influential. Only a dozen states, mostly in the South and the West, do not have some kind of mandatory bargaining law to support public employee unions today.

The constant investment of union resources in political lobbying confirms the difficulty that they have in maintaining their monopoly positions in a dynamic economy filled with substitutes, ingenious entrepreneurs, and responsiveness to relative prices. Unions, continuously battling the erosion of their privileged positions, urge new restrictions, thereby reducing the free flow of capital and labor throughout the economy. Although public-sector unions harm productivity, many government bureaus produce little that is of value to the public anyway. Greater competition and privatization is the key to improved public-sector productivity (see Bennett and Johnson 1981, Pirie 1985, Poole 1980, and Savas 1982). Since most productivity comes from the private sector, this book concentrates on the private sector and ignores whatever costs public-sector unions and public-sector labor laws impose on the public.

International Comparisons

Evidence on the link between productivity and unions is not confined to the United States. Most of the industrialized countries of the world are more unionized than the United States (France is an exception), although the institutional setting and historical traditions of labor relations differ sharply among countries. Although many scholars warn of the hazards of international comparisons, economic propositions must hold across cultures, space, and time if they are to be valid. To ease our task, we can conveniently group countries into three categories: European, Japanese, and British. U.S. unions fall into the tradition of British trade unions, but there is something to learn in all three groups.

European unions have relied on strong working-class identity and easily aroused class antagonisms for their allegiance. These unions, by and large, have embraced socialism explicitly from the start, often with their own political party in tow or else directly linked to a collectivist party—in contrast to the United States, where union-political interdependence has not been so continuously obvious. Some European unions have been religious (mostly Catholic) or communist in ideology rather than socialist. The union agenda has been very broad, encompassing political, social, and economic change, although in recent years the ideological edge of European unions has declined, partly due to the attainment of most of their agenda, including codetermination or industrial democracy. Although unions engage in collective bargaining, it is at the industry or economywide level with employer federations and government. In West Germany, for example, about 40 percent of the labor force is unionized but bargained wage schedules apply to 90 percent of employees. Wage schedules generally apply to all firms in an industry, regardless of degree of unionization. For example, in France,

181

the least unionized industrial country, there is no union-nonunion wage differential (Hennart 1983). Nor do unions participate in the grievance system at the plant level; this is handled by a separate "works council" whose members are elected by employees, a political answer to the presence of multiple, ideological unions in plants, none of which have exclusive (monopoly) representation.

Under these centralized labor-market arrangements, most of the Western European economies did very well in the post–World War II era, apparently defying free-enterprise theory. However, there were at least three good reasons for the rapid growth in Europe: (1) the abnormally low amount of capital per worker at the end of World War II meant that Europe would grow faster and invest larger fractions of income for some time, given modest amounts of economic freedom; (2) the economic burden of the welfare state was modest by today's standards; and (3) in countries where international trade was so large a fraction of economic activity, labor unions were more moderate than in large countries where the international sector was small. Enhancing this comparative moderation and flexibility was the fact that the wage bargains in European countries were floors that usually were not effective labor-market constraints. So-called wage drift (increases) occurred under the twin pressures of rapid growth in the demand for labor and inflation.

Today, however, Europe faces enormous problems that require major economic adjustments to avert stagnation. Although Europe continues to report productivity advances on a par with those of the United States, this fact is misleading. European labor costs have risen to absurd heights through union and state pressures, sharply reducing employment on the demand side. (The higher the labor costs, all else equal, the smaller the number of hours hired.) The result has been persistent double-digit unemployment rates not seen since the 1930s. Twenty million people remain quietly unemployed in Europe. Such massive unemployment is quiet because on the supply side, the willingness to work has been sapped by the lure of generous state benefits and steep marginal tax rates to support the bloated spending by government. Such comfortable unemployment is truly voluntary. Employment has expanded by over 20 million jobs in the United States in the past 10 years, depressing U.S. productivity gains to some extent. In contrast, employment has fallen in Europe, especially in manufacturing, thereby artificially inflating the European productivity figures because there is more capital per employed worker, at least in the short run, and the more productive workers tend to be kept on the job.

Union membership has slowly shrunk in Europe because of lower employment, especially in state enterprises such as steel, mining, shipbuilding, and textiles, in which governments finally began adjusting to rapidly growing and increasingly unaffordable subsidies. The prospects for making profits in such an inflexible environment (job security laws alone discourage new hiring by making it nearly impossible to adjust to economic conditions by laying off or firing anyone) are poor compared to those associated with the virtual frontier or entrepreneurial ethic of the United States. Schumpeter labeled the untidy process of economic progress as "creative destruction." Although there are signs of change, much of Europe seems intent on living with its economic sclerosis for years to come.

The rapid growth of productivity in Japan is too well known to need documentation here. What role have unions played? Unions have played a role similar to government's: step aside and do not hinder progress. Unions essentially have not been the serious impediment to productivity growth in Japan that they have been in Western economies generally. Japan has labor codes patterned after the pro-union, adversarial model of the United States, and it has unionization comparable to that in the United States or a little greater now that U.S. membership has eroded so rapidly. Nevertheless, Japanese unions and their environment are much different. About 80 percent of Japanese unions are enterprise or company unions, and they account for 90 percent of all union members.

A company union is intensely aware that its existence depends on the prosperity of the firm, in contrast to the American-style multifirm unions. Further, a company union has circumscribed monopoly power. More generally, in the postwar environment, the Japanese have considered harmony an overriding social virtue and conflict or confrontation a social evil. From an economic viewpoint, the Japanese occupy islands without substantial natural resources, which has reinforced their awareness that they must compete successfully in international markets if they are to prosper. If foreign markets are closed to Japanese goods, the alternative means to power and prosperity (tried in World War II) is to annex nearby lands rich in natural resources. Hitler called this means of national aggrandizement "lebensraum." Protectionism, in the style of, say, the Hawley-Smoot Tariff Act, can be a prelude to war.

The British tradition of trade unions prevails in Great Britain and in its former colonies, such as the United States, Australia, and Canada. If U.S. unions look bad in terms of hampering productivity, they almost look harmless by British standards. Once the workshop of the world, Britain is now the poor man of northern Europe largely because of the direct and indirect effects of British trade unions. The sheer size of Britain's relative decline is little short of catastrophic, according to two British economists (Addison and Burton 1984). The unique legal privileges of British trade unions, which still control nearly 50 percent of the labor force, have given them quasi-military power, as confirmed by the long, bitter strikes characterized by "flying pickets" (traveling strikers) and similar devices. Britain still retains enormous advantages as a place for international production and trade, but these have been nearly obliterated by unions and the national government, an apparatus often run by the political party owned outright by the trade unions.

The harm to productivity done by British unions is well described in anecdotes, but there are remarkably few statistical studies. Pencavel (1977) found a substantial union drag on productivity in British coal mining in 1900–1913. His data suggested that a wholly unionized coal field would produce 22 percent less output than a similar nonunionized field, all else equal. Addison and Burton (1984) cited a few productivity studies that show negative effects of British unions on productivity, but an interesting aspect is that British inferiority to both West German and U.S. manufacturing productivity stems from wider causes related to unionism. Prais (1981) and his associates found, for example, that British inferiority is worst in automobile production; quantitative analysis showed that value added per employee was only 40 percent of the West German level and an incredibly low 20 percent of the U.S. level. Although British capital expenditure per worker is the same as or only slightly lower than that in West Germany, there is a British deficit in the number of very large manufacturing plants, all else equal. The reason seems to be that relative to the rest of the world, British strike-proneness, which always creates planning problems, is most severe in large plants, and managers respond accordingly. As long as British work-

184

ers are prepared to down tools at the drop of a hat, they will remain poor by the standards of the leading industrial nations.

A great economist of the 20th century, W. H. Hutt, recently put it this way: "It [Britain] is an appalling example of a country ruined by the radicals. Before World War II she was easily ranked second in the world in terms of the average standard of living, but she now ranks way down the list. That is not due to war damage. It is due entirely to the wage structure" (Reynolds 1985a).

Conclusion

This survey of the labor conditions across U.S. industries and across high-income countries confirms the negative association between unions and productivity growth. Within U.S. manufacturing, for example, nondurable goods producers have been less unionized and have enjoyed more rapid productivity advance. Japan's real product (gross domestic product) per person rose from 17 percent of U.S. product in 1950 to 72 percent in 1980. Hong Kong went from 18 percent of U.S. product in 1960 to 51 percent in 1980 and became an area of relatively expensive labor by world standards. No one, to my knowledge, attributes these gains to union wage pressures and adversarial labor relations.

In the United States between 1980 and 1984, the number of employed union members fell by nearly 3 million while nonunion employment rose nearly 8 million (Adams 1985). If U.S. labor unions are to survive as major organizations when the calendar turns to the 21st century, they must make the far-reaching adjustments that they have refused to make thus far. In short, policies that well-meaning people believe help the average worker have made the whole nation, including its workers, poorer.

185

XI. Summary and Conclusion

> Masters are frequently intimidated, and are obliged to comply with the unjust demands of their workmen. The true remedy for combinations is perfect liberty on both sides, and adequate protection against violence and outrage. Wages should be the result of a free compact, and the contracting parties should look to the law to protect them from force being employed on either side; competition would not, I think, fail to do all the rest.
>
> —David Ricardo

The major findings in this book can be summarized as follows:

1. The federal labor laws passed in the 1930s continue to distort the playing field in U.S. labor relations, and they hinder the discovery of superior forms of labor relations at major corporations.
2. The adversarial unions promoted by archaic U.S. labor laws reduce the real income of working people.
3. These unions reduce the size of the economic pie, especially during economic recessions, by
   (a) Diverting labor and capital from higher to lower productivity uses.
   (b) Raising unemployment and reducing the coordinating ability of the price system.
   (c) Discouraging work effort and investment in skills due to wage compression.
   (d) Hindering managerial flexibility in unionized workplaces.
   (e) Opposing new technology.
   (f) Requiring the use of unnecessary labor.
   (g) Fostering adversarial attitudes in the workplace.
   (h) Reducing production by strikes, strike threats, and other adversarial tactics.
4. Unions lower the profit rate in unionized firms and thereby discourage investment.

187

5. Growth in productivity is negatively associated with the degree of unionization.
6. Sick firms and sick industries are associated with unions; deregulation reduces unionization and stimulates productivity.
7. International comparisons confirm the harmful effects of adversarial unions on national output.

A Numerical Tally

No one knows how much U.S.-style (monopoly) unionism and the laws that support it (the collective-bargaining system) really cost the American public. Ultimately, it cannot be quantified with precision. Yet there is something to be learned in an attempt to calculate the general order of magnitude. Uncertain or not, numbers force us to think a little harder about whether unions are a serious problem or only a minor one. If we grapple with the problem, others may be led to improve upon this first effort.

Along with W. H. Hutt, I am led to the conclusion that total output is largest and inequalities in income smallest when competitive markets are allowed to operate freely in balancing supply and demand in both product and factor markets. The counterfactual for the cost estimates below is a U.S. legal system that effectively would permit only free-market labor organizations with no power to fix monopoly wage rates or work practices. This basically depends on repeal of the New Deal labor legislation that props up labor monopolies and collective bargaining. In the absence of these laws, the economic problems of labor monopoly would shrink to insignificance, yielding competitive or quasi-competitive results in labor markets.

Labor monopolies are a serious disharmony that keeps production, employment, and economic expansion below their potentials here and around the world. Table 11.1 summarizes the quantitative results of this study: the cost of unions in the U.S. private sector is at least $126 billion per year, or 3.15 percent of gross national product (GNP), and a good case can be made for much higher estimates. In sum, real GNP would rise 3–4 percent if we adopted a neutral legal regime in the area of labor contracts.

Table 11.1 identifies five types of direct costs. The first is a loss of $10 billion due to the differential in union-nonunion wage rates.

Table 11.1

ESTIMATED ANNUAL COST OF PRIVATE-SECTOR UNIONISM IN THE UNITED STATES, 1986

Source of Loss Due to Union	Amount ($ billions)	Percent of GNP
1. Wage differentials		
Social loss	10	0.25
Forced transfers to union members	(70)	(1.75)
2. Wage inflexibility	52	1.3
3. Work rules, absenteeism, delay of new technology	40	1.0
4. Lost output and damages due to strikes, violence, disruptions	12	0.3
5. Administrative costs of bargaining, negotiating, grievances, arbitration	12	0.3
Total	126	3.15
Total including forced transfers	196	4.9

SOURCE: Author's calculations.

This estimate of social loss is similar to figures in the professional literature. It accounts only for the basic union-nonunion misallocation of labor; it makes no allowance for additional distortions within industries or for the consequences of misincentives due to wage compression. Another aspect of union-nonunion wage differentials is the redistribution of $70 billion from the general community to union members. This is not a social cost in the economist's lexicon, which distinguishes between mere transfers and lower-valued uses of resources. The income that unions extract from the rest of the community each year does not disappear but constitutes a kind of zero-sum game in which the unionists' gains are offset by the losses of union victims. If we assume that the parties to these forced exchanges are not equally blameworthy, then it is not costless to the innocents who lose; from their vantage point, the $70 billion in union plunder is an involuntary loss, whether a transfer or a social loss. Further, the success of unions in political rent-seeking acts as a model for other seekers of monopoly privilege, generating additional social waste.

The second cost of $52 billion is the inflexibility of union wage rates, which limits employment and therefore output. Over the course of the business cycle, union inflexibility combined with the subsidized idleness of the welfare state raises unemployment rates by about 2 percentage points during business slumps and 1 percentage point during business booms, for an average reduction of employment and output of about 1.3 percent. An identity between lower employment and output is warranted if we assume that the average labor quality of the employed and unemployed is the same over the business cycle, that productivity in the unionized sectors is at least as high as productivity in the nonunionized sectors, and that the capital stock is geared to these ups and downs over the long run.

The third cost of $40 billion is the drag on productivity caused by union work rules, absenteeism, protection of lackadaisical workers, and delays in the introduction and use of new technology at unionized companies. Chapter 6 estimates these at a minimum national cost of 0.9 percent of GNP, and Table 11.1 uses a best estimate of 1 percent.

The fourth cost of $12 billion is the lost output directly due to strikes, the vandalism and destruction associated with strikes, and the costs of related disruptions. The cost is conservatively estimated at $12 billion per year, thereby acknowledging the effectiveness of the precautions taken and substitutions made to minimize the harm done by strikes. The threat of strikes—ever present—is much more effective than the actual losses suffered in strikes.

The fifth cost of $12 billion is administrative expenses for union officials, company personnel costs incurred in dealing with unions, and the costs of third-party mediators, fact finders, and arbitrators. Although some of these activities would occur in the absence of laws favoring adversarial unions, the vast majority of these expenses are pure waste associated with wrangling with state-supported labor monopolies. Without the straitjacket of federal labor laws, which protect and encourage adversarial unions, much greater diversity in employer-employee relations would develop. Nonunion companies would be freer to experiment with a richer menu of personnel policies, including the participatory decision making desired by an increasingly well educated work force.

Some readers may find an estimated loss of 3–5 percent of GNP due to adversarial unions too high, but others (especially the front-line managers who deal with unions) may find it too low. Among economists, the lowest figure proposed is the costless unionism envisioned by Richard B. Freeman and James L. Medoff (1984, p. 247), who have claimed that unionism probably raises social efficiency. The highest estimate of loss among economists is a reduction in national output of 50 percent in the long run, as argued by W. H. Hutt, who points to the case of Great Britain. I tend to concur with Hutt—and also with John T. Addison and John Burton (1984), who have described Britain's union- and socialist-caused decline as "catastrophic"—but it would be difficult to statistically document the direct impact of unions as being that great in Britain, much less in the United States.

In *Power and Privilege: Labor Unions in America* (1984a, p. 158), I also speculated on the cost of unions and wrote the following conclusion:

> The real cost of the promotion and imposition of unionism on the U.S. economy by the national government is probably considerably higher [than 1 percent of national income], although difficult to measure. My own unsubstantiated hunch is that real income would rise by 10 percent if the economic power of unions disappeared. Unionism discourages investment, innovation, and entrepreneurial risk-taking. The prospects for extraordinary returns are reduced, and the effects on the dynamics of the economy are substantial, although hard to estimate. The constant threat and fear of strikes, disruption, and instability have untold potency in decreasing investment and productivity. The fear is more important than actual strikes because it is always there. People figure out ways to get around unions, but no one can accurately predict how much ingenuity would be released to reshape and multiply the national wealth if these obstacles to trade were reduced or eliminated.

If we include the all-around political effects of unions in a comprehensive analysis of the impact of unions on the political economy, we stumble into the entire system of state intervention and welfare. To take a modest example, the maritime unions have politically blocked the export of Alaskan oil to Japan, despite the fact that export would be eminently sensible and would narrow the U.S.-Japan trade deficit by nearly $10 billion a year. Intracoastal trade also is reserved for U.S. flag carriers and their union employees. Many trade barriers owe their political life to unions, both here and abroad, adding immeasurably to world poverty. In terms of federal spending, perhaps George Meany, the late AFL-CIO president, summed it up best: "Every piece of social welfare legislation in the last two decades carries a union label" (*AFL-CIO Legislative Alert* 1980).

Public Policy

If unions are privileged monopolists that harm the public and reduce our standard of living—whether by small or large estimated amounts of income—what are we to do about it? What would be promising changes in government policies? David Ricardo said it well nearly 200 years ago in the quotation at the head of this chapter. The answer, in brief, is that government should not help unions or harm them but simply enforce ordinary contract, tort, and criminal law in an impartial manner. Entertaining such an idea involves rethinking the entire labor problem and the current labor policies that we have inherited from the 1930s. Although there have been minor variations on the New Deal theme of promoting labor collectives as Republican and Democratic administrations have come and gone over the past 50 years, there has been little public discussion of the fundamentals of federal labor law. A cliché from public finance probably explains this inattention to the burdens of labor regulation: "An old tax is a good tax."

The wrong approach is to outlaw unions or repress them in any special way. This would only reinforce their carefully cultivated underdog image and their sense of paranoia; it would also be contrary to the idea of a free society and would be ineffective if not counterproductive, as demonstrated by patch-up legislative attempts such as Taft-Hartley and Landrum-Griffin. No one knows how to make government-supported cartels behave responsibly, despite the optimism of some observers (Lande and Zerbe 1985).

The proper remedy is deregulation, as first argued by Dan C. Heldman, James T. Bennett, and Manuel H. Johnson (1981) in modern labor scholarship. The success of deregulation in product markets can be realized in labor markets too. It could be done in either piecemeal or wholesale fashion and would involve the ultimate repeal and abolition of all the special labor legislation that supports labor cartels and collective bargaining in both the private

192

and public sectors. This prescription includes getting rid of the Railway Labor Act of 1926, the Norris-LaGuardia Anti-Injunction Act, the National Labor Relations Act of 1935 (Wagner Act) as amended, and their pro-bargaining counterparts in the public sector, plus dismantling the commissions, boards, executive orders, state laws, rulings, administrative orders, and regulations. The object would be to restore the rule of law in labor relations, which means generality, impartiality, and predictability. Unions and their members would then play on a level field; they would be treated like everyone else under ordinary contract, tort, and criminal law. No longer would Justice peek out from behind the blindfold and say, "Is this a labor matter? Oh, in that case it's different" (Reynolds 1986a).

Those unfamiliar with the Wagner Act may not realize the privileges that it establishes for unions—privileges far beyond those of the firms they bargain with. For example, unions are immune from taxation and the antitrust laws. They can compel a firm to bargain with them "in good faith"—an undefined term—and make its private property available for union use. Unions represent all employees in a bargaining unit, whether all employees want that representation or not. And, by and large, unions are immune from payment of damages for personal or property injury in labor disputes. If we repealed labor legislation, particularly the Wagner Act, union officials and members would lose their state privileges, not their human rights.

Many people still believe that privileged treatment of unions today is justified by the ill-treatment workers received during the last century and early years of this century. However, on no issue of comparable scope do people know so much that just isn't so. As the great American journalist H. L. Mencken said about wisdom, so we can say about the common understanding of labor relations: "What remains to the world is a series of long-tested and solidly agreeable lies." The myth boils down to the proposition that a free economy and a free society impoverish working people. In a free-market system without strong unions, goes the conventional wisdom, each employer retains an awesome power to impoverish the individually helpless people who trade their services for general purchasing power in a private-property, capitalist order. The image of labor's disadvantage is so hopelessly distorted that it is impos-

193

sible to correct in a short space, but special treatment for organized labor cannot help the ill-treated of years ago or the bulk of workers today. Government simply should protect the right of all to search out the highest bidders for their labor services, no matter how much this allegedly harms those better off (union members).

If we dispensed with the legal privileges and immunities for unions, labor disputes would be resolved like other disputes—primarily in private negotiation and ultimately in the courts. Labor disputes would decline because strong unions would shrivel without their special-interest legislation, deunionizing the economy more rapidly than is occurring already. Unions simply cannot prosper within a competitive environment. Direct access to the courts in labor disputes also would reduce strong-arm tactics and threats. People would learn that labor threats and violence are induced by legal privilege and slack law enforcement ("boys will be boys") rather than by alienation from the capitalist system or incipient revolutionary potential.

Things are rarely what they seem. Our labor laws were motivated by humane ideals (to a great extent) but have inhumane effects. Repealing our labor relations laws may appear unrealistic, but political reality keeps changing in unpredictable ways. The duty of economists and other scholars in this area is impartial analysis, as best their disciplines will allow, of the impact of government policies, regardless of the popularity or unpopularity of the policies. Moreover, there are signs that the nation's labor laws are the subject of a growing national debate. Following NLRB rulings in the 1980s unfavorable to labor unions, disgruntled AFL-CIO leader Lane Kirkland and other union officials have declared that they would be better off without the Wagner Act and the NLRB. While these outbursts were for political effect, one thing is clear in today's global markets: the time is ripe for a reexamination of the purpose of our labor laws. Age has not been kind to the 1930s theories of labor exploitation that still underlie our national labor laws.

References

Abramowitz, Moses, and Paul David. 1973. "Economic Growth in America." *De Economist* NR 3.

Adams, Larry T. 1985. "Changing Employment Patterns of Organized Workers." *Monthly Labor Review* 108 (February): 25–31.

Addison, John T. 1985. "What Do Unions Really Do? A Review Article." *Journal of Labor Research* 6 (Spring): 127–46.

Addison, John T., and John Burton. 1984. *Trade Unions and Society*. Vancouver: The Fraser Institute.

AFL-CIO Legislative Alert. 1980. February 11:3.

Allen, Steven G. 1984a. "Trade Unions, Absenteeism, and Exit-Voice." *Industrial and Labor Relations Review* 37 (April): 331–45.

———. 1984b. "Unionized Construction Workers Are More Productive." *Quarterly Journal of Economics* 99 (May): 251–75.

———. 1986. "Union Work Rules and Efficiency in the Building Trades." *Journal of Labor Economics* 4 (April): 212–42.

Apcar, Leonard M. 1984. "Kirkland's Call to Void Labor Laws Ignites a Growing National Debate." *Wall Street Journal*, Nov. 6, 29.

Ashenfelter, Orley. 1978. "Union Relative Wage Effects: New Evidence and a Survey of Their Implications for Wage Inflation." In *Econometric Contributions to Public Policy*, edited by Richard Stone and William Peterson, pp. 31–60. New York: Macmillan.

Baldwin, Carliss Y. 1983. "Productivity and Labor Unions: An Application of the Theory of Self-Enforcing Contracts." *Journal of Business* 56 (April): 155–85.

Barbash, Jack. 1980. "Commentary." In *Collective Bargaining: Contemporary American Experience*, edited by Gerald G. Somers, pp. 553–88. Madison, Wisc.: Industrial Relations Research Association.

Bauer, P. T. 1984. *Rhetoric and Reality*. Cambridge: Harvard University Press.

Baumol, William J., and Kenneth McLennan, eds. 1985. *Productivity Growth and U.S. Competitiveness*. New York: Oxford University Press.

Becker, Brian E., and Craig A. Olson. 1986. "The Impact of Strikes on Shareholder Equity." *Industrial and Labor Relations Review* 39 (April): 425–38.

Beney, M. Ada. 1936. *Wages, Hours, and Employment in the United States, 1914–1936*. New York: Industrial Conference Board.

195

Bennett, James T., and Manuel Johnson. 1981. *Better Government at Half the Price*. Ottawa: Caroline House.

Bluestone, Barry, and Bennett Harrison. 1982. *The Deindustrialization of America*. New York: Basic Books.

Boulding, Kenneth E. 1949. "Collective Bargaining and Fiscal Policy." *Industrial Relations Research Association Proceedings* (December): 52–68.

Bourdon, Clinton C., and Raymond E. Levitt. 1980. *Union and Open-Shop Construction*. Lexington, Mass.: Heath.

Branson, William H., and Julio J. Rotemberg. 1980. "International Adjustment with Wage Rigidity." *European Economic Review* 13: 309–32.

Brown, Charles, and James L. Medoff. 1978. "Trade Unions in the Production Process." *Journal of Political Economy* 86 (June): 355–78.

Brown, Douglass V., and Charles A. Meyers. 1962. "Historical Evolution." In *Public Policy and Collective Bargaining*, edited by Benjamin Aaron, Clyde W. Summers, and Joseph Shister, pp. 1–27. New York: Harper & Row.

Brozen, Yale. 1981. *Revitalizing the American Economy*. Kansas City: University of Missouri–Kansas City.

———. 1982. *Concentration, Mergers, and Public Policy*. New York: Macmillan.

Brunner, Karl, ed. 1981. *The Great Depression Revisited*. Boston: Martinus Nijhoff.

Burner, David. 1979. *Herbert Hoover: A Public Life*. New York: Knopf.

Burton, John. 1979. *The Trojan Horse*. Leesburg, Va.: Adam Smith Institute.

Business Roundtable. 1982. *Construction Industry Cost Effectiveness Project Report*. New York: Business Roundtable.

———. 1983. *More Construction for the Money*. Summary report of the Construction Industry Cost Effectiveness Project. New York: Business Roundtable.

Caldwell, William E., and Michael D. Moskalski. 1982. "The Effects of School District Strikes on Student Achievement." *Government Union Review* Special Education Supplement: 9–30.

Caldwell, William E., Michael D. Moskalski, and Loretta M. Jeffreys. 1983. "The Effect of Teacher Strikes on Student Achievement: New Evidence." *Government Union Review* 4 (Winter): 40–58.

Chowdhury, Gopa, and Stephen Nickell. 1985. "Hourly Earnings in the United States: Another Look at Unionization, Schooling and Unemployment Using PSID Data." *Journal of Labor Economics* 3 (January): 38–69.

Christenson, C. L. 1953. "The Theory of the Offset Factor: The Impact of Labor Disputes upon Coal Production." *American Economic Review* 43 (September): 513–47.

Clark, Kim B. 1980a. "The Impact of Unionization on Productivity: A Case Study." *Industrial and Labor Relations Review* 33 (July): 451–69.

———. 1980b. "Unionization and Productivity: Micro Econometric Evidence." *Quarterly Journal of Economics* 95 (December): 613–39.

196

———. 1984. "Unionization and Firm Performance." *American Economic Review* 74 (December): 893–919.

Connerton, Margaret, Richard B. Freeman, and James L. Medoff. 1983. "Industrial Relations and Productivity: A Study of the Bituminous Coal Industry." Unpublished manuscript, Department of Economics, Harvard University.

Cottle, Rex L., Hugh H. Macaulay, and Bruce Yandle. 1982. *Labor and Property Rights in California Agriculture*. College Station: Texas A&M University Press.

Crandall, Robert W. 1985. "What Have Auto-Import Quotas Wrought?" *Challenge* (January/February): 40–47.

Darby, Michael R. 1984. "The U.S. Productivity Slowdown." *American Economic Review* 74 (June): 301–22.

DeFina, Robert H. 1983. "Unions, Relative Wages, and Economic Efficiency." *Journal of Labor Economics* 1 (October): 408–29.

Denison, Edward F. 1979. *Accounting for Slower Economic Growth: The United States in the 1970s*. Washington: Brookings Institution.

Diewert, W. E. 1976. "Exact and Superlative Index Numbers." *Journal of Econometrica* 4 (May): 114–45.

———. 1978. "Superlative Index Numbers and Consistency in Aggregation." *Econometrica* 46 (July): 883–900.

Duncan, Gregory J., and Frank P. Stafford. 1980. "Do Union Members Receive Compensating Wage Differentials?" *American Economic Review* 70 (June): 355–71.

Eckstein, Otto. 1968. "Money Wage Determination Revisited." *Review of Economic Studies* 35 (January): 133–43.

Economic Report of the President. 1986. Washington: Government Printing Office.

Ehrenberg, Ronald G. 1979. *The Regulatory Process and Labor Earnings*. New York: Academic Press.

Ehrenberg, Ronald G., Leif Danziger, and Gee San. 1983. "Cost-of-Living Adjustment Clauses in Union Contracts: A Summary of Results." *Journal of Labor Economics* 1 (July): 215–45.

Ehrenberg, Ronald G., Daniel R. Sherman, and Joshua C. Schwarz. 1983. "Unions and Productivity in the Public Sector: A Study of Municipal Libraries." *Industrial and Labor Relations Review* 36 (January): 199–213.

Epstein, Richard A. 1983. "A Common Law for Labor Relations: A Critique of the New Deal Labor Legislation." *Yale Law Journal* 92 (July): 1357–1408.

Feldstein, Martin, ed. 1983. *Capital Taxation*. Cambridge: Harvard University Press.

Ferguson, C. E. 1969. *The Neoclassical Theory of Production and Distribution*. Cambridge, England: Cambridge University Press.

Flanagan, Robert J. 1984. "Wage Concessions and Long-Term Union Wage Flexibility." *Brookings Papers on Economic Activity* 1: 183–216.

Fortune. 1986. "A Man with a Screwdriver Operates on AT&T." June 23, 122–25.

Freeman, Richard B. 1983. "Unionism, Price-Cost Margins, and the Return to Capital." National Bureau of Economic Research, Working Paper no. 1164.

———. 1984. "Longitudinal Analyses of the Effects of Trade Unions." *Journal of Labor Economics* 2 (January): 1–26.

Freeman, Richard B., and James L. Medoff. 1984. *What Do Unions Do?* New York: Basic Books.

Friedman, Milton. 1962. *Capitalism and Freedom.* Chicago: University of Chicago Press.

Furstenberg, George M. von. 1980. *The Government and Capital Formation.* New York: Pergamon Press.

Goldsmith, Raymond W. 1982. *The National Balance Sheet of the United States, 1953–1980.* Chicago: University of Chicago Press for the National Bureau of Economic Research.

Gollop, Frank M., and Dale W. Jorgenson 1980. "U.S. Productivity Growth by Industry, 1947–73." In *New Developments in Productivity Measurement and Analysis,* edited by John W. Kendrick and Beatrice N. Vaccara, pp. 17–124. Chicago: University of Chicago Press for the National Bureau of Economic Research.

Gordon, Robert J. 1982. "Why U.S. Wage and Employment Behaviour Differs from That in Britain and Japan." *Economic Journal* 92 (March): 13–44.

Grubb, Dennis, Richard Jackman, and Richard Layard. 1983. "Wage Rigidity and Unemployment in OECD Countries." *European Economic Review* 21: 11–39.

Haber, William, and Harold M. Levinson. 1956. *Labor Relations and Productivity in the Building Trades.* Ann Arbor: University of Michigan Press.

Haggard, Thomas R., and Armand J. Thieblot, Jr. 1983. *Union Violence: The Record and the Response by Courts, Legislatures, and the NLRB.* Philadelphia: Industrial Research Unit, Wharton School, University of Pennsylvania.

Harris, Ralph, ed. 1979. *Job 'Creation'—or Destruction?* London: Institute of Economic Affairs.

Hartman, Paul T. 1969. *Collective Bargaining and Productivity: The Longshore Mechanization Agreement.* Berkeley: University of California Press.

Hawley, Ellis W., ed. 1981. *Herbert Hoover as Secretary of Commerce.* Iowa City: University of Iowa State Press.

Hayek, Friedrich A. 1960. *The Constitution of Liberty.* Chicago: University of Chicago Press.

———. 1972. *A Tiger by the Tail.* London: Institute of Economic Affairs.

———. 1976. *Law, Legislation, and Liberty.* Vol. 2. Chicago: University of Chicago Press.

Heldman, Dan C., James T. Bennett, and Manuel H. Johnson. 1981. *Deregulating Labor Relations.* Dallas: The Fisher Institute.

Hennart, Jean-François. 1983. "The Relative Wage Effect of French Unions." In *The Economics of Trade Unions: New Directions,* edited by Jean-Jacques Rosa, pp. 63–81. Boston: Kluwer Nijhoff.

Higgs, Robert. 1985. "Crisis, Bigger Government, and Ideological Change: Two Hypotheses on the Ratchet Phenomenon." *Explorations in Economic History* 22: 1–28.

———. 1987, forthcoming. *Crisis and Leviathan.* New York: Oxford University Press.

Hirsch, Barry T., and John T. Addison. 1986. *Economic Analysis of Labor Unions—New Approaches and Evidence.* Boston: George Allen and Unwin.

Hirsch, Barry T., and Robert A. Connolly. 1984. "Union Effects on Profitability and R&D Intensity." Unpublished manuscript, Department of Economics, University of North Carolina.

Hirsch, Barry T., and Albert N. Link. 1984. "Unions, Productivity, and Productivity Growth." *Journal of Labor Research* 5 (Winter): 29–37.

Hoover, Herbert. 1951, 1952. *The Memoirs of Herbert Hoover, The Cabinet and the Presidency.* Vol. 2. New York: Macmillan.

Houston Chronicle. 1985a. "Miners Continue Strike." Jan. 1, sect. 1, p. 3.

Houston Chronicle. 1985b. "ILA Making Concessions Due to Non-union Labor Pressures." June 4, 1.

Houston Post. 1985. "No Hard Times for These Hard Hats." June 13, 4F.

Hutt, W. H. 1930. *The Theory of Collective Bargaining.* London: King. Reprinted by the Institute of Economic Affairs, London, 1975.

———. 1973. *The Strike-Threat System.* New Rochelle, N.Y.: Arlington House.

———. 1982. "Every Man a Capitalist." *Policy Review* 22 (Fall): 141–53.

Industrial Relations. 1983. "The Future of Industrial Relations: A Conference Report." Vol. 22 (Winter): 125–31.

Jackman, Michael. 1984. *The Macmillan Book of Business and Economic Quotations.* New York: Macmillan, p. 121.

Johnson, George E. 1984. "Changes over Time in the Union-Nonunion Wage Differential in the United States." In *The Economics of Trade Unions: New Directions,* edited by Jean-Jacques Rosa. Boston: Kluwer Nijhoff.

Johnson, George E., and Kenwood C. Youmans. 1971. "Union Relative Wage Effects by Age and Education." *Industrial and Labor Relations Review* 24 (January): 171–79.

Johnson, Harry G., and Peter Mieskowski. 1970. "The Effects of Unionization on the Distribution of Income: A General Equilibrium Approach." *Quarterly Journal of Economics* 84 (November): 539–61.

Jones, Larry M., et al. 1982. *Management and Employee Relationships within the Federal Aviation Administration*. Washington: Federal Aviation Administration.

Kalt, Joseph P., and Mark A. Zupan. 1984. "Capture and Ideology in the Economic Theory of Politics." *American Economic Review* 74 (June): 279–300.

Kearl, J. R., et al. 1979. "What Economists Think: A Confusion of Economists?" *American Economic Review* 69 (May): 28–37.

Kendrick, John W. 1983. *Interindustry Differences in Productivity Growth*. Washington: American Enterprise Institute.

————. 1984a. *Improving Company Productivity*. Baltimore: Johns Hopkins University Press.

————. 1984b. "U.S. Economic Policy and Productivity Growth." *Cato Journal* 4 (Fall): 387–400.

————, ed. 1984c. *International Comparisons of Productivity and Causes of the Slowdown*. Washington: American Enterprise Institute.

Kendrick, John W., and Elliot S. Grossman. 1980. *Productivity in the United States: Trends and Cycles*. Baltimore: Johns Hopkins University Press.

Kirkland, Lane. 1986. "It Has All Been Said Before. . ." In *Unions in Transition*, edited by Seymour Martin Lipset. San Francisco: Institute for Contemporary Studies.

Klamer, Arjo. 1984. *Conversations with Economists*. Totowa, N.J.: Rowman & Allanheld.

Kosters, Marvin H. 1984a. "Disinflation in the Labor Market." In *Essays in Contemporary Economic Problems: Disinflation*, edited by Wm. Fellner, pp. 247–86. Washington: American Enterprise Institute.

————. 1984b. "Comment on Flanagan." *Brookings Papers on Economic Activity* 1: 217–20.

Koziara, Karen S. 1980. "Agriculture." In *Collective Bargaining: Contemporary American Experience*, edited by Gerald G. Somers, pp. 263–314. Madison, Wisc.: Industrial Relations Research Association.

Kreinen, Mordecai E. 1984. "Wage Competitiveness in the U.S. Auto and Steel Industries." *Contemporary Policy Issues* 4 (January): 39–51.

Labor Relations Reporter. 1985. Washington: Bureau of National Affairs. June 24, 6.

Lande, Robert H., and Richard O. Zerbe. 1985. "Reducing Unions' Monopoly Power: Costs and Benefits." *Journal of Law & Economics* 28 (May): 297–310.

Lawrence, Robert Z. 1984. *Can America Compete?* Washington: Brookings Institution.

Lazear, Edward P., and Robert L. Moore. 1984. "Incentives, Productivity, and Labor Contracts." *Quarterly Journal of Economics* 94 (May): 275–96.

Lebergott, Stanley. 1984. *The Americans: An Economic Record*. New York: Norton.

Lee, Dwight R. 1984. *Union Myopia and the Taxation of Capital.* Los Angeles: International Institute for Economic Research.

————, ed. 1986. *Taxation and the Deficit Economy.* San Francisco: Pacific Research Institute for Public Policy.

Leigh, J. Paul, 1984. "Unionization and Absenteeism." *Applied Economics* 16: 147–57.

Leiserson, William. 1959. *American Trade Union Democracy.* New York: Columbia University Press.

Lewis, H. Gregg. 1963. *Unionism and Relative Wages in the United States.* Chicago: University of Chicago Press.

————. 1986. *Union Relative Wage Effects.* Chicago: University of Chicago Press.

Lieberman, Myron. 1981. "The Costs of Collective Bargaining in the Modesto City School Districts: A Case Study." *Government Union Review* 2 (Winter): 73–103.

Link, Albert N. 1981. "Basic Research and Productivity Increase in Manufacturing: Some Additional Evidence." *American Economic Review* 71 (December): 1111–12.

————. 1982. "Productivity Growth, Environmental Regulations and the Composition of R&D." *The Bell Journal of Economics* 13 (Autumn): 548–54.

Linneman, Peter, and Michael L. Wachter. 1986. "Rising Union Premiums and the Declining Boundaries among Noncompeting Groups." *American Economic Review* 76 (May): 103–8.

Lipset, Seymour Martin, and William Schneider. 1983. *The Confidence Gap: Business, Labor, and Government in the Public Mind.* New York: The Free Press.

Lloyd, Craig. 1972. *Aggressive Introvert.* Columbus: Ohio State University Press.

Lyons, Eugene. 1964. *Herbert Hoover: A Biography.* Garden City, N.Y.: Doubleday.

Macaulay, Hugh. 1982. "Lessons from PATCO: The School of Hard Knocks." *Pathfinder.* Center for Education and Research in Free Enterprise, Texas A&M University.

Maki, Dennis R. 1983. "The Effects of Unions and Strikes on the Rate of Growth of Total Factor Productivity in Canada." *Applied Economics* 15: 29–41.

Mandelstamm, Allan B. 1965. "The Effect of Unions on Efficiency in the Residential Construction Industry: A Case Study." *Industrial and Labor Relations Review* 18 (July): 503–21.

Mansfield, Edwin. 1980. "Basic Research and Productivity Increase in Manufacturing." *American Economic Review* 70 (December): 863–73.

Martin, Philip L., and Alan L. Olmstead. 1984. "Sprouting Farm Machinery Myths." *Wall Street Journal,* May 14, 24.

McFadden, Daniel. 1966. *Cost, Revenue, and Profit Functions: A Cursory Review*. Berkeley, Calif.: Institute for Business and Economic Research, Working Paper no. 86.

———. 1978. "Cost, Revenue, and Profit Functions." In *Production Economics: A Dual Approach to Theory and Applications*, edited by M. Fuss and Daniel McFadden. Amsterdam: North Holland Publishing.

McKenzie, Richard B. 1981. "The Case for Plant Closures." *Policy Review* (Winter): 130.

———. 1984a. *Fugitive Industry: The Economics and Politics of Deindustrialization*. San Francisco: Pacific Institute for Public Policy Research.

———, ed. 1984b. *Plant Closings: Public or Private Choices?* 2d ed. Washington: Cato Institute.

McKenzie, Richard B., and William F. Shughart II. 1986. "Has Deregulation of Air Travel Affected Air Safety?" Washington University, St. Louis, Center for the Study of American Business, Working Paper no. 101.

Melvern, Linda. 1986. *The End of the Street*. London: Methuen.

Miernyk, William. 1980. "Coal." In *Collective Bargaining: Contemporary American Experience*, edited by Gerald G. Somers, pp. 1–48. Madison, Wisc.: Industrial Relations Research Association.

Mills, C. Wright. 1948. *The New Men of Power: America's Labor Leaders*. New York: Harcourt, Brace.

Mincer, Jacob. 1962. "On-the-Job Training: Costs, Returns, and Some Implications." *Journal of Political Economy* 70 (part 2, supplement) (October): 50–73.

———. 1983. "Union Effects: Wages, Turnover, and Job Training." In *New Approaches to Labor Unions*, edited by Joseph D. Reid, Jr., pp. 217–52. Research in Labor Economics, supplement 2. Greenwich, Conn.: JAI Press.

Mises, Ludwig von. 1922. *Socialism*. Indianapolis: Liberty Classics. Reprinted in 1981.

———. 1963. *Human Action*. Chicago: Regnery.

Mitchell, Daniel J. B. 1980. *Unions, Wages, and Inflation*. Washington: Brookings Institution.

———. 1982. "Recent Union Contract Concessions." *Brookings Papers on Economic Activity* 1: 165–201.

———. 1985. "Wage Flexibility in the United States: Lessons from the Past." *American Economic Review* 75 (May): 36–40.

Monthly Labor Review. 1985. "Employment Cost Index." February: 101.

Monthly Labor Review. 1986. "Employment Cost Index." August: 80.

Moore, Thomas Gale. 1978. "The Beneficiaries of Trucking Regulation." *Journal of Law & Economics* 21 (October): 327–43.

Moore, William J., and John Raisian. 1983. "The Level and Growth of Union/Nonunion Relative Wage Effects, 1967–1977." *Journal of Labor Research* 4 (Winter): 65–79.

National Labor Relations Board. 1979. *Forty-Fourth Annual Report.* Washington: Government Printing Office.

Neftci, Salih N. 1984. "Are Economic Time Series Asymmetric over the Business Cycle?" *Journal of Political Economy* 92 (April): 307–28.

Neumann, George R. 1980. "The Predictability of Strikes: Evidence from the Stock Market." *Industrial and Labor Relations Review* 33 (July): 525–35.

Neumann, George R., and Melvin W. Reder. 1984. "Output and Strike Activity in U.S. Manufacturing: How Large Are the Losses?" *Industrial and Labor Relations Review* 37 (January): 197–211.

Newman, Patty. 1983. "Harvest of Power." *Reason*, Sept., 19–26.

Newman, Robert J. 1983. "Industry Migration and Growth in the South." *Review of Economics and Statistics* 65 (February): 76–86.

New York Times. 1983. "Bell Unions Assail Offer of 'Bounty.'" Sept. 4, sect. 11, p. 17.

Noam, Eli M. 1983. "The Effect of Unionization and Civil Service on the Salaries and Productivity of Regulators." In *New Approaches to Labor Unions, Research in Labor Economics,* edited by Joseph D. Reid, Jr., pp. 151–70. Greenwich, Conn.: JAI Press.

Norquist, Grover. 1984. "Four Million New Jobs." *Policy Review* 28 (Spring): 27–29.

Northrup, Herbert R. 1984a. *Open-Shop Construction Revisited.* Philadelphia: Industrial Relations Unit, Wharton School, University of Pennsylvania.

———. 1984b. "The Rise and Demise of PATCO." *Industrial and Labor Relations Review* 37 (January): 167–84.

O'Brien, Anthony. 1985. "The Cyclical Sensitivity of Wages." *American Economic Review* 75 (December): 1124–32.

Office of Management and Budget. 1985. *Budget of the United States Government, FY 1986.* Washington: Government Printing Office.

Olsen, Randall J. 1978. "Comment on 'The Effect of Unions on Earnings and Earnings on Unions: A Mixed Logit Approach,'" *International Economic Review* 19 (February): 259–61.

Olson, Mancur. 1982. *The Rise and Decline of Nations.* New Haven: Yale University Press.

Peltzman, Sam. 1976. "Toward a More General Theory of Regulation." *Journal of Law & Economics* 19 (August): 211–40.

Pencavel, John H. 1977. "The Distributional and Efficiency Effects of Trade Unions in Britain." *British Journal of Industrial Relations* (July): 137–56.

Pencavel, John H., and Catherine Hartsog. 1984. "A Reconsideration of the Effects of Unionism on Relative Wages and Employment in the United States, 1920–1980." *Journal of Labor Economics* 2 (April): 193–232.

Perloff, Jeffrey M., and Michael L. Wachter. 1984. "Wage Comparability in the U.S. Postal Service." *Industrial and Labor Relations Review* 38 (October): 26–35.

Personnel Management. 1986. Washington: Bureau of National Affairs. June, 35–38.

Pirie, Madsen. 1985. *Dismantling the State.* Dallas: National Center for Policy Analysis.

Poole, Robert W., Jr. 1980. *Cutting Back City Hall.* New York: Universe.

———, ed. 1982. *Instead of Regulation.* Lexington, Mass.: Heath, Lexington.

———. 1986. *Privatizing the Air Traffic Control System.* Santa Monica, Calif.: Reason Foundation.

Posner, Richard A. 1973. *Economic Analysis of Law.* Boston: Little, Brown.

———. 1984. "Some Economics of Labor Law." *University of Chicago Law Review* 51: 988–1011.

Pound, Roscoe. 1958. "Legal Immunities of Labor Unions." In *Labor Unions and Public Policy,* edited by Philip D. Bradley, pp. 122–73. Washington: American Enterprise Association. Reprint. *Journal of Labor Research* (Fall 1979): 46–97.

Prais, S. J. 1981. *Productivity and Industrial Structure: A Statistical Study of Manufacturing Industry in Britain, Germany, and the United States.* Cambridge: Cambridge University Press.

Raisian, John. 1983. "Contracts, Job Experience, and Cyclical Labor Market Adjustments." *Journal of Labor Economics* 1 (April): 152–70.

Reder, Melvin W. 1984. "Strike Cost and Wage Rates: Cross-Industry Differences." In *The Economics of Trade Unions: New Directions,* edited by Jean-Jacques Rosa. Boston: Kluwer Nijhoff.

Rees, Albert. 1963. "The Effects of Unions on Resource Allocation." *Journal of Law & Economics* 6 (October): 69–78.

———. 1977. *The Economics of Trade Unions.* 2d ed. Chicago: University of Chicago Press.

———. 1979. "Trade Unions and Productivity: Job Preservation by American Unions." In *Job 'Creation'—or Destruction?* edited by Ralph Harris, pp. 61–71. London: Institute of Economic Affairs.

Review Symposium. 1985. "What Do Unions Do? by Richard B. Freeman and James L. Medoff." *Industrial and Labor Relations Review* 38 (January): 244–63.

Reynolds, Alan. 1979. "What Do We Know about the Great Crash?" *National Review,* Nov. 9, 1416–21.

Reynolds, Morgan O. 1982. "An Economic Analysis of the Norris-LaGuardia Act, the Wagner Act, and the Labor Representation Industry." *Journal of Libertarian Studies* 6 (Summer/Fall): 227–66.

———. 1984a. *Power and Privilege: Labor Unions in America.* New York: Universe.

———. 1984b. "Union Violence: A Review Article." *Journal of Labor Research* 5 (Summer): 237–46.

———. 1985a. "An Interview with W. H. Hutt." *Journal of Labor Research* 6 (Summer): 307–22.

———. 1985b. *Taxation and Economic Growth: The Emerging Consensus among the Experts.* Dallas: National Center for Policy Analysis.

———. 1985c. *The History and Economics of Labor Unions.* College Station: Center for Education and Research in Free Enterprise, Texas A&M University.

———. 1986a. "The Case for Ending the Legal Privileges and Immunities of Trade Unions." In *Unions in Transition,* edited by Seymour M. Lipset, pp. 221–38. San Francisco: Institute for Contemporary Studies.

———. 1986b. "Trade Unions in the Production Process Reconsidered." *Journal of Political Economy* 94 (April): 443–47.

———. 1986c. "Unions and Jobs: The U.S. Auto Industry." *Journal of Labor Research* 7 (Spring): 103–26.

———. 1987a, forthcoming. "Review of Union Relative Wage Effects." *Journal of Labor Research.*

———. 1987b, forthcoming. "A Critique of *What Do Unions Do?*" *Review of Austrian Economics.*

Reynolds, Morgan O., and Mary E. Edwards. 1985. "The Receipts, Spending, and Net Worth of Sixty Unions, 1976–83." Unpublished working paper, Department of Economics, Texas A&M University.

Ricardo, David. 1821. *The Principles of Political Economy and Taxation.* Reprint. 3d ed. New York: Dutton, Everyman's Library, 1969.

Robinson, Chris, and Nigel Tomes. 1984. "Union Wage Differentials in the Public and Private Sectors: A Simultaneous Equations Specification." *Journal of Labor Economics* 2 (January): 106–27.

Rogge, Benjamin A. 1979. *Can Capitalism Survive?* Indianapolis: Liberty Press.

Rose, J. Curtis. 1980. "The High Price of Bargaining." *Government Union Review* 1 (Fall): 104–10.

Rosenberg, Nathan, and L. E. Birdzell, Jr. 1986. *How the West Grew Rich.* New York: Basic Books.

Rothbard, Murray. 1983. *America's Great Depression.* New York: Richardson and Snyder.

Rothstein, Lawrence E. 1985. *Plant Closings: Power, Politics, and Workers.* Dover, Mass.: Auburn House.

Ruback, Richard S., and Martin B. Zimmerman. 1984. "Unionization and Profitability: Evidence from the Capital Market." *Journal of Political Economy* 92 (December): 1134–57.

Sachs, Jeffrey, 1980. "The Unchanging Cyclical Behavior of Wages and Prices: 1890–1976." *American Economic Review* 70 (March): 76–90.

Salinger, Michael A. 1984. "Tobin's q, Unionization, and the Concentration-Profits Relationship." *Rand Journal of Economics* 15 (Summer): 159–70.

Savas, E. S. 1982. *Privatizing the Public Sector*. Chatham, N.J.: Chatham House.

Schlossberg, Stephen I., and Steven M. Fetter. 1986. *U.S. Labor Law and the Future of Labor-Management Cooperation*. Washington: U.S. Department of Labor, BLMR 104.

Schmidt, Peter, and Robert P. Strauss. 1976. "The Effect of Unions on Earnings and Earnings on Unions: A Mixed Logit Approach." *International Economic Review* 17 (February): 204–12.

Schumpeter, Joseph A. 1962. *Capitalism, Socialism, and Democracy*. 3d ed. New York: Harper & Row.

Shenfield, Arthur. 1977. "The Rise of Trade Union Power in Britain." *Journal of Social and Political Studies* 2 (Summer): 73–89.

———. 1986. *What Right to Strike?* London: Institute of Economic Affairs, Hobart Paper no. 106.

Shepherd, R. W. 1953. *Cost and Production Functions*. Princeton: Princeton University Press.

———. 1970. *Theory of Cost and Production Functions*. Princeton: Princeton University Press.

Simons, Henry C. 1944. "Some Reflections on Syndicalism." *Journal of Political Economy* 59 (March): 1–25.

Simpson, Wayne. 1985. "The Impact of Unions on the Structure of Canadian Wages: An Empirical Analysis with Microdata." *Canadian Journal of Economics* 18 (February): 164–81.

Sloan, Frank A., and Killard W. Adamache. 1984. "The Role of Unions in Cost Inflation." *Industrial and Labor Relations Review* 37 (January): 252–62.

Smith, Adam. 1776. *The Wealth of Nations*. Reprint. Indianapolis: Liberty Classics, 1981.

Solow, Robert M. 1957. "Technical Change and the Aggregate Production Function." *Review of Economics and Statistics* 39 (August): 312–20.

Sowell, Thomas. 1980. *Knowledge and Decisions*. New York: Basic Books.

———. 1981. *Pink and Brown People and Other Controversial Essays*. Stanford, Calif.: Hoover Institution Press.

———. 1984. "The Economics and Politics of Race." *Policy Report* 6 (January). Cato Institute.

Sraffa, Piero, ed. 1952. *The Works and Correspondence of David Ricardo*. Vol. 8, p. 316: Letter from Ricardo to McCullough, Dec. 4, 1820. London: Cambridge University Press.

Staten, Michael E., and John Umbeck. 1982. "Information Costs and Incentives to Shirk: Disability Compensation of Air Traffic Controllers." *American Economic Review* 72 (December): 1023–37.

Stein, Herbert. 1983. "Industrial Policy à la Reich." *Fortune*, June 13, 201–8.

Stigler, George J. 1971. "The Theory of Economic Regulation." *Bell Journal of Economics* 2 (Spring): 3–21.

206

Summers, Robert, and Alan Heston. 1984. "Improved International Comparisons of Real Product and Its Composition: 1950–1980." *Review of Income and Wealth* 30 (June): 207–62.

Sveikauskas, Catherine Defina, and Leo Sveikauskas. 1982. "Industry Characteristics and Productivity Growth." *Southern Economic Journal* 48 (January): 769–74.

Taft, Philip. 1964. *Organized Labor in American History.* New York: Harper & Row.

Taylor, D. E. 1981. "Absences from Work among Full-time Employees." *Monthly Labor Review* 104: 8–70.

Terlecky, Nestor E. 1974. *Effects of R&D on the Productivity Growth of Industries: An Exploratory Study.* Washington: National Planning Association.

———. 1980. "What Do R&D Numbers Tell Us About Technological Change?" *American Economic Review* 70 (May): 55–61.

Thomas, R. L. 1977. "Unionization and the Phillips Curve—Time Series Evidence from Seven Industrialized Countries." *Applied Economics* 9 (March): 33–49.

Tobin, James. 1980. "Stabilization Policy Ten Years After." *Brookings Papers on Economic Activity* 1: 19–72.

Toffler, Alvin. 1986. "Labor Pains: Giving Birth to a New Social Order." *Washington Post,* Aug. 31, D1, D4.

Toner, Bill. 1985. "The Unionisation and Productivity Debate: An Employee Opinion Survey in Ireland." *British Journal of Industrial Relations* 23 (July): 179–202.

Troy, Leo, C. Timothy Koeller, and Neil Sheflin. 1980. "The Three Faces of Unionism." *Policy Review* 14 (Fall): 95–109.

Troy, Leo, and Neil Sheflin. 1985. *Union Sourcebook.* West Orange, N.J.: Industrial Relations Data Information Services.

Tullock, Gordon. 1967. "The Welfare Costs of Tariffs, Monopolies, and Theft." *Western Economic Journal* 5 (June): 224–32.

U.S. Department of Agriculture. 1984. *Agricultural Statistics.* Washington: Government Printing Office.

U.S. Department of Labor. 1974. *Characteristics of Construction Agreements, 1972–73.* Bulletin 1819.

———. 1983. *Trends in Multifactor Productivity, 1948–81.* Bulletin 2178 (September).

———. 1985a. *Trends in Manufacturing: A Chartbook.* Bulletin 2219.

———. 1985b. *Productivity Measures for Selected Industries, 1954–83.* Bulletin 2224.

———. 1985c. *How Workers Get Their Training.* Bulletin 2226 (February).

U.S. Department of Transportation. 1970. *The Career of the Air Traffic Controller—A Cause of Action.* Washington.

U.S. Department of the Treasury, Bureau of Alcohol, Tobacco, and Firearms. 1979. "Explosive Incidents." *1978 Annual Report*. Washington: Government Printing Office.

Uzawa, H. 1964. "Duality Principles in the Theory of Cost and Production." *International Economic Review* 5: 216–20.

Voos, Paula B. 1984. "Trends in Union Organizing Expenditures, 1953–1977." *Industrial and Labor Relations Review* 38 (October): 52–63.

Voos, Paula B., and Lawrence R. Mishel. 1986. "The Union Impact on Profits: Evidence from Industry Price-Cost Margin Data." *Journal of Labor Economics* 4 (January 1986): 105–33.

Wall Street Journal. 1982. "Louisville Frets Over Labor Strife Record As Companies Depart and Jobs Disappear." Aug. 16, 15.

Wall Street Journal. 1984. "Resurgence of Private Participation in Urban Mass Transit Stirs Debate." Christopher Conte. Nov. 27, 33.

Wall Street Journal. 1985a. "Massey Coal Strike Is Testing UMW Strategy." June 3, 6.

Wall Street Journal. 1985b. "International Efforts Revive a Steel Factory Kaiser Had Shut Down." June 4, 1.

Wall Street Journal. 1986a. "Big Railroads Watch as Regional Line Tries to Overpower Unions." May 30, 1.

Wall Street Journal. 1986b. "Work Rules Shape Up as Major Battleground in U.S. Labor Disputes." June 4, 1.

Wall Street Journal. 1986c. "AT&T Earnings Decreased 8.5% in 2nd Quarter." July 18, 2.

Wall Street Journal. 1986d. "For Fired Air-Traffic Controllers, Life's OK, but Not Like Old Times." Aug. 1, 15.

Warren, Ronald S. 1985. "The Effect of Unionization on Labor Productivity: Some Time-Series Evidence." *Journal of Labor Research* 6 (Spring): 199–208.

Washington Post. 1984 "Editors Claim Firing by Nader Based on Unionization Attempt." June 28, B3.

Waters, Craig. 1984. "Born Again Steel." *Inc.*, Nov., 52–64.

Weidenbaum, Murray L. 1979. *The Future of Business Regulation*. New York: AMACOM.

Weitzman, Martin L. 1984. *The Share Economy*. Cambridge: Harvard University Press.

Welch, Stephen W. 1980. "Union-Nonunion Construction Differentials." *Industrial Relations* 19 (Spring): 152–62.

Wessels, Walter J. 1985. "The Effects of Unions on Employment and Productivity: An Unresolved Contradiction." *Journal of Labor Economics* 3 (January): 101–8.

Witte, Edwin. 1932. *Government in Labor Disputes*. New York: McGraw-Hill.

Wolff, Edward N. 1985. "The Magnitude and Causes of the Recent Productivity Slowdown in the United States: A Survey of Recent Studies."

In *Productivity and U.S. Competitiveness*, edited by William J. Baumol and Kenneth McLennan, pp. 29–57. New York: Oxford University Press.

Wolman, Leo. 1931. *Wages in Relation to Recovery*. Chicago: University of Chicago Press.

Zeisel, Rose N. 1983. "Productivity Challenge in Bituminous Coal Industry, 1950–79." In U.S. Department of Labor, *A BLS Reader on Productivity*. Bulletin 2171: 56–57.

Index

Chrysler Corp., 9, 73, 172
Civil Service Commission, 128
Civil Service Reform Act of 1979, 129
Class resentments, America's lack of, 6
Clayton Antitrust Act of 1914, 25
Coal Mine Health and Safety Act of 1960, 165
Collective bargaining: in agriculture, 163; costs of, 141–45, 144tbl; labor consultants, 143; mandated by law, 8, 22; neutral parties, 124, 143–45, 144tbl; repeal of laws, effects of, 3–4
Common law: efficiency promoted by, 32–33; labor relations governed by, proposal re, 3–4, 11, 16, 31, 192–93; rules of, 28
Communications industry, 178
Communications Workers of America (CWA), 133, 134, 178
Company unions, 3, 174; employees, appeal for, 31; in Japan, 183; legal restrictions on, 22
Competitive model of general equilibrium, 43
"Competitive unions," definition of, 3
Congress of Industrial Organizations (CIO) (*see also* American Federation of Labor–Congress of Industrial Organizations), 8
Conrad, Joseph, 126
Construction Industry Stabilization Committee, 110
Construction industry unions, 70, 75, 165–67; work rules of, 111, 115, 116tbl, 117, 121–22
Consumption as purpose of economic activity, 38
Corporate executives' responsibility for strikes, 125–26
Corson Report, 127
Cost-of-living adjustments (COLAs), 95, 96
Criticism of unions, hesitancy re, 1, 2
Current Population Survey, 114, 164

Davis-Bacon Act of 1931, 8, 33–34, 92, 167
"Deadweight loss triangle," 80
Decline of unions, psychological effects of, 10
Democratic party, union ties of, 24
Deregulation of industry, 15, 176–77
Deregulation of labor, 16–17, 25;

consequences of, 30–32; equality of income concerns, 28–29; feasibility of, 33–34; justice concerns, 26; liberty concerns, 27–28; in the 1920s, 25; political opposition to, 83–84; profit sharing and, 100; proposals re, 30–31, 192–94; prosperity concerns, 29–30; union support for, 33, 194; wage inflexibility, effect on, 99
Digital Equipment Corp., 162
Disadvantaged workers, unions' impact on, 28–29, 45, 46
Douglas, William O., 23–24
E. I. du Pont de Nemours & Co., 174

Economics: principles of, 37–41; as scientific discipline, 35
Economists, public image of, 37
Edison, Thomas A., 40
El Salvador, 51tbl
Employee-owned enterprises, 101
Employment Standards Administration, 143, 144tbl
Entertainment unions, 70, 110, 112
Entrepreneurs and inventors, 40, 56
Ethiopia, 51tbl
European unions, 181–83
Extended Negotiating Agreement (ENA), 139, 173

Fair Labor Standards Act of 1938, 8, 20
Farrell, James A., 92
Federal Aviation Administration (FAA), 126–27, 128, 129, 132, 136
Federal Labor Relations Authority, 128, 144tbl
Federal Mediation and Conciliation Service, 144tbl, 145
Federal Reserve Board, 97
Federal Surface Mine Control and Reclamation Act of 1977, 165
Fink, David, 111
Firestone Tire & Rubber Co., 175
Fishery unions, 164
Food retailing unions, 75
Ford, Henry, 40, 42–43
Ford Motor Co., 172
Ford Motor v. NLRB, 22
Forestry unions, 164
France, 51tbl, 169tbl; unions in, 181, 182

About the Author

Morgan Reynolds, a professor of economics at Texas A&M University, received his Ph.D. from the University of Wisconsin in 1971. He has published many articles in academic journals, edited *W. H. Hutt: An Economist for the Long Run* (1986), and authored *Power and Privilege: Labor Unions in America* (1984), *Crime by Choice* (1985), and *Public Expenditures, Taxes, and the U.S. Distribution of Income* (1977). He has been a consultant for the National League of Cities, the U.S. Department of Labor, and many private organizations. He also serves on the board of the *Journal of Labor Research* and the *Review of Austrian Economics* and is a member of the Mont Pelerin Society and an adjunct scholar of the Cato Institute.

Cato Institute

Founded in 1977, the Cato Institute is a public policy research foundation dedicated to broadening the parameters of policy debate to allow consideration of more options that are consistent with the traditional American principles of limited government, individual liberty, and peace. Toward that goal, the Institute strives to achieve a greater involvement of the intelligent, concerned lay public in questions of policy and the proper role of government.

The Institute is named for *Cato's Letters*, pamphlets that were widely read in the American Colonies in the early eighteenth century and played a major role in laying the philosophical foundation for the revolution that followed. Since that revolution, civil and economic liberties have been eroded as the number and complexity of social problems have grown. Today virtually no aspect of human life is free from the domination of a governing class of politico-economic interests. A pervasive intolerance for individual rights is shown by government's arbitrary intrusions into private economic transactions and its disregard for civil liberties.

To counter this trend the Cato Institute undertakes an extensive publications program dealing with the complete spectrum of policy issues. Books, monographs, and shorter studies are commissioned to examine the federal budget, Social Security, regulation, NATO, international trade, and a myriad of other issues. Major policy conferences are held throughout the year, from which papers are published thrice yearly in the *Cato Journal*.

In order to maintain an independent posture, the Cato Institute accepts no government funding. Contributions are received from foundations, corporations, and individuals, and other revenue is generated from the sale of publications. The Institute is a nonprofit, tax-exempt, educational foundation under Section 501(c)3 of the Internal Revenue Code.

CATO INSTITUTE
224 Second St., S.E.
Washington, D.C. 20003